Advance praise for ***Transforming Race Conversations***

"This book is a comprehensive guide to promoting a greater understanding of the complexities of race and our society's endless struggles to come to terms with it. Ellis offers a wealth of helpful insights and suggestions for not only how we can talk more effectively about race, but how we can *transform* and transcend it as well. *Transforming Race Conversations* is a must-read for those with lingering questions about race and race relationships, those who struggle to talk about it, and those with a passionate commitment to changing the prevailing racial order and need guidance on how to do it. This book offers answers and should be required reading for all of us!"

—**Kenneth V. Hardy, PhD**, author of *Racial Trauma: Healing Invisible Wounds* and editor of *The Enduring, Invisible, and Ubiquitous Centrality of Whiteness*

"Eugene Ellis's *Transforming Race Conversations* offers a profound perspective on dismantling racism. Confronting the inherent discomfort in these discussions, Ellis emphasizes finding one's voice to challenge racial paradigms. Delving into embodied cognition and advocating for internal decolonization, Ellis guides readers through a transformative process. Grounded in neuroscience, psychology, and personal narratives, this book is a compelling call to engage in meaningful conversations, providing a roadmap for personal and societal change."

—**Linda Thai, LMSW,** trauma therapist and educator

"The book describes, in an easily digestible way, the historical, social, and economic forces that make deep connections and healing across race so difficult to sustain; the symbolic and economic value of whiteness that allows for a disengagement from basic morality. I highly recommend this book to anyone. Even if they think they don't need to read it, they do."

—**Julia Samuel,** psychotherapist and author

"Eugene Ellis's book, *Transforming Race Conversations,* is a remarkable piece of literature written with skill, compassion, and experience. This book provides invaluable insights and practical strategies that are essential for fostering racial understanding in today's diverse world. It is a must-read for anyone who is committed to meaningful change and inclusive discourse."

—**Keisha Siriboe, PhD,** chief equity and engagement officer for The Master Series

Further praise for *Transforming Race Conversations*

"Ellis invites us to tune into our cognitive and physiological triggers in conversations about race, so that we can listen and understand our own and others' experience and move away from cycles of defensive and fearful discourses towards a more informed, open and ethical dialogue . . . an enriching resource for trainers, therapists, educators, and anyone who wants to develop the compassionate awareness that offers hope for meaningful change." —*Therapy Today*

"This timely, moving book captures in an accessible and practical way the essence and depth of the trauma and psychodynamics of race. Over eight chapters the book maps the construction of race through the centuries, the language and social constructivism around race, the nature of embodied trauma and how it manifests in the here and now." —*New Psychotherapist*

"Whether you consider yourself informed in this area, or new to cross-racial conversations, this book will have much to offer. It speaks to all forms of oppression . . . I cannot recommend it highly enough." —*The Transactional Analyst*

"This fascinating read dives into a world of new vocabulary coined to initiate conversations around race. . . . If creative language, thought-provoking theories, and an honest breakdown of how we can all participate in race conversations is what you're after, then this is the read for you. Its forward-thinking narrative aims to normalize conversations about race, highlights the significance of historical oppression, and proposes different solutions to healing from race-related trauma"

–**Aaliyah Harris**, *The Canary*

"This is a beautifully written and highly accessible book on one of the most challenging subjects in modern discourse. It is superb in its cultural sensitivity and succeeds in taking us beyond familiar places in the race conversation, keeping the reader's mind open and encouraging a sense of curiosity. Ellis, a gifted psychotherapist, guides us through the immense pain of racial injustice and offers a solution nested in human experience and the growth of knowledge. This is a brilliant book, and the message is in the title. It is indeed an essential guide."

—**Peter Fonagy, OBE**

"This book has been written to help us take an honest look at who we really are. It is here to help us dig deep. It is here to heal the nation. I'm no psychotherapist, but I get it. After years of experience on the frontline helping people like me, Eugene has written a book that I believe can change the way we relate to each other, and the way we relate to ourselves."

—**Benjamin Zephaniah**, author, poet, lyricist, and musician

"Launched from his personal and professional experience as a therapist, Eugene Ellis presents an insightful and empirical text. He addresses rage, vulnerability, and trauma across racial minds and creates a pathway to the understanding of racial dialogue. The book emphasizes the multi-faceted positions of racism, mindfulness, and body connections that trigger 'racial arousal.' Language with a slight bite and examples of dialogue prompt further understanding and unravel 'race construction.' . . . This book is an important contribution to keeping the race conversation alive."

—**Isha Mckenzie-Mavinga,** psychotherapist, and author of *The Challenge of Racism in Therapeutic Practice*

"In this comprehensive text, Eugene Ellis describes a pathway to racial understanding, speaking to both the history of racism and the psychology of race relations, interwoven with a mindfulness-based, somatically-informed model for addressing the effects of this history on all of us. He leaves us with much to converse about!"

—**Janina Fisher, PhD,** author of *Transforming the Living Legacy of Trauma* and *Healing the Fragmented Selves of Trauma Survivors*

"Eugene Ellis has powerfully captured the nuances and fractures of trauma, where our minds and bodies have been dehumanised for far too long, and takes us towards reclaiming our sanity and positive growth. This is a 'must have' book for all therapists working with people of African and Asian diaspora heritage who want to understand the impact of historical and modern-day racism on the Black British psyche."

—**Patrick Vernon, OBE,** social commentator, and coauthor of *100 Great Black Britons*

"It would be impossible to exaggerate how important this book is for our times. Written, as it was, in the wake of Brexit, the election of Donald Trump, and Black Lives Matter, it tells of the damaging way that conscious and unconscious ideas of race are woven into society. . . . Race is a construct with a terrible history that is held deep within the body of individuals and in communities, both white and nonwhite. Eugene Ellis brings both personal experience and psychotherapeutic insight into this often fraught area with compassion, thoughtfulness, and rigor."

—**Judy Ryde,** author of *White Privilege Unmasked: How to Be Part of the Solution*

"How the mental construction 'race' affects the inner life, the very bodies, of individuals is little recognized and less explored. *Transforming Race Conversations* is a groundbreaking and timely study that brought me, a white English Buddhist, new awareness of my own inner experience and has already benefitted my participation in the 'race conversation' through greater understanding of how the construction of race impacts on the psychic and somatic experience of people of color."

—**Subhuti,** member of the Triratna Buddhist Order, president of the London Buddhist Centre, and author of *Mind in Harmony: The Psychology of Buddhist Ethics*

TRANSFORMING RACE CONVERSATIONS

TRANSFORMING RACE CONVERSATIONS

A HEALING GUIDE FOR US ALL ‹ ‹ ‹

› EUGENE ELLIS

W. W. NORTON & COMPANY
Independent Publishers Since 1923

Note to Readers: Standards of clinical practice and protocol change over time, and no technique or recommendation is guaranteed to be safe or effective in all circumstances. This volume is intended as a general information resource for professionals practicing in the field of psychotherapy and mental health; it is not a substitute for appropriate training, peer review, and/or clinical supervision. Neither the publisher nor the author(s) can guarantee the complete accuracy, efficacy, or appropriateness of any particular recommendation in every respect. As of press time, the URLs displayed in this book link or refer to existing sites. The publisher and author are not responsible for any content that appears on third-party websites.

For information about special discounts for bulk purchases, please contact W. W. Norton Special Sales at specialsales@wwnorton.com or 800-233-4830

Manufacturing by Marquis Book Printing
Book design by Amanda Weiss
Production manager: Gwen Cullen

ISBN: 978-1-324-05389-7 (pbk)

W. W. Norton & Company, Inc., 500 Fifth Avenue, New York, NY 10110
www.wwnorton.com

W. W. Norton & Company Ltd., 15 Carlisle Street, London W1D 3BS

1 2 3 4 5 6 7 8 9 0

Dedicated to my wife, Jayakara,
who has kept me out of confusion, brought
me back to Earth time and again, and
given me her unwavering support.

CONTENTS

APPENDICES

ACKNOWLEDGMENTS

I feel honored to have had many fruitful race conversations with those who have given their permission to be featured in this book and thankful for their candidness and honesty.

Cathy Ingram, Gary Baron, Kam Sanghera, Maitrinita, Mickey Peake, Nandaraja, Patrick Harrison, Dr. Phil Cox, Roshmi Lovatt, Ruth Calland, Sabina Khan, Sharon Beirne, Sujhayini, Tali Lernau, and Warren Davis.

I want to thank members of the Black, African, and Asian Therapy Network (BAATN) and the attendees of BAATN trainings and forums over the years for their contribution to my thinking and process.

I am grateful to the BAATN Leadership and Advisory Team who, for many years, helped me stay sane and process the many corridors of the race construct.

Carmen Joanne Ablack, Dennis L. Carney, Dr. Isha Mckenzie-Mavinga, Kris Black, Ian Thompson, Poppy Banerjee, Jayakara Ellis, Karen Minikin, Mickey Peake, Ngozi Fofah, Robert Sookhan, Rotimi Akinsete, and our beloved brother Arike who passed in June 2020.

I am indebted to Manjusiha and George Bunting for their support with the manuscript and to Catherine Jackson for her encouragement over many years.

Finally, I am thankful for the teachings and friendships within the Triratna Buddhist Community and my safe base within their People of Color Sangha.

PREFACE

Since the original publication of *Transforming Race Conversations* back in March 2021, it has been heartening to receive numerous comments from individuals and institutions who have found the ideas within the book both accessible and impactful. In the many race conversations I have had or witnessed over the years, the predictable and defining features are fear, discomfort, and the loss of clear thinking and compassion. The framing of race and racism in relation to interpersonal and intergenerational trauma has been particularly useful for many readers in helping them make sense of this discomfort. The trauma-informed ideas and theories I talk about in this book have sowed the seeds of belief in the possibility of connecting with the impact of race and racism in much more profound ways, along with the belief that it is possible to move towards undoing racism on a personal and institutional level.

In the short time since the first edition of *Transforming Race Conversations*, much has happened that continues to highlight a global phenomenon that obscures the humanity of racialized people. The UK government issued their long-awaited report from the Commission on Race and Ethnic Disparities, which declared there was no evidence of structural racism in the police or in education. This assertion devastatingly denies the reality of many racial and ethnic minorities. Amid the Ukrainian refugee crisis, African students, who make up a sizeable percentage of overseas students in Ukraine, were denied fair passage to neighboring countries even after the declaration from the EU that anyone coming from Ukraine would be welcomed. The Child Q safeguarding report was also published. This report stated that a black 15-year-old girl was taken out of an exam and strip-searched by police, including having to remove her sanitary towel, with no appropriate adult present and no one informing her parents. Teachers had wrongly suspected her of carrying cannabis. This incident has changed a "top of the class" student, according to her parents, into a shell of her former self.

On one level, it would appear that not much has changed and that racism continues unabated. On another level however, there are expanding pools of grief and rage and a growing number of dissenting voices, which are becoming louder and more urgent. The opening up of consciousness that has taken place has blossomed into a chorus of voices that pressingly need to continue their momentum until the hearts and minds of significant numbers of individuals are impacted enough for cultural and behavioral change to take place. This book is about listening to, understanding and amplifying these voices. It is also about mindfully attending to how we are conditioned to react around race and being creative in our responses. I feel honored to be able to contribute in words and ideas to the continuing struggle.

TRANSFORMING RACE CONVERSATIONS

› 1 ‹

BEING COLOR CONSCIOUS

EVERYDAY RACISM

When I started writing this book, the electorate in the United Kingdom had just voted to leave the European Union. It was Obama's last week in office, after serving two terms as president of the United States, and Donald Trump had just been elected president. For me, and for many others, the social narrative of the U.K. and U.S. had shifted decidedly away from equality and connection and toward division, separateness, and protectionism. Shifting narratives of connection versus disconnection were taking place in other countries also, as feelings that had previously laid dormant were once again given license to be expressed.

Whatever you thought of his policies, Obama brought with him a level of hope and possibility to the idea of a nonracial world. His very presence, however, placed a mirror up to the myth of a post-racism society. Obama's visibility and very existence brought to the surface hidden thoughts, feelings, and behaviors that had been hiding in plain sight. Among other conversations around inequality, the world, it seemed, was in the grip of a race conversation that few people knew what to do with.

Like many others, I went through a phase of dislocation and mourning, even paranoia, as these narratives played out on the world stage. Before these events took place, I had done a considerable amount of research regarding race and its traumatic effects on past and present generations. I had steeped myself in the historic horror and brutality of it all. What was happening in the U.K., U.S., and other countries around the world triggered something inside me. I felt linked very personally to the atrocities directed at past generations, even though I was not a direct part of it. I have not experienced old-time racism in an overtly hostile way my lifetime, yet I could feel it in my bones. The range of feelings stirring within me could be summed up as fear, and from that fear came rage, along with a sense of helplessness and intense inner discomfort. Nothing material had changed in my world, yet there I was with all this emotional turmoil. It was the charged narrative and the threat behind the narrative that had brought me to where I was.

My vulnerability as a person of color had been exposed, and the race construct had been activated within me. It was troubling to observe the breaking down of clear thinking in those I heard in the media. Sweaty lipped politicians, desperate to recapture a sense of superior identity that they felt they had lost, frequently appeared on the news. On one side of the street, there seemed to be a drive to redefine British identity as something ahead of the pack that needed to reassert itself; on the other side, there was a cry from those who experienced cold alienation.

As I wrote the final chapter of this book, George Floyd had just been killed by a police officer in the U.S. The calmness with which this police officer took George Floyd's life and the undisturbed nature of the other officers involved was genuinely shocking to witness. The subsequent sharing of testimonies of acts of race brutality on social media swept aside the seduction of the post-racism narrative. If you have never thought about racism before and you watch or listen to these videos and testimonies, you will begin to understand what the stakes are and what it means for you as a person of color or as a white person. Although it is very hard to watch and listen to these stories, this type of impactful engagement with race is a vital part of a particular journey. For some, it can be what flips the script. An understanding might begin to emerge that we are living in a system—from this understanding, we can start to orient toward what we really need to be thinking about. For others, there may be an experience akin to waking up from slumber with a renewed energy to refocus and recommit.

My personal experience of George Floyd's killing and the subsequent Black Lives Matter protests was, once again, dislocation and mourning; this time, however, it was on a whole different level. I could actually feel my body bristling under the collective weight of distress. There were so many other people I knew who were experiencing something similar. It wasn't just that racism had woken up in the present, there was also an awakening of historical distress from the past. Talking about race had always been hard work, but after George

Floyd's killing, it had somehow become hard work not to. The race construct had become glaringly evident in our collective heightened state of awareness. People of color, in particular, were either being asked about race by white people or feeling compelled to call out the racism they saw in their places of work or even in their own homes. People of color experienced the intense feelings of discomfort that the race conversation brought up for them and were also exposed to the intense feelings of discomfort that the race conversation brought up for white people and white institutions. In 2021, with the new administration in the White House, we were spared the daily threats and toxic insults, but what does this mean going forward? What do we need to do to sustain the level of awareness required to move into the type of action that dismantles the structures of racism and reduces suffering? The ideas and narratives in this book are my small contribution to this effort.

This book's central idea is about the discomfort that appears to be the abiding experience of the race conversation, for both people of color and white people. Looking at the title of this book for the first time would have predictably elicited a response and probably an uncomfortable one. Perhaps images may have come to mind about how this book would be experienced as it was read. In our minds, we might imagine this book will be tough-going or, for some, not tough enough. Our expectations might lead us to imagine the tone of the book to be a pointy-fingered diatribe or maybe way too optimistic. There might be images in your mind of previous race conversations where things didn't go as well as planned. Perhaps you've never had a race conversation and you wonder why, given how influential race is in people's lives. When we enter into the race conversation, we are entering into the territory of trauma, of the good/bad binary. Our most present experience is often one of confusion. What complicates the race conversation, as we have all probably experienced, is the emotional soup that gets evoked that plays havoc with our cognitive and rational minds. The left side of our brain is eager for understanding and is brilliant at it, but with emotions running high, instead of our cognition helping us, it just appears to make things worse.

I'm using the term "race conversation" to describe the many narratives that happen within us and between us. Most race conversations happen internally, within the confines of our minds and bodies. These internal conversations are typically activated when we hear casual racism or when we witness or experience the grosser acts of racism out in the world. This internal conversation is generally in the form of conscious, competing voices in our heads, which result in confusion or a truce-making silence. Typically, there is also a nonverbal, physiological struggle between the drive to act, which feels dangerous, and the drive to be still, which feels safe. A challenge for all of us is communicating this internalized conversation to others, especially across racial lines.

The aim of the book is not necessarily to make changes to the external world directly. Instead, it is about making an internal shift that honors and validates our experiences and gives us more opportunities to discover our voices. This would then ultimately lead us to challenging the paradigm of race in our places of work, our places of study, and our personal lives. With an eye on ending racism somewhere in the distance our present focus needs to be on our relationship with the construct of race itself, which comes only through dialogue with ourselves and with others. Race conversations between individuals and between groups offer great potential for change and healing, and there are many contexts for the race conversation to take place. These conversations can happen between people of color and white people, between people of color and other people of color, and between white people and other white people. Each context offers various levels of perceived safety or danger and different overall perspectives on living in a society deeply embedded in the race construct.

"Our present focus needs to be on our relationship with the construct of race itself, which can only come through dialogue with ourselves and with others."

Toward the end of the book, I will present race conversations I have had with people from white, black, brown, and mixed-race backgrounds. My initial hope with these conversations was to present examples that would illuminate the ideas I wanted to present; what I received, however, was so much more. I was opened up to further important strands of exploration and was taken to new places of understanding. In addition to mirroring the everyday places the mind and body move toward in the race conversation, each conversation contains other areas of possible interest and speaks for itself. Although the focus for these conversations is on race, the individuals' intersecting identities inevitably give rise to experiences that are not merely the sum of each of them. The idea of intersectionality, coined by Kimberlé Crenshaw (1991), would make it very unlikely that, say, a black gay man and a black gay woman would have the same experience.

There are many stories that we tell ourselves around race that keep us stuck. For instance, there is the story that understanding race is too far out of reach, too other, too strange, and too complicated. Another might be that to make contact with the impact of race, you would need to develop a previously undiscovered part of the self. Another story might be that only a lived experience of racial discrimination can bring real understanding. These stories are trauma response stories. They are stories of protection from possible pain and stories that are, at least in part, an attempt to keep us safe emotionally and to move toward comfortable ground. To counter these stories, I could say that the process of understanding the impact of race is more about removing the clouds to see the sky than developing new eyes. I might also say that although being a person of color is the most direct route to understanding, this does not necessarily mean a person of color is more equipped to navigate the type of understanding that brings about healing and change.

"The process of understanding the impact of race is more about removing the clouds to see the sky than developing new eyes."

The seemingly global discomfort with having the race conversation makes sense when seen through the lens of trauma. During the writing of this book, I have been very conscious of a fundamental principle in working with race trauma or, in fact, any trauma. For individuals to move beyond where they currently are and into a place of healing, they need to be within what is called their window of stress tolerance (Siegel, 1999).[1] Being within a window of arousal that is not too high and not too low allows coherence of thinking. This state also allows individuals to remain reflective and compassionate toward themselves and others. For this to happen, people need to feel a measure of safety—but they cannot feel too safe, as we need some level of challenge if things are to change and heal. If people are activated to the point of pulling away, never to return, this is retraumatizing, and there will be no moving forward and no healing, merely a replaying of the old story.

Parts of the book will be intellectually stimulating, perhaps allowing you to make connections with what you see in the real world, in terms of behavior, and what you see in yourself. In other parts of the book, you might be "witnessing the racial wound" more directly. This more direct witnessing will be harder to reflect on and make sense of in a coherent way. When thinking has lost its coherence and you are moving toward confusion and incomprehension, there are often accompanying visceral experiences within the body. These inner sensations are what we normally try to move away from. The invitation is to stay connected as you investigate your experience. Just allow your body to be, without trying to put together a coherent narrative, which will take you back into your head and continued confusion. I will be saying a lot more about how trauma works and how this type of attention to the body can support healing beyond words. Our bodies have their own wisdom, which we would do well to heed.

I will be focusing on everyday racism, which might be called micro acts of racial bias. On their own, these micro acts have a certain impact, but when experienced throughout a lifetime, they contribute significantly to our identities and a sense of belonging or not belonging. I will also be focusing on people who would not identify themselves as having strong racial biases and who are well-intentioned, even energized, around engaging with these issues. In my mind, these parts of the racial landscape are the most fruitful doors to engage and the most direct route toward action and changing the lived experience of people of color. Engaging with these more open doors will, hopefully, lead us to engaging with more challenging and hard-to-reach doors in the future.

The language of race carries with it the history of struggle and oppression, and along with this comes fear. The words of racism are designed to bludgeon someone into retreating into the status quo or bludgeon someone into waking up. I want the reader to have the experience that they are being taken beyond these familiar places of confusion and fear in race conversations toward a place of clarity and curiosity. No doubt, fear and uncertainty will still be there, but the aim is to lessen that particular experience and bring about much-needed aha moments to what is usually a challenging and unforgiving landscape. I also want to use language in such a way that it applies to everyone, no matter who you are and where society places you in the hierarchy of race.

On the topic of language, I am very aware of having been educated in the U.K., with Oxford English being the proclaimed standard. I have also been trained (some might say groomed) in a particular style that demands precise and researched arguments that relate to previously valid arguments. I am aware that this style often alienates those who have no connection with these rules of the game and that this proclaimed standard can be off-putting and inaccessible for many. I'm left with the dilemma, then, of who am I aiming to be acceptable and accessible to?

I was also trained in the psychotherapy profession, with its requirement to reference valid sources. This led to another either/or impasse, where the race-construct itself invalidates the many sources that I would deem extremely relevant, even essential. More recently, however, an increasing number of books on the subject of race and racial trauma have attained academic validity, and the issue is being talked about and referenced increasingly in the media.

Throughout this book, I alternate between the style I have been trained in, of academic rigor, and a more personal and accessible style. My main goal was to write in such a way as to awaken the ethical values of the reader, whatever the style they value. I also wanted to give alternative and more plausible narratives to counter the negative-cycle narratives that are part of the race construct. My hope is to bring to the surface progressive narratives that give our ethical values more of an opportunity to bloom. The sources I have referenced are from people of color and white people who have something important to say about their side of the race divide. Whether these references are seen as valid sources is a matter of personal judgment.

In the coming chapters, I will explore race through the lens of science. Science is a dominating force that determines much of reality ("it's in a book and scientifically proven, so it must be true"). Science, however, is both friend and foe within the race construct. It has been instrumental in shaping the race narrative, on the one hand bringing us such titles as *Some Racial Peculiarities of the Negro Brain* (Bean, 1906). On the other hand, we need to exercise caution and use science that is not based on hate or a need to justify racial superiority. Science can be a landscape where unconscious biases roam free. Science can also be a landscape that uncovers what has been staring at us in plain sight and can also overturn once-believed "certainties."

In addition to hard science, I will be offering some formulations based on western psychological theories. From a western psychological perspective, the pathway to good mental health includes knowledge of the self and the turning inward to understand what motivates and drives our behaviors. Let us take the concept of attachment theory, which I say more about in future chapters. This theory asserts that when a parental figure and infant turn toward each other and interact, the parent's internal representation of the infant is communicated to the infant. If all goes well, the infant gets to know themselves through the parent's eyes, and a sense of security develops in the relationship. This knowing of self that comes from a secure connection then creates a sense of internal safety and an understanding of emotional regulation and trust. As a psychotherapist, I have based treatment on attachment theory and can see that it works to a degree. However, it's not always the case that having a secure attachment to a significant caregiver (usually the mother, as the theory is typically presented) automatically translates into feeling safe in the world. Many western psychological therapies assume that good caregiving is wholly within the realm of parental or family relationships. There is, however, an essential element that is missing regarding whether individuals feel safe and experience trust. What is missing is that caregiving is not just the responsibility of parents or family. Caregiving that affects the child's sense of security is also the responsibility of the community, and how the community around the family behaves toward the child and their caregivers. In the case of the infant in attachment theory, there is not just the turning inward toward the parental figures; there is also a turning outward toward the immediate community and the wider world. Both are important for a felt sense of safety and good mental health. Children are sensitized not just to parental figures' recognition of their wants and wishes but also to the communities' wants and wishes for the child. It is both the sensitive responses from significant caregivers along with sensitive responses from the broader community that foster trust in children. Many western psychological theories attempt to make sense of human experience but rarely include an understanding of racialized people and the political landscape in which they live. Unless these theories include the impact of whiteness on people of color, the theories as practiced will continue to offer few pathways to explore the impact of racism on trust and mental health.

Another point of reflection when writing this book has been the side of me that feels a duty to "tell it like it is" and "speak truth to white people." The side of me that understands trauma, however, is highly aware that we all have nervous systems that get triggered when race is on the table. If there is going to be any integration and change, then the body needs slow and steady rather than fast and furious. I want to tell the raw truth, but respect race triggers that have us pull away or bring about confusion. I have come to believe that the best we can do is familiarize ourselves with the dynamics of race in the present, understand the dynamics of race through history, and explore our personal, generational, and genetic connections to it. We can then develop an inner sense of safety that would drastically increase our ability to bring our best thinking and our best selves to this vital area.

Exploring the history of race and its impact on the present inevitably brings us to the question of blame. We blame ourselves, and we blame others, and then blame moves us out of relationship and into confusion. As we begin to explore race, the paradigm of wealth accumulation and the loss of that accumulation is something that becomes increasingly apparent. The focus that the British Empire and the West have on amassing as much wealth as possible in one lifetime was not the paradigm in which countries in Africa or India based their social societies. These societies were less about the accumulation of wealth and more about spiritual ascendance through many lifetimes. At present, we are seeing a serious challenge to the wealth accumulation paradigm in western countries through movements like Extinction Rebellion. We are also witnessing an equally robust reinvigoration of the accumulation paradigm via populism's need to perpetuate a state of crisis in society in an attempt to reassert a culture of fear and blame. The race construct is just one example of the consequences of the wealth accumulation paradigm—there are many more examples, like class and gender divides. My interest is more about how we got here than on who is to blame. Of course, there will be some measure of blame, which is inevitable when we delve into our relationship with race. In relationships, gross errors are often made, as we might have experienced for ourselves; however, apportioning blame or taking the blame does not often take us to where we want to go. It is more helpful to keep the focus on repair and on finding ways to take the sting out of the debilitating emotion of blame and set it aside. Instead of attempting to heal through blame, I want to foster a sense of responsibility and active redress. Instead of attempting to sidestep responsibility through criticism, I want to foster a sense of relational engagement and active repair.

"I have come to believe that the best we can do is familiarize ourselves with the dynamics of race in the present, understand the dynamics of race through history, and explore our personal, generational, and genetic connections to it."

As I am a therapist, many of the examples within this book come from the world of therapeutic practice, but this isn't a therapy book for therapists. I hope that these ideas are accessible to everyone, including those in the world of therapy. Given that the therapy profession specializes in working with all aspects of the human condition, it should be the ideal place to bring some of the ideas in this book to life. With therapy's promise of liberation from oppressive experiences, you might imagine that having the race conversation in these conditions would be more comfortable. As you will see in the coming chapters, this is not necessarily the case. My own experience, however, is that I have had more fruitful and healing conversations within the world of therapy than I have had outside of it.

Within the race construct, race hurt is inflicted on people of color by those who I'm going to call perpetrators of race hate. The perpetrators consciously and proactively seek to spread hate and to denigrate and oppress the racial groups they see as below them. This group, by far, is the main engine of racism's continued presence. Within the race construct, there are also the witnesses. The witnesses are in the position of being both spectators to perpetrators' indefensible acts and also spectators to the harm they themselves unconsciously or ignorantly inflict. Witnesses, through firsthand accounts, images, or narratives, are indirectly exposed to race trauma and are aware, to some extent, of their own discomfort as active and unwilling agents of racism. Within psychotherapy and outside of it, I have met many witnesses who feel an internal compulsion to work on their conscious and unconscious racism and to go on a personal journey to overcome their fear of the race conversation. Far more witnesses, however, experience their discomfort levels rise, sometimes exponentially, to the point where they lose their ability to think within a race conversation. It is as if their thinking has become paralyzed. There is then the inevitable quick escape, away from the discomfort. People of color can go this route also, but I have found this is far less likely.

James Baldwin, American novelist and social critic, said, "History is not about the past, it's about the present. We are our history" (Peck, 2016, 1:22:37).[2] Racism is not going away any time soon but within the backdrop of racism, we can have the race conversation and at the same time transcend aspects of the race construct. I came into this world with a body, a beautiful body capable of a vast range of expression, from intense hatred to great acts of generosity. I came into this world with a body that could be shaped, restricted, and limited in its expression. I, along with many others, have been on a journey to regain access to my body. This journey has entailed navigating through what were once immoveable blocks and expressing more of what my body is capable of. The more I journey, the more I express; and the more I express, the more I really live.

"Whether you describe yourself as white, a person of color, mixed heritage, or a citizen of the world, there is work to be done."

I have sought to illuminate what often appears hidden and impenetrable to communicate a sense of hope for those who are disheartened to the point of not even taking the first steps to understanding. Whether you describe yourself as white, a person of color, mixed heritage, or a citizen of the world, there is work to be done. In the words of Ben Okri, in his epic poem *Mental Fight*, "You can't remake the world, without remaking yourself. Each new era begins within. It is an inward event, with unsuspected possibilities for inner liberation" (Okri, 1999, p. 66).

RACE, THE BODY, AND THE MIND

Here is a functional definition of racism, as offered by Dr. Francis Cress Welsing[3]:

> The local and global power system structured and maintained by persons who classify themselves as white, whether consciously or subconsciously determined; this system consists of patterns of perception, logic, symbol formation, thought, speech, action and emotional response. (Welsing, 1991, p. ii)

Conversations about race inevitably bring to the surface patterns of perception, thought, emotion, and action that Cress Welsing points toward. Race oppression separates individuals from their bodies; this separation is the crux of oppression, according to social activist, bell hooks (Ensler & hooks, 2014).[4]

An important idea in my exploration of race is the idea of finding your voice. Finding your voice within a race conversation is an essential antidote to the construct of race itself, which silences and perpetuates negative conscious and unconscious patterns within us and between us. Finding your voice might initially present as a purely mental activity, but it is also about nonverbal body-to-body communication and nonverbal body-to-mind communication.

Communication between body and mind, what might be called embodied cognition, is where the body influences thoughts as well as where thoughts influence the body. Within the social construct of race, power and oppression act first on the body and then are communicated, unconsciously and nonverbally, body-to-body. Stories and narratives are then played out in the mind that either feed the continued embodiment of oppression or provide a platform for healing the body. This book is an attempt at a coherent narrative for these processes. I want to support individuals to reorganize, repattern, and reexperience their body's responses to race oppression so that they can find their voice.

An important idea in all of this is the concept of black bodies and white bodies and what Carla Sherrell calls "the demand to simulate white bodies" (Sherrell, 2018, p. 146). Sherrell brings our attention to an essential element of the race construct when she says, "If I am allowed in white spaces, I must communicate in white styles on white terms. I must simulate white bodies and not explicitly communicate that I'm doing so. . . . I am reminded every day that my livelihood, and indeed my life, may depend on simulating well" (Sherrell, 2018, p. 148).

What Sherrell is communicating here is that there is systematic pressure on the black body to simulate white bodies and that this pressure is embedded in white institutions. This pressure is also there to remove control from black bodies. Sherrell further goes on to say, "When I have studied and engaged in experimental learning exercises associated with embodiment, I have run headlong and body long into the violence and violation of racism and white supremacy on and in my Black [*sic*] body" (Sherrell, 2018, p. 149).

If you are of the view that we are in a post-racist society, then how possible is it to meet what arises in the black and brown body? How safe is it for black and brown bodies to truly embody their experience in white spaces if they are assumed, encouraged, or required to be like white bodies? There is a process of internal decolonization here that needs to happen on many levels: historical, psychological, cognitive, and also in the body. I want to explore the ways we might support ourselves to become more internally flexible within the race conversation, which can then allow change to take place.

I will put forward ideas from the field of mindfulness, which talks directly of the body–mind connection. I will also be exploring other ways that might support us to become more internally flexible within the race conversation. The race conversation is far from being unknowable and confusing and is, in fact, a very predictable landscape. In the chapters that follow, I explore why the race conversation is so activating as well as what happens in our minds and, particularly, our bodies when issues of race are on the table. By exploring the race conversation through the lens of intergenerational trauma and the body, I employ ideas from neuroscience and psychology. These ideas, for me, offer opportunities for challenging our patterns and bringing some measure of change. For me, change is about listening, awareness, sensitivity, and healing.

"For me, change is about listening, awareness, sensitivity, and healing."

I will not be telling people what could-or-should be done or what could-or-should be said in response to any particular race conversation that feels uncomfortable or confusing. Instead, I will be attempting to articulate what drives the experiences people have in the race conversation and to present a frame of reference that is partly about the mind but mostly in the body. This frame of reference will include historical and present moment facts, along with the use of the imagination and listening to personal stories that bring these facts to life. The invitation is to stay in listening mode, not just in the mind but also in the body, and to witness the wounds of racism. When there is a witnessing and a compassionate *staying with* the wounds of race, there is no need to ask what to do or what to say, as it will be obvious. What you do and say will simply be what you would do or say with any other human being in distress. Just the act of staying with the distress in a particular way is life-changing. If enough of us do this, perhaps it will be world-changing.

A DANCE PARTNER DESIGNED TO TRIP US UP

Jay Smooth is the host of New York's longest running hip-hop radio show, the Underground Railroad, and a commentator on politics and culture. In a talk he entitled "How I Learned to Stop Worrying and Love Discussing Race," he examines the sometimes thorny territory of how we discuss issues of race and racism. In his TEDx Talk (2011), Smooth offers us some insightful suggestions for expanding our perception of the subject.[5] He says:

> We are dealing with a social construct that was not designed to make sense. To the extent that it is the product of design, the race constructs that we live by were shaped specifically by a desire to avoid making sense. They were shaped for centuries by a need to rationalize and justify indefensible acts. So, when we grapple with race issues, we are grappling with something that was designed for centuries to make us circumvent our best instincts. It's a dance partner that is designed to trip us up. (TEDx, 2011, 6:15)

I think the description of race being a dance partner designed to trip us up is very apt. Making mistakes and feeling bad about it are part of the territory. The idea that this tripping up is by design allows us to let ourselves off the hook a little. We can know that if we do trip up, it's as much about the nature of the territory as it is about our competence.

Another point that Smooth makes, which is also an important one to make at this point, is how easily feeling bad equates to being a racist. The two don't necessarily go together. This is how Smooth (TEDx, 2011) puts it:

> You want to tell someone that they have said something racist and has had an impact on someone that they were not aware of. It's a conversation we sometimes have and a conversation that usually goes horribly wrong, because no matter how clear you are about your intention to not attack the person but offering a critique of what they just said, the recipient of the critique tends to deeply personalize it and take it as a personal attack. "Are you saying I am a racist? I'm a good person." They try to talk about the specific thing, and the conversation comes back to "I am not a racist." What started out as a "what you said" conversation turned into a "what you are" conversation or "what I am" conversation, which is a dead end. (TEDx, 2011, 1:40)

The race conversation is hard work. The success rate seems to be about ten percent, according to Smooth's (2011) reckoning. The invitation from Smooth is this: if you have received a critique that you might have done or said something racist, don't freak out. Take it in your stride and do not assume that the whole world thinks you're a bad person.

THE LANGUAGE OF RACE

The first thing we need to navigate in the race construct is language. The language of race has several faces. On one face is a need to respect the power of language and to be mindful of the language we use because of the personal and collective history of hurts that it can evoke. The adage "sticks and stones may break my bones, but words will never hurt me" can be useful, in principle, as something to tell children as a playground survival strategy. In the race conversation, however, as we all know, this adage does not hold so true.

Another face of language is the tendency to either cling to certain words and claim them as our own or assign them no value or relevance at all. For instance, the word "black" can elicit a sense of pride that can become overly central to a person's identity. Black can also be dismissed as invalid in an attempt to somehow escape or transcend the boundaries of race. Both ends of this continuum move us away from the hurt.

The third face of language is a tendency to want to deconstruct the words in an attempt to get a definitive handle on the problem. Here, the cognitive mind tries hard to work it out logically when, in fact, the confusing nature of the words is another aspect of the dance-partner-designed-to-trip-us-up. The drilling down into the meaning of words in an attempt to get to the kernel of truth keeps us stuck and generally moves us away from where we need to be going. The image I have in my mind is of holding a small bird in the cup of your hands. You need to hold the bird lightly but not so lightly that it flies away. At the same time, you don't want to hold on to the bird so tightly that you restrict movement and cause suffering.

Throughout this book, I will be using the words *black* and *white*. Even if you do not identify with these terms, you understand their meaning in an instant. These terms relate to important concepts of whiteness and blackness, which I will explore more fully later, that fundamentally shape racial discourse. I have no particular attachments to these terms or to any of the other names that apply to people's skin color beyond their ease of understanding. There is also the issue of whether to capitalize these terms or not: Black or black, White or white. The case for capitalizing black is to symbolize its importance in black people's lives and to assert black power. By contrast, white supremacists might capitalize white to signify their importance over black people. I will be using lowercase for black and white throughout the book in order to both speak into the experience of race and at the same time be reminded that black and white are social constructs. I want to bring some sense of hope for a future wherein the importance of these constructs diminishes. Where I have quoted someone else's work, I keep the source's choice of capitalization style.

I will also be using the term "brown" to represent a particular type of experience of racism. Those who consider themselves brown would typically be from south Asian countries such as Pakistan, India, and Sri Lanka or the Middle East.

"People of color" is another term I will be using to define anyone of any race who isn't white. It is a term that acknowledges how racism and white supremacy affect people of color all over the world and recognizes their collective experiences. It should be understood, though, that using the term "person of color" for those who could also be seen as black could be conveying a message of toning down their blackness—being "less black"—and could be interpreted as a concession to the need to be "more white" to be more acceptable. The term "BIPOC" (Black, Indigenous, and People of Color) is another term in use that originated in the U.S. and Canada. The placement of the word *black* at the beginning of BIPOC highlights the operation of color banding in the race construct where the darker you are, the less likely you are to be able to insulate yourself from racism. It is also meant to acknowledge and begin to undo Native peoples' invisibility.

I am going to use the term "mixed race" to describe people who sit between two or more racial identities simultaneously and those who are trying to carve out a space to exist between them. This term appears to be the most popular term used by young people in the U.K. whose parents are of different racial backgrounds, usually some mixture of black or brown and white.[6] The mixed-race diaspora extends far beyond this definition, however, and includes one of the child's parents coming from a mixed heritage themselves. Other terms that individuals might use to identify themselves include "biracial," "multiracial," "dual heritage," and "multi heritage."

Lastly, I will be using the term "nonwhite" if I am referring to its use in someone else's work. It should be noted however, that the term "nonwhite" nods toward the idea of lacking something wholesome that white signifies.

THE GENETICS AND RACE QUESTION

Attempts to divide human characteristics and assign them based on race have been going on for centuries, and the searching hasn't ended.

So, where has the genetics and race question gotten to? How diverse is the human gene pool? And is it diverse enough to merit biological classification beyond merely "human"?

Recently I came across a radio science and comedy program called *The Infinite Monkey Cage*[7] (this title has no racist connotation, I promise). The title of this particular episode was "What is Race?" The program's focus was on whether our genes reveal racial differences. The presenters started by saying that this was a comedy show and they wanted to write material that wasn't racist. They could then only come up with jokes about Norwegians and Scandinavians and confessed that it was like walking on eggshells. They were also expecting a large sack of mail after the program aired that would challenge them on the show's content, particularly as they don't link genes and race. They also expected the comments to highlight that whatever they had to say would be typical of what liberals think.

Concerning what genes reveal about racial differences, the presenters noted that physical differences were the worst measure imaginable for how related we are biologically. For instance, people from the Melanesia region and people from Central Africa have the same skin color, but you couldn't find two more genetically different groups in the world.

The presenters did a good job of articulating the genetics and race question but then sidestepped the hurt inflicted in the name of race. The time of colonialism they described as "a transient phase in our history when identity did line up with a perceived notion of race" (*The Infinite Monkey Cage*, 2016, 40:48) was also accompanied by the idea that people just *met each* other. This description of that moment of meeting belies the terror and suffering in that coming together. Also, the noted "transient moment in our history," where physical and mental characteristics were equated with race, is still very much with us in some quarters. The presenters of the program were unquestionably

"According to science, there are no genes or gene clusters which are common to all those who might be identified as being of a separate race. It's true, then, to say that race has no biological element."

anxious about awakening the wrath of the far right. We are reminded, then, that despite indisputable evidence, even the genetics and race question is not dead and buried.

According to science, there are no genes or gene clusters that are common to all those who might be identified as being of a particular race. It's true, then, to say that race has no biological element. There is a problem with this statement, however, as race clearly exists. For some, race needs to continue to exist as a social construct to bring some sort of order to their lives. Ta-Nehisi Coates, a journalist and social commentator, aptly notes, "Race does not need biology. Race only requires some good guys with big guns looking for a reason" (Coates, 2013, para. 24).[8]

SHARED JOURNEYS

As we go through the journey of examining the race construct, we need to stay tethered to some kind of reality and truth. Truth does not reside in one single place or position, but we do need a set of organizing principles to keep us grounded and connected. The organizing principle that I will be using is neuroscience's understanding of the body and the nervous system as a result of human-inflicted traumas.

Enquiring into race demands we tolerate a certain measure of bodily discomfort. This discomfort cannot be easily avoided, even though that is our overwhelmingly preferred route. If we are to go beyond a shallow understanding of race and remain connected with what is important, we will need strategies for managing discomfort. In my experiences working with race trauma, what seems to be most important is keeping connected to the hurt that race inflicts on people of color, predominately, but also on white people. I am referring to hurt transmitted over generations that continues to be inflicted in the present. It is this focus within the race conversation that I believe will bring about healing and change.

To support this journey with you, it's important that you have a sense of who I am and what makes me tick. What are my beliefs and sensibilities? What are my experiences, and where am I coming from?

What you make of my life and my experiences is essential to how this conversation is going to play out. From my experience, when it comes to going on this type of journey together, who I am is just as important as what I have to say. You need to get a sense of whether you will be in safe hands—or not. My journey is also a shared journey with others. I encourage you to share this journey with others, too, as exploring race is not something you can do very easily on your own.

Some time ago, I read Ben Okri's book, *A Way of Being Free*. I remember being blown away by what he had to say about the power of story in our lives, embracing cultural differences and evoking a new political language. Okri's writing initiated me into a way of being that was both hopeful in its outlook and at the same time grounded in the reality of the world as it is. He writes, "It is easy to forget how mysterious and mighty stories are. They do their work in silence, invisibly . . . beware the stories you read or tell; subtly, at night, beneath the waters of consciousness, they are altering our world" (Okri, 1998, p. 120).

The story that I want to tell is about the possibility of transcending aspects of the race construct while having the race conversation and, in doing so, finding a measure of liberating freedom. Coming back to who I am, I'm going to give a brief account of the experiences in my life that have shaped how I relate to the race construct and how I feel less confused within it.

When I was growing up, I felt very strongly that people didn't know what to do with me. I was quiet and introverted and didn't have the kinds of interests that other people around me seemed to have. I don't know whether the place I found myself in allowed me to develop my love of ideas or whether that was something that was naturally there, but I became fascinated by how people worked and what motivated them to do the things they did. I was very interested in the human condition, mainly through science fiction and philosophy. These were the things that I spent a lot of time on.

When I was growing up, I also felt fear much of the time and a kind of unease. As a young man, I experienced myself as not fitting in. I disengaged from the relationships in my life and focused on my work, which was recording music. I started my working life in the early 1980s as something called a tape operator in a studio owned by the recording artist Pink Floyd. I worked alongside the sound engineers who were recording and mixing many of Britain's pop and rock artists. I was there 24/7, and would basically watch other people living their lives.

After a time, I got involved with what was called the British soul explosion of the late 1980s and early 1990s, in particular with a band called Soul II Soul, and I became their chief engineer. Their motto was "a happy face, a thumping bass, for a loving race." At its core, Soul II Soul was a group of young black men. Their songs pointed toward personal growth and betterment as well as a positive state of mind and a vision of hope. One of their early signature tracks was called "Feeling Free."[9] The lyrics spoke to me:

> *Well, feeling free, release your inhibitions*
> *Go forth, achieve your ambitions*
>
> HOOPER & ROMEO, 1989

I was there alongside Soul II Soul at the time of their first U.K. number one hit and their triple-platinum first album. The Soul II Soul collective, as it was called, had made it. I felt the power of the collective and was inspired and energized by everything that was going on around me. Lodged in my mind and my being was the possibility of a black-owned business that could transcend expectations and at the same time keep a strong sense of its identity.

Somewhere along the line, after many years in the music business, something shifted inside me. I couldn't give voice to this shift, but it brought about a decision in me to be more active with my mental health rather than let it drift. A story I remember that aided this shift is of sitting in a studio in my early thirties watching a sound engineer in his late fifties going through the motions. He lit one cigarette after another in a chain-smoking frenzy as he stared into space. To me, it felt as if he was going through some unconscious ritual of self-preservation. That image, of the slow burning away of life energy, was a metaphor for my life up until that point. My body also gave me a sign that something was wrong. I developed back pain from both the stress of relentless sound engineering and the feeling of being trapped inside my race conditioning. I would not, however, have put my experience in those terms at that time.

I took some time out of the studio life off, and this was where I felt my life began, in terms of being a conscious participant in it. I started to attend self-development groups, encountering all kinds of people from all walks of life along the way. Like me, they were on a journey to have more influence over their own lives. I went through a transformative process and, through that process, I became aware that I was living in a world of competing stories that kept me stuck. The story that everyone is the same was running alongside the story that our racial identities make us different from each other. The story that we can self-construct our own identities was running alongside the story that our identity is thrust upon us—willing participants or not. I also experienced first hand that even though white people embody conscious and unconscious race privileges, it doesn't necessarily mean that they are free from pain and suffering.

I also began a journey of personal psychotherapy. I did this because I wanted a loving relationship, a soulmate and partner. I also wanted to raise children, and I needed to feel confident that I could do that with emotional positivity. I wanted to break what felt like a repeating cycle of trauma that I could see happening inside me. My parents came to England from the Caribbean, bringing the brutal history of racism in their wake. They were saddled with emotions that no one seemed interested in listening to and that they themselves struggled to contain. They tried to make a life in the U.K. while being burdened with this history, and they struggled. Through my explorations, I began to see how painful and detrimental historical racism was to them and the impact that this had on us, their children. The childhood feelings I had of the adults not knowing what to do with me finally made sense. In wanting to understand who I was in relation to the history of unspoken emotions that my parents had inherited, I came to a place of real understanding and respect for them as people and as parents.

The life I have now would not have been possible without that internal journey, without journeying through these issues with myself and with others. There have been aspects of the journey that have been very painful, but I have since come to realize that pain is part of the human condition. We can try to avoid the pain, which I had attempted to do for some time, or hold on to it for dear life. Alternatively, we can attend to the pain with compassion for ourselves and others. The other side of suffering can then reveal itself; that is where we become more alive. My journey through therapy led me to make better choices, feel more in control, feel my power, and become more in touch with my creative self. I also became more consciously aware that there is deep-rooted suffering in having dark skin, which society negatively projects upon. As I went deeper into my experience, I really inhabited the pain of the toxic gaze that I received from the world.

I also found out that there was much to reconcile within the race construct. I had to reconcile that for white people, acknowledging and responding to the hurt of race is a monumental task. I had to reconcile that white people have a choice to engage or not engage with race and that people of color don't have that choice. People of color have to engage, even if that engagement is denial. I had to reconcile that the race construct, by design, is there to dial down empathy toward people of color and that the darker you are, the more empathy is dialed down. I had to reconcile that the race construct has an array of universal stories that can be picked from its shelves and that these stories aid the dampening of empathy. These stories include: "We are all the same, aren't we?" and "You have the same rights as everyone else, so I don't get why you feel so aggrieved" and "You need to integrate more" and "You need to be less angry." I also had to reconcile that the race construct has very few universal stories that dial *up* empathy for people of color or that speak to the potential for healing.

As part of integrating my healing and supporting others to do the same, I trained as an integrative arts psychotherapist. This training led me to work with adoptive families. The children in the adoptive families I worked with had been severely traumatized within their families of birth and then placed for adoption after spending some time in the British care system. I was working with the impact of what is called *developmental trauma*. Developmental trauma evolves from recurring stress that impacts infants while in the womb and during the early months after birth, while their nervous systems and brains are still in the process of developing and adapting to their environment. I was using what is termed a trauma-informed approach to support not just the child but also the people supporting the child, including the adoptive parents and the wider network. My experience of working with these adoptive families, where the child has experienced developmental trauma or what could be called relational trauma, relates directly to what I am proposing within this book around race trauma.

I will depart from my personal story for a moment to say a little about this trauma-informed approach, and then make links with how this relates to having the race conversation. A trauma-informed approach to working with adoptive families and their children with developmental trauma is typified in a book entitled *Beyond Consequences, Logic, and Control* by Heather Forbes and Bryan Post.[10] Forbes and Post (2014) proposed a new model of supporting children with trauma and their adoptive or foster families. This approach moved away from what might be called "normal parenting," which was not working for a significant number of these families.

Forbes and Post see normal parenting as a series of imposed consequences following poor behavior that would help the child to make better behavioral choices next time. They also see normal parenting as laying out for the child the cause-and-effect logic of their poor behavior. Cause-and-effect explanations are given to children in an effort to support their cognitive understanding of how their behavior has impacted on others. Normal parenting, then, is about imposed consequences, parental control, and logical explanations given to the child about the consequences of their mistakes. After dealing with the child's poor choice of behavior, there can then be the possibility of making up and being relaxed with each other again. However, in children with developmental trauma, it is very common to find a compulsion to turn toward aggression as a means of managing relationships.

This is especially so for children whose early caregivers were both scared and scary, which then formed a template for what to expect in relationships.

The reason for using a new parenting approach with children with developmental trauma is that these children are very susceptible to feeling high levels of danger within a normal parenting model. This susceptibility to feeling danger can have severe consequences on the adoptive parent's ability to sustain empathy and compassion toward the child. This sense of danger can also breed a kind of toxic shame in both the caregivers and the child, which then disables logical thinking, making the normal parenting model ineffective. Forbes and Post's new trauma-informed approach puts the carer's ability to be calm (called *internal regulation*) and the carer's relationship with the child first. Consequences and logic come afterward, when the child's internal regulation is established and clear thinking is once again possible.

Relationship disruptions caused by trauma within the field of adoption that leave both the parent and the child frustrated translate directly into the race conversation experience. What is typical in both an adoptive family with a child with developmental trauma and the experience within the race conversation is threefold: First, the symptoms of trauma become the focus, leaving historical hurts unacknowledged. Second, connection is difficult due to the sense of danger, which eclipses all other considerations. Third, it is incredibly challenging to stay with the experience of hurt, which lies behind a wall of anger and shame for both parties.

Continuing with my personal story: In 2006, I started a network for therapists with the primary aim of addressing the inequality of access to appropriate psychological services for black, African, Asian, and Caribbean people. The network, called the Black, African, and Asian Therapy Network (BAATN) continues today. I was initially motivated to create BAATN out of self-interest. I wanted to commune with other therapists of color and to feel more connected with people like me because I imagined it would bring me into a closer relationship with myself. I wanted to shake off the anxieties I felt about being that rare combination of black, male, and a psychotherapist. My initial motivations for the network were most definitely met and continue to be met. As the network grew, however, I began to feel the weight of the task we were trying to undertake. Beyond serving my personal needs, BAATN came to be about living and practicing psychotherapy in a society that is deeply damaged by the legacy of racism. For BAATN, this means bringing our collective intergenerational wound to the attention of those involved with mental health, highlighting the impact of the race construct on our lives and communicating ways to address our healing.

In the U.K., efforts have been made to make mental health services accessible to more people of color, but to date, this has not been very successful. From the many forums I have attended that address race issues and mental health, I have come to believe that it is the internal discomfort of mental health professionals, as well as their profound feelings of not feeling safe talking about race, that is the problem. This discomfort and feeling unsafe is then picked up on in a heartbeat by people of color. With mental health practitioners experiencing race in this way, it is easy to understand why people of color would stay away, with the consequence being that they do not get the safe emotional support they need. Beyond the world of mental health, this internal sense of not feeling safe creates interpersonal and institutional environments of fear, objectification, and defensiveness, along with the metaphorical elastic band of tolerance being stretched that bit too far.

The creation of spaces where therapeutic practitioners as well as those commissioning their services could develop some measure of internal felt safety would enable them to stay empathic to the victims of racism. Internal felt safety is essential for healing and breaking the "circles of fear."[11] These circles of fear cause people of color to wait until their mental health condition is so acute that the only options available are medication or admission into a psychiatric ward.

For many of its members, BAATN is an island within a sea of others' discomfort. This separation is sometimes framed in people's minds as part of the separation that the race construct pushes us into, but this is not the frame in which BAATN operates. BAATN members come together, not to separate, but to heal themselves. That healing enables them to become as much of their ideal as their ability and passion allow and go on to heal others. BAATN came into being because the profession that claims to meet distress in all its forms cannot meet distress when that distress is around race.

› 2 ‹

TOWARD A TRAUMA-INFORMED UNDERSTANDING OF RACE

Our Quest for Safety

Being Trauma Informed

The Nonverbal

Safety and Danger (The Polyvagal Theory)

OUR QUEST FOR SAFETY

For many people of color, there is a specific hurt that adds to the hurts accumulated by personal family experiences and from the stresses of everyday life. This hurt has to do with living lives that are highly influenced by the race construct. For healing to take place, this aspect needs to be addressed and witnessed for what it is. Once our hurt is witnessed, addressed, and worked through, we can experience liberation. This liberation can carry us beyond the constraints that race places on us, even if the race construct is ever present and continues to put up unjust barriers.

I want to focus on three questions about the race conversation in this and subsequent chapters. What prevents the hurt of racism from being addressed? What impedes the race conversation from being a fruitful experience? And what might prevent us from being retraumatized by it?

"The psychological pain of racism is complex. We are all part of it, willing participants or not, and our part in it is the bit that's hard to work through."

I am a psychotherapist, and along with other practitioners in this field, I meet people in their pain, and in this meeting, something happens that transforms it. There are plenty of techniques to get closer to the hurt but not so close that people feel overwhelmed. Therapists know that to stay with distress, we also need to work on the parts of ourselves that want to close down. There are parts of us that want to move away from the pain through deflection, denial, silence, rage, or boredom.

The psychological pain of racism is complex. We are all part of it, willing participants or not, and our part in it is the bit that's hard to work through. Race conversations make us feel unsafe because who we are as individuals is also part of the conversation. The race conversation challenges seem to focus around the questions: "Can I be a good person with good intentions and still be part of the system of oppression?" and "Is it possible to create safe spaces in which the race conversation can happen?" These questions, as you may have noticed, take us away from the hurt of racism and into our beliefs about ourselves as people of good and honorable intentions. We are also brought into an un-nameable sense of our bodies being under threat.

In an article I wrote for the journal *Therapy Today* entitled "Silenced: The Black Student Experience,"[1] I detailed a conversation between myself and Niki Cooper, who is a white therapy practitioner. At that time, Niki was a therapy training course leader and, among other things, the article discussed the training space she offered to her students. Niki describes her painful journey toward recognizing the impact that the race construct had on her and her three black students and on their relationships.

> EUGENE: What tends to happen with black trainees is that they enter into the spirit of inquiry that is encouraged on any counseling or psychotherapy training course, but when they do so in the area of their culture and their race, there is all this silence and it's like you've just opened a huge hole in the floor. Somehow it becomes your fault. You can then choose either to say nothing, because it's too painful, and focus on just getting your qualification, or you insist that your voice is heard, get labeled as the troublemaker, and risk not making it to the end because you're worn out by the fighting.
>
> It's so sad to see this happen and I have heard this from so many black and Asian students. It all goes on under the surface. Just naming what's going on becomes almost impossible and everyone gets defensive and blaming. It's normally the student of color who gets the rougher end of things because that's how oppression works . . .
>
> NIKI: What was painful was realizing that they [the three black students] hadn't been able to say anything. The students had all been invited to work in groups to do a sculpt of their experience of the training. These three women had ended up together, apparently serendipitously, and they made a sculpt of "Hear no evil, speak no evil, see no evil." I don't know how to describe it . . . even thinking about it now gives me goose

> pimples. The whole room completely froze. Kelli, my cotutor, as another woman of color, was the only person who was able to name what had happened. She reflected the painfulness of the image and the importance of the moment for those students. She was the person who, in that instant, enabled the students to feel heard and understood. I was, very uncharacteristically, struck dumb. It was a real turning point for the group and for us as tutors . . .
>
> Up until that point I felt the participants were choosing not to speak. With their sculpt, the students had articulated that their silence wasn't something they had chosen necessarily. It swivelled the lens round to point at us, and made me think "Maybe there is something about this course that is silencing and having a silencing impact," and that was very troubling; that was horrible and shocking, but it also represented a turning point for me personally because I could have those conversations and they were probably not as difficult as before. (Ellis & Cooper, 2013, pp. 14–19)

What Niki is describing here is a very important moment that many people of color would recognize. It's that moment when everything freezes. It's like so many other kinds of trauma where people become triggered, frozen, and then preoccupied by their side of the story. What Niki was pointing toward when she imagined the participants had chosen not to speak was the perpetrator side of the race construct. She noticed that there was some active agent in the room that created the conditions for silence and that this active agent was her whiteness and the other students' whiteness. Niki was shocked and horrified by what she noticed. I know that Niki felt a great deal of discomfort, but this incident also led her on to a journey to explore her whiteness and its impacts on blackness.

For the black students, I imagine that they were preoccupied with the victim side of the racism story. The victim side of the story is often backed up by personal experience, even if just on the microaggression scale, over many years. When a white person says all the right things and clearly thinks they believe them but has not recognized or seen their part in what's happening, people of color are left with the option of either colluding with that denial, which is a painful act in itself, or challenging the denial and risking being more of a victim than they already feel. It's not a great place to be, to feel silenced by that denial and also silenced by the denial inside yourself. So how can we organize and make sense of that moment of freezing, of not knowing what to do or say and being, to use Niki's words, struck dumb? For me, I couldn't put these experiences into words until I came into contact with new concepts that helped me to organize the landscape of race and make sense of it.

There is something important about trauma and how it impacts us in the race conversation that we really need to pay attention to. That moment of being frozen is very characteristic of the body's preparation for danger and its desperate search for a way back to safety. Scientist and author Stephen Porges talks about humans as being on a "quest for safety" that overrides every other consideration (Porges, 2015).

In the rest of this section and the next, I will introduce important ideas within the field of neuroscience that help our understanding of how the brain and the nervous system work and how experiences of extreme discomfort in having the race conversation come about. I will also be unpacking the various aspects of the race construct, including the two socially constructed realities of blackness and whiteness along with the mixed-race experience, both historically and how they play out in the current context of our lives. The various aspects of the race construct will then be summarized into a concluding definition before exploring how the race construct came about and the reasons for racism's lingering effects.

BEING TRAUMA INFORMED

The brutality of historic racism and its legacy on its victims and its witnesses bring us to the world of intergenerational trauma. Our first response to even the idea of the race conversation sets the frame within which the conversation plays out. Our first response also dictates whether there is a moment of connection or of disconnection along with further retraumatizing. To help us navigate the race conversation, we will need to have in our minds a familiarity with some basic concepts regarding the functioning of the nervous system. In essence, we will need to be what could be called "trauma informed."

When the word *trauma* is used, we think we have a reasonably good idea of what it is. For most of us, however, our understanding of trauma is quite limited. We might think of traumatic experiences as being physical abuse, sexual abuse, extreme neglect, or torture. These types of events are, without a doubt, traumatic, but trauma is not limited to just types of experiences. Trauma also results from any stressful event that is prolonged, overwhelming, or unpredictable.

The field of trauma differentiates between two types of trauma: The first is single event traumas. We hear about people being attacked, being in car accidents, coming back from a war zone. We can see that they're traumatized; they're perhaps more quiet than usual, they seem preoccupied, more shutdown. They don't want to talk about what happened. If they do, it seems to bring back the traumatic incident in their minds and makes it feel like it's happening all over again. If they were in a car accident, they are not too keen to get back in the driving seat. They might insist on staying inside their homes if they were attacked in their neighborhood. They overreact in situations that, to others, seem trivial.

"Trauma is actually any stressful event which is prolonged, overwhelming, or unpredictable."

People generally don't know what to do to help someone who is in this state. The person who experienced the trauma seems to communicate that they don't want help anyway, to leave them be. But if you care for them, you feel that you can't just leave them alone. They seem like they are suffering, and the suffering is painful to witness. There are effective therapy treatments for this type of trauma. And with traumas that were not too impactful, people may find that over time, the trauma symptoms fade. They may also avoid situations similar to the traumatic event and go on with their life that way.

The impact of trauma begins to get more confusing and more complicated, even for clinicians who treat trauma, with what is called *relational trauma.* Relational trauma occurs when an individual's trauma was caused not by an accident in a car or from being trapped in a cave but by people who have or had primary roles in their lives. By far the most challenging type of trauma to integrate and make sense of is relational trauma from infancy and childhood, which can have a lifelong impact on future relationships.

As noted earlier, I have worked for many years with adoptive families in which the child experienced severe trauma within their family of birth before being placed with an adoptive family. I have become increasingly aware that the emotional and behavioral characteristics of children with severe trauma and their new families are very similar to the emotional and behavioral characteristics of those who enter into the race conversation. I want now to outline this similarity to give further context to the concepts I will define in future chapters.

Humans are hardwired at birth to form relationships with important caregivers. If these caregivers are actually a threat or a perceived threat to our safety and we are unresourced to foster a sense of safety, then the sense of being in danger becomes hardwired. Children then direct themselves toward not making connections with others, not exploring the world with curiosity and ease, and not even connecting with themselves.

The ongoing experience of not feeling safe has been shown to literally rewire children's brains and nervous systems. The nervous systems of children with early chronic relational traumas are different from other children's brains in that they are wired in such a way that the children cannot easily regulate their emotional experiences. When children grow up with enough safety, they naturally turn to others when they have feelings that are hard to handle. There is something about turning toward others and being attended to that soothes us and brings us back to feeling okay again. Children with early relational traumas develop defensive impulses that turn them away from others as a source of support. They are then on their own to manage the often overwhelming ups and downs of their emotional lives. For these children, sadness can quickly turn into despair, anger into rage, joy into delirium, and fear into terror. Many of the children I have worked with would like nothing more than to escape their wired impulses. For them, however, the link between thought and the body has been compromised. It's as if the body has a mind of its own.

Caregivers, who are witnesses to their adopted child's struggles, begin to develop an emotional life similar to that of the child. The caregivers begin to develop easily triggered fight, flight, or freeze responses. They experience difficulty sustaining empathy for the child and behave in ways that they later feel ashamed about. Those outside the family, who observe the goings on between the child and adoptive parent, find it difficult to understand how the child can manage perfectly well in some social situations but completely unravel in others. For these witnesses, blame is close at hand. They blame the new carers, judging that they should be able to get a grip on this unruly child. They blame those who are meant to handle the situation, like the social workers, for not doing the right thing at the right time. They also blame the child, whom they judge to no longer be living in a threatening environment and, given that the child has been living in a good home with good people for years, that they should have gotten over their trauma by now.

"When you really understand the causes and the legacy of trauma, you can begin to open up the possibility of taking a less defensive stance."

You might be starting to see the parallels between the adoptive family situation and the race conversation. Trauma symptoms are rampant throughout the system; there is blame, shame, and dialed-down empathy and compassion. There is also the parallel with intergenerational trauma between the adoptive situation and race, as relational trauma moves from one generation to the next in both cases. The adoptive families I have just outlined represent extreme cases, but they highlight the dynamics of all types of relational trauma, including what may be seen as less intense experiences. When you really understand the causes and the legacy of trauma, you can begin to open up the possibility of taking a less defensive stance, which offers more potential for engagement and corrective experiences.

The race construct carries within it the shadow of dehumanizing, traumatizing, and brutal acts inflicted on both victims and witnesses. From birth, both people of color and white people have had their expectations and assumptions about themselves and others influenced and shaped by the race construct, both inside and outside of the home. For many communities, there is also the transmission of unresolved trauma, passed on from one generation to another. This generational transmission of racial trauma within families needs far more attention than it receives and holds an important key for understanding the challenges of the race conversation. What I am proposing is that the difficulties in the race conversation are a direct result of relational trauma in the past that has been passed on intergenerationally and then triggered in the present.

Coming back to the idea of taking a trauma-informed approach, Porges's idea that humans are on a quest for safety (Porges, 2015)[2] that overrides every other consideration is an important one. What, then, does feeling safe actually mean? As a society, we are encouraged to believe that we are in control of all our behaviors and in control of how we respond. There is a vast disconnect between our social and cultural definitions about what should be deemed safe and how our nervous systems and our bodies actually react in real life. It's common to think that the absence of danger naturally brings with it safety. Politicians promise to remove dangerous elements in society to make us feel safe, but you don't have to look too deeply to discover that removing danger doesn't necessarily bring about the kind of safety that we would all like to see. Some people are scared of spiders. By any logical, social, or cultural measure, these individuals are safe, but that isn't how they feel inside their bodies. Some bodies just feel unsafe and don't appear to have any reason for being so. Being trauma informed means reframing the

"There is a vast disconnect between our social and cultural definitions about what should be deemed safe and how our nervous systems and our bodies actually react in real life."

idea of safety very differently from how we usually frame it. Two concepts that will help us to do this are the concepts of implicit memory and neuroception. Although you don't need to have an in-depth knowledge of what these are, it is important to have a sense that they are operating, especially given that most people's experience of the race conversation is one of feeling unsafe.

THE NONVERBAL

Implicit Memory

We will now look at the ideas of implicit memory and neuroception to further explore what it really means to feel safe. In neuroscience, it is well known that two memory systems exist, each with a different function. One system deals with explicit memory and the other with what is called implicit memory. Explicit memory can be retrieved consciously and can be verbalized. It contains memories of specific events that can be recalled and spoken about, which allows someone to give meaning to their experience. Explicit memory also allows, through remembering, the reconstruction of a coherent personal history.

Implicit memories, by contrast, are memories that are unconscious; they can't be brought to mind or verbalized because of the way that they are encoded in the brain. The way implicit memory works is that people "remember" on a subliminal level, which primes their future choices. Implicit memory is also how skills, habits, and automatic behaviors are stored. These implicitly stored behaviors are, however, disassociated from content and context. Often, we don't recognize the extent to which past experiences have steered our conscious judgments. These influences are where biases and stereotypes come in: as unconscious and unremembered associations create our conscious values and beliefs. Implicit memory was popularized in the late 1980s by Professor Dan Schacter of Harvard University (Schacter & Graf, 1986).

A book entitled *Blind Spot: Hidden Biases of Good People*, by Dr.

Mahzarin Banaji and Dr. Anthony Greenwald, explored some of these biases (Banaji & Greenwald, 2013). We all carry with us a lifetime of experiences with various social groups that might be considered targets of oppression, like gender, race, or social class. Banaji and Greenwald wanted to explore these oppressions in relation to the many people who were striving to align their behavior with their good intentions, hence the words "good people" in the book's title. The book references something called an Implicit Association Test. The authors, in association with another colleague, Brian Nosek, created a test that measures biases individuals are not aware of having.

One of these tests, developed in 1995, is called the Race Test.[3] The Race Test is a two-part test that involves responding to a series of words and faces that appear on a computer screen. The words are either pleasant or unpleasant, and the faces are faces of black or white people. In the first part of the test, you are asked to press one key when presented with either a white face or a pleasant word, and another key when presented with a black face or an unpleasant word. In the second part of the test, you press one key when presented with either a white face or an unpleasant word, and another key when presented with either a black face or a pleasant word. The difference between the time it takes to respond to both parts is then a measure of preference.

If, like many people, you are faster when white faces are keyed with pleasant words, than when black faces are keyed with pleasant words, you have an automatic bias in favor of viewing white faces. Surprisingly, among black people in the U.S. there were an equal number of subjects who demonstrated a preference for white faces over black and subjects who demonstrated a preference for black faces over white.

I took the Race Test, and you can imagine my surprise when I was met at the end with "Your data suggest a moderate automatic preference for European American children, compared to African American children." In a way that result was not a big surprise. Given all the messages I have received about race since the day I was born, it makes sense that I would have these implicit biases within me.

The biases revealed by the Implicit Association Test often contradict what people would say if they were asked questions directly about their racial bias. What both black and white people honestly believed about themselves as well as their conscious preferences and values often differed from their implicit preferences. You might be thinking that people simply lied about their biases and were caught in that lie, but apparently this isn't the case. They were just not aware of the automatic associations that their implicit memories had made as a result of their lifetime of experiences. What these tests tell us is that the more blatant expressions of racism from yesteryear may have changed, but there hasn't been a significant change in implicit associations. For me, this doesn't necessarily constitute hostile race discrimination, but it does point toward how the race construct works—outside our awareness and despite our good intentions. All is not lost, however. Even though implicit biases are accompanied by a neural signature in the brain underlying the preference, implicit biases are malleable. They can gradually be unlearned and replaced with new mental associations (Staats, 2014).

So how does this relate to our sense of safety within the race conversation?

In our brains, we have a pair of almond-shaped structures collectively called the amygdala; there is one in each hemisphere. The amygdala is one of the key brain structures involved in evaluating fear, threat, and danger and in preparing our bodies to respond automatically for fight or flight. The amygdala is also involved in the organization of implicit memory. In the race conversation, our acquired implicit memories and racial biases can clash discordantly with our beliefs about ourselves as good, honest people with values of fairness, honesty, and integrity. This disconnect between our beliefs and values and our implicit biases causes the amygdala to trigger the threatened state in the rest of the body, and we quickly lose our sense of safety.

"This disconnect between our beliefs and values and our implicit biases causes the amygdala to trigger the threatened state in the rest of the body, and we quickly lose our sense of safety."

Neuroception

Let's now turn to the concept of neuroception. There's a bit to unpack here. Again, it's not necessary to know everything in detail, but it is useful to know that these processes are happening in the background. We have just looked at implicit memory, to the extent that within us there is unconscious historical information that reveals itself outside our awareness in the form of unconscious biases. These unconscious biases may directly conflict with our beliefs and values, and this conflict triggers the amygdala and the fight–flight–freeze response. Our felt sense of safety, however, is not just affected by our implicit biases. There is also another aspect that is more rooted in the present.

A crucial aspect of the nervous system's role is to quickly decide if another mammal is safe or dangerous to be around. Porges's research has brought to light a process he calls neuroception. Porges asserts that neuroception enables us to confront the world's current concept of safety. Ordinarily, people focus their attention on the removal of threat to create safety. As we know, however, this does not necessarily make us feel safe. Porges is instead interested in how to foster a sense of safety.[4]

We all have a sense of the word *perception*, where we take on board what is happening around us in a conscious way that we can later recall. Neuroception is similar to this but without awareness and without the ability to recall what happened. When two people are together in a conversation, there are two nervous systems with their own independent ebbs and flows. The concept of neuroception in neurobiology is the ability of our nervous systems to detect unintentional and unconscious behavioral cues of safety, danger, or threat to life in others and the environment without our having any awareness that this might be happening. Muscles of the face, especially around the eyes, the upper face, and the larynx, which affect our tone of voice, play major roles in this unconscious communication. We don't necessarily register consciously that we have, through neuroception, picked up a cue about another's internal state. Our physiology nevertheless changes, either relaxing because we have registered a cue of safety or preparing the body for danger.

How does all of this then relate to the race conversation? Consider this scenario: Someone with whom you are in a race conversation looks, on casual inspection, the same as they did before the conversation began, but internally, a lot could be going on. For instance, they might be caught between their implicit biases and values and be triggered into a state of fear through the amygdala. At the same time, through neuroception, you might have picked up the unconscious cue of danger. Your internal physiology has changed in response to the cue even though nothing noticeable has happened. Your body's physiology has shifted and, even though the reason for the shift may be outside your awareness, your brain still wants to make sense of it. What typically happens is that we disengage because the situation feels dangerous. Afterward, we put a cognitive narrative to the event to explain the experience. A narrative to describe the experience might be something like "I'll need to be clearer about what I'm saying next time so that we can avoid what happened." The internal narrative on the other side of the conversation might be something like, "They needed to be clearer about what they were saying because I'm confused."

"Neuroception gives us an understanding that there are spontaneous, nonverbal cues that our nervous system receives from other people's nervous systems."

Neuroception gives us an understanding that there are spontaneous, nonverbal cues that our nervous system receives from other people's nervous systems that are outside our awareness. These out of awareness signals inform us whether a person is safe to be with, and if they are not, inwardly prepares the nervous system for defense against potential danger. From an evolutionary point of view, this makes perfect sense: The last thing you want to do to successfully escape a perceived threat is to start thinking about it. Neuroception is much more efficient: Just act, and think about things later. Escaping from a dangerous predator is a rare event in ordinary modern life. What we are more likely to encounter are social threats, which could be something like a challenge to our identity or someone catching us in a lie. As far as the nervous system is concerned, social threats and the threat of actual physical danger are the same.

From a trauma-informed perspective, our task in the race conversation is to understand our stress response, understand our triggers from the past, and find ways to stay reflective and nondefensive. You cannot learn the nonverbal cues of danger or safety in an attempt to get around them. To send out the cues of safety, you need to be in the physiological state where these cues of safety are naturally there. This means experiencing the race conversation mental state and, at the same time, creating the conditions where the nervous system's defenses are not overly activated. There can be, in effect, a decoupling from the fear-driven mental representations inherent in the race construct while remaining anchored in the reality of the race conversation.

SAFETY AND DANGER (THE POLYVAGAL THEORY)

I want to outline Porges's model (Porges, 2009)[5] of how the nervous system works in a little more detail so that you have enough of a picture to make sense of the information in the chapters to come. Porges's model of the nervous system is built on the idea of evolution and that living things have changed and developed over time. Humans have inherited biological structures from our reptilian and mammalian ancestors that allow us to quickly evaluate danger and swiftly respond to it. Our nervous systems have developed to evaluate safety, danger, and threat to life from other mammals and the environment through neuroception, and then shunts us to one of three major neural circuits.

The first circuit developed alongside our reptilian ancestors, whose only defense was to shut down and immobilize. This type of passive defense includes reducing the heart rate, slowing down breathing, and even feigning death. The second neural circuit developed alongside early mammals and added mobilizing fight–flight behaviors on top of the shutdown/immobilizing behaviors. The third neural circuit developed alongside more social mammals and linked social communication with physiology and physiological states. This third circuit brought with it an ability to come together in social groups and to socially signal to one another that conditions are safe.

In this model, the first circuit is called the immobilizing circuit, the second the mobilizing circuit, and the third the social engagement system. All three systems are used to negotiate and confront potential threats. If the nervous system evaluates that there is no risk, it will spontaneously engage other people socially. While in the social engagement system, there is a sense of cooperation and easy communication. If the nervous system detects danger, it mobilizes the body in preparation for fight–flight. If the nervous system detects a life-threatening situation in which the fight–flight system cannot produce safety, it triggers a spontaneous immobilizing response. This immobilizing response comes from our distant evolutionary past, and our bodies literally go into a shutdown state. All of these systems are cued implicitly, without any conscious or intentional intervention on our part. Typically, we spend our lives alternating between the social engagement system and the mobilizing system. Throughout the day we might feel an internal sense of being safe at one moment and then internally unsafe the next, moving from one state and back again as we confront the normal ebbs and flows of everyday life. If our lives are threatened or we are seriously injured, we use the third neural circuit of shutdown. The nervous system evaluates this shutting down on its own and produces a dissociation from the pain and immobilizes the body.

Neurologically, there is a direct connection between our physiological state and the muscles of the face and head, in particular, the muscles around the eyes and the upper face and the muscles around the larynx. These muscles send out cues to other mammals as to whether the environment is safe and whether we, as an individual, are safe to be around. Muscle movements around the eyes and changes to the tone of voice as the muscles around the larynx change are all part of the efficient and unconscious neuroceptive communication of our physiological states.

The archetypal image for the social engagement system is of the caregiver and the baby. The caregiver is regulating the baby's physiological state through soft eye contact, a lullaby, a sing-song type of voice, and gentle rocking. Rocking also stimulates and promotes social engagement. Through all of these gestures, the caregiver is signaling that they are feeling safe, and the baby, through neuroception, is calmed. This is not just a one-way street, however; the baby is also sending cues to the caregiver. The formation of a positive feedback loop of feeling good together is called coregulation. This is where each regulates the other. In this coregulating mode, the caregiver and the baby are at their most curious, accepting, playful, and engaged—ideal conditions for learning from and communicating with each other.

The three neural circuits work together to generate either a socially engaged state or a defensive state. But, when we are cued for social engagement, the mobilizing and immobilizing systems are not turned off, as you might expect. What happens is we just don't use the mobilizing and immobilizing systems for defense. In social engagement, the mobilizing and immobilizing systems are used instead to support health, growth, and restoration. We exercise, we relax, we flop into someone's arms, we sleep. On the other hand, when our mobilizing and immobilizing circuits are cued for defense, compassion and curiosity (the characteristics of social engagement) disappear.

Simply put, what activates the social engagement system is a stance of acceptance, and what activates the defensive system is evaluation. If you have a good relationship with someone, you could evaluate them without necessarily triggering them into being defensive, but even then you're on the edge. Also, evaluation is not always negative. As you might have experienced for yourselves, being positively evaluated and praised isn't always comfortable, and sometimes we push it away. The bottom line here is that if you want to activate someone's defensive neural circuits, evaluate them.

I want to bring in the experience of shame at this point, as the discomfort in the race conversation is sometimes associated with this often-debilitating emotion that is very unhelpful to people of color. Through the process of socialization, we typically come to believe that our behavior is under our control. Although some of our behavior is under our control , a lot of it sits within these three neural circuits. It is my view that, in the race conversation, the hijacking of our behavior by our neuroception contributes significantly to this sense of shame, because the discrepancy between how we would like to behave and what our triggered bodies actually do is something we believe should be in control of and therefore take total responsibility for.

As I noted previously, it's not necessary to have a thorough working knowledge of all this. We simply need to have in our mind the nervous system's way of quickly deciding whether things are safe or dangerous and that the nervous system is often out of step with our deeply held values and beliefs. This knowledge frees us up a little, as we can more readily accept that there is no binary good or bad. There are only how we want to be as a person and how our unconscious falls short of that. With potential cues of danger all around us, what then can we do to hold our corner?

"There is no binary good or bad. There are only how we want to be as a person and how our unconscious falls short of that."

There is no way to directly manipulate the cues of safety we give out or the cues that we receive. We are, however, able to influence our physiology through less direct means to get ourselves back to social engagement. We can work toward developing a sense of safety inside us over time, and being cued more of the time from this internal source, even though there are external cues of danger coming at us from outside. We will be exploring these ways of influencing our physiology in a later chapter.

› 3 ‹

WITNESSING THE WOUND

Pause

The Need to Be Heard

Hiding in Plain Sight

Are All White People Racist?

Whiteness and Blackness

Mixed Race: Walking the Line

The Race Construct

Race Construct Shame and Black Rage

PAUSE

As you proceed through the rest of the book, you will find that I occasionally invite you to pause and focus on the breath if you find that you are trying hard to "work it out," whatever "it" might be, or if you are feeling strong sensations in your body. Initially, you will have to train yourself to do this, as it is not something that comes naturally. To aid this practice, I have placed occasional pause reminders throughout the rest of the book to invite you to pause and breathe whenever you feel it necessary.

Remember, when we are having the race conversation, we are working with trauma that is experienced first in the body (whether we choose to notice) and then in the mind, as the mind tries to make sense of what the body is doing. During the pause, the ever-present breath can anchor us to the present moment and also keep us present to the sensations of the body, so that body and mind can once again find their connection.

When working with trauma, the real work happens within these pauses, where the invitation is to let go of analysis and "putting things together" and just experience what we are experiencing. We are simply bringing our awareness to what the race conversation activates in the body. What muscles contract? What muscles are relaxed? What do we notice about our reaction to pull away or grasp onto the experience we are having? What is it like to just sit with what is?

› › › PAUSE . . . *and breathe* ‹ ‹ ‹

You can try this body scan exercise for five to ten minutes before continuing:

Find a place to sit quietly.

- Close your eyes; this allows you to focus more on your internal world and your body. If this is too intense, keep your eyes open.

- If sitting still is not working for you, get up and walk around instead.
- Whether you are sitting or walking, notice your breath; feel the breath as it comes in and out of the body; feel the sensations of the lungs filling with air and then releasing it.
- Notice any constriction in the muscles of the face: around the jaw, around the forehead. Notice where there is no muscle tension. Allow the muscles of the face to relax, if possible. Notice what is happening in your arms, your lower back, your legs, the contact you are making with the ground through your feet. Just notice what is there without judgment and without adding a story to your experience.
- Notice the quality of your thoughts. Are your thoughts focused on one thing? Are they moving from one thing to the next? Is there a theme to your thoughts? Whatever your thoughts are doing, just notice them. What happens when you describe your cognitive experience: "My thoughts are moving from one thing to the next," "My thoughts are on one thing at the moment," "The thoughts I'm having are critical about me."

Remember, just the very act of noticing will change something. It can be helpful to have someone lead you through short body scan exercises by downloading a mindfulness or body scan app on your mobile phone, some of which are free.

THE NEED TO BE HEARD

I'm often in the position of relaying the experience of race on people's lives. Within any given audience, some people connect with the experiences I am trying to communicate, and some struggle or feel no connection at all. In my conversations with others who find themselves in a similar position of trying to convey the paradigm of race and its impact, this is not an unusual state of affairs. Many of the people who find it hard to connect with the experience of race on people's lives would also see themselves as signed-up members of multiculturalism, or at least not causing others harm. For reasons we will be exploring in this chapter, many people still find it hard to connect with the experience that people of color have daily. Here I'm talking about a range of experiences, from small, almost undetectable messages about an individual's status within the race construct to lived and witnessed experiences that are grossly dehumanizing and life threatening.

It is a perplexing mystery to many people of color how what is in plain sight for them is not noticed by white people. In her book *Why I'm No Longer Talking to White People about Race*, Reni Eddo-Lodge[1] brings to the fore this sense of exasperation of not being able to get through what appears to be an impenetrable veil that separates the white experience from the experiences of people of color. In her book, she writes:

> Entering into conversation with defiant white people is a frankly dangerous task for me. As the hackles rise and the defiance grows, I have to tread incredibly carefully, because if I express frustration, anger or exasperation at their refusal to understand, they will tap into their prescribed racist tropes about angry black people who are a threat to them and their safety. (Eddo-Lodge, 2017, p. xi)

Eddo-Lodge then goes on to say: "I stopped talking to white people about race because I don't think giving up is a sign of weakness. Sometimes it's about self-preservation" (2017, p. 15).

Paradoxically, since sending this message out into the world, Eddo-Lodge has done a lot of talking about race, and talking about race with white people. There is a pressing need for people of color to be heard and, more importantly, acknowledged, which Eddo-Lodge articulated so well in the title of her book. She had put herself right in the middle of the race conversation and, in doing so, received some measure of acknowledgment for her concerns. Through the process of engaging in the race conversation and being heard in a particular way, I imagine she developed more of an internal sense of safety. Eddo-Lodge had, in effect, recalibrated how she neurocepts cues of safety, danger, and threat to life within the race conversation.

HIDING IN PLAIN SIGHT

In a previous chapter, I quoted from my article entitled "Silenced: The Black Student Experience." The article pointed toward a dilemma for counseling and psychotherapy students of color. As a part of the training, students of color are typically invited to examine aspects of their identity and who they are as individuals as a first step toward understanding others. When they do so, however, they are met with silence and defensiveness by trainers and students alike.

After that article was published, two opposing responses in the form of letters, which typify the reactions to the race conversation, were posted in the comments section of the same journal. One response was from someone who was, the name suggested, of south Asian origin, and the other I presumed to be from a white person.

The response from the person of south Asian origin started off:

> The article "Silenced: The Black Student Experience" in Therapy Today (December 2013) really resonated with my recent experience on the supervision training course of which I have been part for three years. After sharing my personal and professional reflections, I heard the facilitator say, "I didn't know you were black . . . just different." The majority of the experienced counselors in the group looked on in silence, with only two querying this comment. . . . Eugene Ellis's comments in his interview for the journal were a painful reminder of the five years before qualifying as a therapist that I spent hiding in plain sight. (comments section, Siddique, 2014, p. 45)

The rest of the letter continued with this tone of connectedness to what the article was trying to express.

The response from the white person began: "I am writing to express my anger at the discussion 'Silenced: The Black Student's Experience,' published in your December 2013 issue—specifically the contributions of Niki Cooper" (*Therapy Today*, 2014, pp. 14–19).

In the rest of the response, Niki was labeled as unenlightened and the idea that the slave trade could have an impact on the present was questioned. It also included a reference to the notion that the west African kingdoms were complicit with the European slave trade. (I will delve into this particular claim in Chapter 4, section "The Past and the Present.") The letter then finished by saying: "Incidentally, if you're going to capitalize the 'B' in 'Black people,' you really should capitalize the 'W' in 'White people.' We're human too, you know" (*Therapy Today*, 2014, p. 44).

The tone of this response could be argued to be rational and logical, but underneath the supposed logic, there is a sense of a disintegrating self. This disintegrated self then initiates a sense of disintegration within the reader. Both stories above orient us toward hurt, pain, and fear. Within race conversations, it is very challenging for the victims of racism, the witnesses, and the perpetrators to attend to these emotions. There is, without a doubt, something hidden in plain sight that generates these emotions. Is a lack of information the key to illuminating what is behind the veil, or some lack of shared emotional connection?

"The race construct and our identities are deeply woven together."

As anyone who has a passing familiarity with psychological processes knows, orienting yourself to aspects of your identity that, consciously or unconsciously, inflict hurt on others is a deep challenge. The race construct and our identities are deeply woven together. It is a complicated task to untangle the parts of our identity that give us a sense of belonging and safety from the other aspects of our identity that are embroiled in the system of race and that continue to cause hurt and harm.

As noted earlier, the central experience in having the race conversation is discomfort. Seeing through the veil that is hiding in plain sight is not something that can be attained through information alone. Nor is it something that can be achieved purely through an emotional emergence into people's stories and experiences, although both of these are useful parts of the journey. There is the body's experience in the race conversation that needs to be paid attention to. There is also something about the history that has brought us to where we are that needs further exploration. More importantly, however, we need to decide to go on a journey that will inevitably involve a particular type of discomfort. Ordinarily, unless there is an equal or larger discomfort waiting in the wings, both the victims and the witnesses are very wary about beginning the race conversation and integrating what emerges into their personal identity. Particularly for the witnesses, the discomfort is seen as way too much to bear, especially as the race construct itself gives them a way out through rationalizations, such as thinking "we are all the same," or clinging to the idea of a post-racism society.

Racism is often considered to be a set of beliefs and ideas that organize our actions. Underlying all the conceptions of racism for white people and people of color is the more visceral experience of racism—the ever-present threat to the physical boundaries of our bodies and the threat of physical violence. The raw experience of the race conversation is less about ideas and concepts and more about the easily triggered sense of danger we feel and the accompanying threat to the integrity of our physical bodies. In the race conversation, we must also contend with a heightened preoccupation with the boundaries of our identities. At the extremes, we feel the fear, real or imagined, of transgressing the constraints of the race construct, with the possible consequence of being socially ostracized or even losing our life. As we go about our lives, aspects of the race construct are normally more hidden and unconscious. With the prospect of dialogue around race, however, the visceral experiences inherent in the race construct begin to emerge and make themselves known more explicitly.

The race construct encompasses the raw, visceral feelings of danger, fear, and threat to life. With these internal sensations is a complicated cocktail of rationalizations that create the bias that white people are more human than people of color. For white people, it is not necessary to remove all biases to meet people of color where they are. However, if your cognitive narrative rationalizes that you are not part of the threat encoded in the race construct, then all you are left with is the visceral feelings of fear. From this comes an overwhelming urge to purge the discomfort through endless cognitive somersaults.

ARE ALL WHITE PEOPLE RACIST?

Currently, we are living in an era dubbed "the post-racist society" and, for people of color, there has undoubtedly been material change. Psychologically, however, things appear not to have changed that much over the years. In 1971, the BBC talk show host Michael Parkinson posed the "Are all white people racists?" question to Mohammed Ali in the second of four interviews they did together (Parkinson, 1971). Parkinson referred to a statement made by Elijah Mohammed, who was then the leader of a religious movement called "The Nation of Islam,"[2] of which Ali was a member. The statement posed to Ali was that Elijah Mohammed had gone on record as saying that white men are devils. Ali responded by saying that he doesn't hate anyone, and then went on to say:

> Many white people mean right and want to do right but they are so few. If 10,000 rattlesnakes was coming down that aisle now, and I had a door here that I could shut, and in that 10,000, 1,000 meant right. 1,000 rattlesnakes didn't want to bite me, I knew they were good. Should I make all these rattlesnakes come down, hoping that the 1000 will get together and form a shield, or should I just close the door and stay safe? (Parkinson, 1971, 24:35)[3]

A typical response to what Ali said is that you can't generalize and say that because most "white" people are racist, they should all be damned, because this is itself racist. Somehow, in this response, staying safe equals being racist. Ali was expressing the action he needed to take, based on his experience, to protect his body from possible harm and distress. By posing Elijah Mohammed's statement to Ali in the way that he did, Parkinson was, in effect, asking him to turn off his defense system and once again expose his body to the potential violence of racism.

Accusing someone of racism, who himself is the victim of racism, is often the inevitable go-to response for those who want to deny that their whiteness in any way oppresses. The psychological aspect of the race construct, it appears, has not disappeared. Instead, in the minds of many individuals, the race construct continues to do its work of covering up the hurt that is hiding in plain sight.

WHITENESS AND BLACKNESS

To engage in the race conversation in any meaningful way, the two central socially constructed identities—of blackness and of whiteness—that are embedded in the race construct need to be brought out of their hiding places. These identities become embodied in the way we move, interact, communicate, and perceive, both consciously or unconsciously. They then spring to life in a form based on the situation and the internal or external triggers that brought them about. Blackness and whiteness are far from the only identities we carry, but these identities are thrust upon us, willing participants or not.

"Blackness and whiteness are far from the only identities we carry, but these identities are thrust upon us, willing participants or not."

Legal scholar and columnist Patricia Williams, in the first of a series of radio broadcasts entitled "The Genealogy of Race," (Williams, 1997) relays a metaphorical sense of the concepts of blackness and whiteness over time and the feelings of being trapped in these conceptions without hope:

> Two centuries ago, or perhaps only a few decades ago, the lake was solidly frozen; and if for those skating across the surface things seemed much more secure, it was a much more dismal

> lot for those whose fates were frozen at the bottom of the pond. Over time, the weather of race relations has warmed somewhat, and some few of those at the bottom have found their way to the surface. We no longer hold our breath, and we have even learned to skate. The noisy racial chasm still yawns darkly beneath us all, but we few brave souls glide gingerly above, upon a skim of hope, our bodies made light with denial, the black pond so dangerously and thinly iced with the conviction that talking about it will only make things worse. (Williams, 1997, 14:56)[4]

The idea of blackness and whiteness certainly brings with it the kind of hopelessness and despair that Williams has communicated in her frozen lake metaphor. The race construct has the feeling of hopelessness built into it, unconsciously laying the ground for our thoughts and behaviors. It is important to realize, though, that the more we become aware of the race construct, the more we break its spell. Along with despair, an equally powerful energy can arises that takes us away from repeating cycles of confusion and toward a more proactive sense of engagement. As we continue to explore, the race construct's unconscious influence on our lives can be broken down.

"The more we become aware of the race construct, the more we break its spell."

Blackness

Since the late seventeenth century, there have been many attempts to classify humans. From these attempts, the concepts of blackness (black skin) and whiteness (white skin) emerged. Blackness was conceived of as a physiological sign that predetermined psychological inferiority. Blackness represented a debilitating state of being that was paralyzed by its own nature. Those with black skin were also assumed to be incapable of creating institutions and civilization unless there was a "mingling of the blood" with those of white skin. These conceptions have infiltrated scientific thought, social discourse, social policy, and law ever since. Blackness, then, represents psychological and intellectual limitations and an impediment to being fully human.

The unconscious form of blackness is very much like an act that has been rehearsed. Like an actor who brings a script to life through practice and repetition, the person of color comes to perform the imposed identity unconsciously and with belief. Blackness also has a more conscious form that emerges from an aware relationship to whiteness. People of color who live in the West are, at some point in their lives, put in circumstances where the boundaries of their race are presented to them. This encounter could be conceptualized as "the realization of blackness." People of color then seek to transcend their situation and find themselves in an identity struggle, which inevitably leaves an emotional scar.

For the person of color in the West, transcendence has a central dilemma. One path leads toward integration with dominant European ideals that relate to whiteness, which comes with the consequence of estrangement from their racial group. The other path leads toward identification with their racial group, which has the consequence of suffering estrangement from the majority society. No matter which path is taken, there is the sobering discovery that there is, in fact, no transcendence out of the blackness construct. Instead, there is a struggle with a state of alienation. Author Toni Morrison (1997), in her book *Tar Baby*,[4] eloquently brings this dilemma to life in story form.

Another aspect of the blackness construct is that, having taken one path or the other toward transcendence, the two positions look across the aisle at each other with disappointment and disapproval. The people of color on the other side of the aisle are accused of not making the "right and proper" choice. They are either a "sellout," rejecting the community's values, or they are "angry and separatist," living out the race construct, which advocates separation of the races. These aspects of blackness represent polar opposite positions, and it is important to acknowledge that there are many positions and spectrums within these poles. The main point I want to emphasize here is: whichever position is taken, there is a psychological cost to mental health.

Although at first glance it appears that exploring one's blackness might end up being a crippling experience, doing so often provides or assists someone in accessing their power. For many people of color, becoming conscious of the story of blackness and whiteness is central to the idea of progress and self-actualization. More recently, the concept of blackness has gone through a transition into what has been termed "post-blackness."[5] Post-blackness is a sense that a deep understanding of the blackness construct can be such that you are liberated into your power rather than disempowered under the weight of the construct's ability to oppress.

Whiteness

The concept of blackness, from the late seventeenth century, emerged alongside and in relation to whiteness. Blackness was seen as inferior; whiteness was conceived of as a physiological sign of predetermined psychological superiority. White skin was deemed an external signifier of thoughtfulness, a sense of unity, great physical strength and beauty, and an extraordinary instinct for order and love of freedom. Those with white skin had a monopoly on beauty, intelligence, and strength and could lose these characteristics with "the mixing of blood" from unions with the nonwhite races. White skin was an external sign that signified the capacity for civilization. It was thought impossible for the nonwhite races to arise without the white race's help.

These early conceptions were central arguments for the continued existence of the slave trade. The conceptions of blackness and whiteness were built on the terms "black" and "white," which were incorporated into law in certain parts of the world beginning in the late 1600s. Black was a term used for Africans, which then extended to other people of color. White was a term used for Europeans. In the sections entitled "Race and the Law" and "Race, Class, and Gender," I will outline some of these early laws and the consequences of those laws on the development of the race construct. Post slavery, the influence of these constructs on the white psyche created the psychological conditions of emotional distance and objectification that allowed colonization, apartheid, and other horrors to take place unchallenged.

More recently, whiteness has gone underground and is more hidden and subtle. It is more or less unnamed and might even be seen as beyond the realm of race. Because whiteness has gone underground, blackness can go underground also, into a kind of colorblindness where all have apparent equal status. As parents or teachers, we might repeatedly assure our children that color makes no difference—it doesn't matter whether you're black or white or green. Although well intentioned, it is also a very clean and tidy resolution of internal discomfort, and a message to young people to do the same. The impetus behind imparting these reassurances, however, is the certainty that it *does* matter what color you are, and it matters in very predictable ways. The tension within these reassurances for people of color is that they are pulled between the clarity of their own experience and how to live in a world where these experiences are edited out of normal conversation.

In the white imagination, race lives on the other side of the street, in nonwhite bodies. Whiteness is rarely implicated as part of the racial landscape, which then leaves the race conversation doomed to frustration. The conversations we do hear about race often speak to the idea of recognizing and accepting differences and acknowledging the right to be different. At the same time, however, the right to be different does not always translate into being treated equally.

"Whiteness is rarely implicated as part of the racial landscape, which then leaves the race conversation doomed to frustration."

The late Peggy McIntosh was, from the 1960s onward, the first white academic to write on the subject of white privilege. McIntosh's paper "White Privilege: Unpacking the Invisible Knapsack" (McIntosh, 2003) is essential reading for those who want to know how white privilege works. Although people of color understand the necessity of being able to read the white system, being defined as white and therefore having white privilege is far from straightforward.

Some white people say they hate being called white. They have never judged or shamed anyone because of the color of their skin. They might have grown up poor and have not risen through affirmative action, yet they are told they have white privilege. This is seen as profoundly unjust and a perfect example of racism.

For many white people, having the label "white" thrust upon them is a real struggle. This is especially so if they have lived their lives knowing very little of the experiences of people of color.

Hating being defined as white, along with hating being defined by race, could be seen as a legitimate position to take. By doing so, however, you are sidestepping the uncomfortable and denying the reality of the collective race construct that organizes vast aspects of our lives.

Francis E. Kendall, author of *Understanding White Privilege*, defines white privilege as

> an institutional (rather than personal) set of benefits granted to those of us who, by race, resemble the people who dominate the powerful positions in our institutions. One of the primary privileges is that of having greater access to power and resources than people of color do; in other words, purely on the basis of our skin color doors are open to us that are not open to other people. (Kendall, 2013, p. 62)

Being labeled as white, and therefore having white privilege if you choose to claim it, means that you also have the privilege to either engage or not engage in the messy and uncomfortable business of race.

An experience that brought the experience of white privilege to the fore very simply was relayed to me by a white individual who accessed the BAATN website. When signing up as a member of the network, an alphabetical list of heritages to choose from are presented to you. Asian, then, is at the top of the list and white at the bottom. This simple reorganization of heritages, where white is usually at the top, was very noticeable and impactful for this particular person and a subtle but relevant reminder of their white privilege.

"Being labeled as white, and therefore having white privilege if you choose to claim it, means that you also have the privilege to either engage or not engage in the messy and uncomfortable business of race."

More recently, white American educator and author Dr. Robin DiAngelo (2018) articulated the concept of *white fragility*. White fragility refers to the tendency of white individuals who consider themselves non-racist to become defensive when confronted with the realities of racism, which prevents them from acknowledging their involvement in the continued existence of racism. Within this concept, DiAngelo states:

> In the dominant position, whites are almost always racially comfortable and thus have developed unchallenged expectations to remain so. We have not had to build tolerance for racial discomfort and thus when racial discomfort arises, whites typically respond as if something is "wrong," and blame the person or event that triggered the discomfort (usually a person of color). This blame results in a socially-sanctioned array of responses toward the perceived source of the discomfort, including: penalization; retaliation; isolation and refusal to continue engagement. Since racism is necessarily uncomfortable in that it is oppressive, white insistence on racial comfort guarantees racism will not be faced except in the most superficial of ways. (DiAngelo, 2017, para. 14)

It's important to remember that white privilege and white fragility are conceptions built around the race construct. The conception of race has no biological validity, yet it shapes the lives of white people and people of color. Even under the most casual of examinations, any perceived solidity in the constructs of whiteness and blackness breaks down. There is no doubt, however, that these two conceptions hold power and influence lives, often tragically. I invite you to think of all these conceptions not as fixed all-or-nothings, but as narratives. These narratives then become embodied in our minds, our gestures, our body postures, and our gazes in unconscious and implicit ways. Unfortunately, the cold glare of the race construct does not offer the possibility of jumping off onto safe islands of comfort and neutrality, even if in our minds we feel we can.

MIXED RACE: WALKING THE LINE

Having just looked at the concepts of blackness and whiteness, I want to turn our attention to mixed-race individuals where the "Who am I?" question brings other unique challenges. To usefully get a handle on the present day mixed-race experience, it is helpful to take into account the various histories of relationships across race lines. Karis Campion's (2017) PhD thesis on mixed-race identities highlights the importance of social histories of time and place as serving "a useful vantage point, to unpack both the pre-configurations and the potential reconfigurations of mixed race, in the future" (Campion, 2017, pp. 198–199).

In this section, I will outline some of this time and place history and also explore the racialized social and political landscapes that mixed-race individuals have to negotiate. I will be specifically looking at black/white and south Asian/white individuals. I do, however, recognize that the term "mixed race" covers many other mixes of racial categories, including minority mixed individuals, who all experience varying degrees of misrecognition.

One of the many challenges of mixed-race individuals is being engaged with by family, friends, and strangers as simply Asian, black, or white when this is not necessarily how they see themselves. It can sometimes be experienced as others policing the boundaries between blackness and whiteness, where one heritage or another is shunned. The rejected heritage can then be a source of isolation and hurt. In her article "Between Black and White," Yvon Guest (2019), a mixed-race counselor in the U.K., reveals that:

> When I was a child, the white people around me wanted me to embrace my white side and reject my black. When I came into contact with black people, they wanted me to embrace my black side and reject the white. There has been an intense tug of war going on in my psyche for most of my life. I was stuck in a binary world created by other people and expected to take sides. It has taken me a long time to embrace what I

> really am, which is both white and black: I am mixed race. (Guest, 2019, p. 27)

Being mixed raced does not automatically lead to an internal tug-of-war, as has been Guest's experience. Mixed-race individuals do, however, have to contend with a curious and sometimes critical gaze toward their family structures. There is also sometimes a questioning of their racial identity by others. Questions from the outside can lead to an internal interrogation of personal identity in relation to what people perceive them to be. Present-day experience of mixed-race individuals, as well as the social interactions these individuals have, has its genesis, just like racism itself, inside the economic and social structures of slavery and colonialism.

I now want to look at some of the historical aspects of the North American colonies, the subcontinent of India, and the British West Indies to explore some of this time and place history. This history will, I hope, give some context to the complexity of the mixed-race experience.

In the North American colonies of the early 1600s, all those who were free of indentureship or enslavement faced the same opportunities, as a matter of law. The prevailing system was indentureship and slavery. Indentureship was served for a specified term, while enslaved people were permanently denied their freedom unless they could obtain the means to purchase themselves or successfully escape. The proximity of social status between European indentured servants and enslaved Africans meant that marriages between them were not uncommon. During the mid-1600s, a system of chattel slavery began to take root, where Africans and their children became property. A series of laws were enacted, beginning with outlawing mixed relationships. This law punished English or other freeborn women who married enslaved Africans. These women would receive punishment, while male enslavers would still have access to black females without consequence. The mixed-race offspring would take on the status of the mother and, as a consequence, not be free in the eyes of the law. The one-drop rule meant that any individual with African ancestry would be considered a member of the Negro race and therefore a slave. I will be exploring these North American colony laws further in the section "Race, Class, and Gender" in Chapter 4.

Turning to the subcontinent of India in the early 1600s, relationships between Indian women and white British traders were, again, not perceived as particularly problematic. As the British presence in India became more militaristic, British soldiers, like the British traders, continued to have relationships with Indian women. The children of these relationships were known as Eurasian. "Eurasians were educated to believe that British rule was essential to India and that public services and utilities were to everyone's benefit bringing modernity, wealth and progress" (Hall, 1831, as cited in Anderson, 2015, p. 141).

The British chose Eurasians to work in these essential public services and utilities, which gave them a sense of status within British rule. Moving forward to 1870, a Parliamentary statute referred to the Eurasian community as "Statutory Natives of India," which effectively set them further apart from Europeans. Several years on, in 1911, the term "Anglo-Indian" was sanctioned to describe the Eurasian community.

For economic purposes, the Anglo-Indian community was called upon to work alongside fellow Indians. For defense purposes, this same community would miraculously be transformed into British European subjects and be liable to serve in the Indian Delta Force, India's second line of defense. The Indian Delta Force was called upon to maintain order during communal riots. Having this role, meant you incurred the "hostility of the major communities as often the suppression of communal riots meant shooting down, impartially, both Hindu and Muslim miscreants" (Anthony, 1969, p. 3). For the Anglo-Indian community, "the most damaging problem for them was their ill-defined and flexible dual status" (Anderson, 2015, p. 141). Anglo-Indians were caught in the unenviable position of being associated with Europeans but excluded from the benefits in order to appease nationalists along with alienation from other Indian communities at times of unrest.

In the British West Indies, mixed descendants were initially produced through violent sexual unions between enslaved women and planters. Great care was taken to catalog and codify the future generations of these descendants and the degrees of mix. William Lawrence, Professor of Anatomy and Surgery at the Royal College of Surgeons in London, published *Lectures on Physiology, Zoology, and the Natural History of Man* in 1822. Lawrence introduces his book with a rousing exposition of his love of science and liberal values. He notes that:

> the philosopher should make the world his country; and should trample beneath his feet those prejudices, which the vulgar so fondly hug to their bosoms. He should sweep away from his mind dust and cobwebs of national partiality and enmity, which darken and distort the perceptions, and fetter operations of intellect. (Lawrence, 1822, p. 16)

Having said all of this, however, he succumbs to the race construct in how he organizes the mixed-race community of the British West Indies. In the chapter entitled "Varieties of Color in the Human Species," Lawrence catalogs the varying mixes of black and white unions. Mulattos are half black and half white. To describe a mulatto he says, "In cleanliness, capacity, activity and courage, they are decidedly superior to the Negroes" (Lawrence, 1822, p. 273). Europeans and mulattos produce tercerons (three-quarters white and one-quarter black). Lawrence describes tercerons in very stark terms:

> the hair and countenance of these resemble the Europeans; the former has nothing of the grandmother's woolly hair; the skin has a light brown tint, and the cheeks are red. In the Dutch colonies, they often have blue eyes and fair hair. The stain of the black blood is principally visible in the organs of generation. The scrotum is blackish in the male, and the labia pudenda dark or purplish in the female. (Lawrence, 1822, p. 273)

For tercerons, the corrupting drop of black blood is honed in on. Even though blackness can sometimes be found only in the most private of places, the mere trace of black blood represents complete contamination. Politically, this places tercerons in the same position, and with the same rights, as mulattos.

Lawrence goes on to describe quarterons, who are produced when Europeans and tercerons have children. Quarterons are indistinguishable from whites but

> they are not entitled, in Jamaica at least, to the same legal privileges as the Europeans or white Creoles,[6] because there is still a contamination of dark blood, although no longer visible. It is said to betray itself sometimes in a relic of the peculiar strong smell of the great-grandmother. (Lawrence, 1822, p. 274)

Here again, blackness is assumed even though not visible. Lawrence says nothing about the political rights of quarterons, but it can only be assumed that they are the same as mulattos.

Other categories of mixed offspring are offered in Lawrence's book, including European and American Indians (mestee) and mixed offspring from European and American Negroes (zambos or sambos). What is evident here is that one drop of black blood, even if entirely invisible, meant that you were categorized as black. Lawrence, in his lectures, references the work of Johann Friedrich Blumenbach, who in the late 1700s wrote on the science of humans. Blumenbach believed that other races could transform themselves to meet the European standard. I will say more about Blumenbach and some of the other early writers of the human sciences in the section "Nonrelational Being" in Chapter 5.

In contrast to Lawrence's "one drop of black blood and you were black," black people in the British West Indies often felt that mixed individuals had distinct advantages in being slightly removed from being black. After slavery ended, these mixed descendants were "the primary inheritors of the plantation legacies of their European grandparents and forefathers, the 'Brown' Jamaican's inheritance meant real social and economic power" (Hope, 2011, pp. 167–168). In post-slavery North America, the one-drop rule continued, and mixed individuals were folded into the general category of black. Despite statistical realities, mixed individuals in North America also had to negotiate the perception that they were disproportionately successful. They were also perceived to have the upper hand in terms of beauty, which also has social currency. A similar two-sided conflict was also the experience of Anglo-Indians. Their flexible status marked them as builders of nations and suppressors of uprisings and positioned them as being both rulers and as being ruled.

In North America and the Caribbean, the legacy of mixed races within slavery and colonialism has left behind a color comparison system that equates skin color with power. This comparison system is called shadism, or colorism in the U.S. Because of colorism, members of the same family grade each other on the racial hierarchy based on skin tone and then behave toward them in ways that met the racial expectations of society.

In the Indian subcontinent, Britain's preoccupation with racial purity wove itself into the caste system. Through the censuses of the early 1900s, British officials endeavored to know the caste system, but only to the extent that they could then imprint their own values on it, their values of the social sciences, of categorization, and of racial hierarchy. In his book *The Truth About Us*, Sanjoy Chakravorty (2019b) argues that precolonial social identities in India had flexible boundaries. He also notes that individuals could move between social identities relatively easily and that there was little evidence, in precolonial times, of systematic caste oppression. Throughout the eighteenth and nineteenth centuries, the caste system became increasingly strict in terms of categorizing people in terms of religion, tribe, and the shade of skin. In the article "How the British Reshaped India's Caste System," Chakravorty (2019a) notes:

> A very large, complex and regionally diverse system of faiths and social identities was simplified to a degree that probably has no parallel in world history, entirely new categories and hierarchies were created, incompatible or mismatched parts were stuffed together, new boundaries were created, and flexible boundaries hardened. (para. 25)

Place and time have created many and various preconfigurations of the mixed-race, light-skinned–dark-skin experience. What an individual mixed-race person experiences at any one time will most likely vary based on where they are and what is happening at that particular moment in time.

After the second World War, there was a lull in the attention paid to the problem of mixed races. Postwar Britain was characterized by the dismantling of colonialism and mass migrations to fill labor shortages. The race problem shifted from the mixed-race problem in the colonies where "they" were over "there" to the problem of mass migration into Britain where "they" were over "here." Enoch Powell's "Rivers of Blood"[7] speech in 1968 summed up this "urgency" to protect Britain from the insurgence of workers from the Commonwealth of Nations, which were the territories of the former British Empire. Powell gave his speech days before Parliament was due to vote on the Race Relations Bill. He described the bill as "throwing a match onto gunpowder" (Powell, 1968, as heard in Rajan, 2018). At this moment in history, the mixed-race question, which had preoccupied policymakers for centuries, became subsumed once more under the general heading of "black."

In the U.S. before the 1980s, mixed-race individuals were assumed to adopt the same race as the parent of color, based on the historical one-drop rule. Challenges to this assumption led to the development of ideas around multiracial development; and in the 1990s, a movement emerged that campaigned to have mixed race as a legitimate identity. Cynthia Nakashima, in her book chapter entitled *Voices From the Movement*, articulated the struggle of mixed-race individuals for inclusion and recognition. Nakashima (1996) identified three positions mixed-race individuals expressed that dominated the mixed-race discourse in the 90s. There were:

- Individuals who want all of their racial/ethnic communities to accept mixed-race people as full members of the community, without erasing the differences in their mixed-race identity.

- Individuals who identify with one of their racial/ethnic communities to the exclusion of others (mono-racial identity).
- Individuals who identify as citizens of the world. (p. 82)

Occupying any one of these positions creates tension with the others. For monoracial-identity individuals, it was felt that the mixed-race movement held a bias toward identifying as multiracial. If they did then identify as monoracial, they would then be open to being pathologized by the multiracial community for not identifying in *that* way (Nakashima, 1996). Citizens of the world individuals saw race ideology as inherently oppressive and rejected it in its entirety. Similarly, they saw the idea of mixed race as being racially constructed. Mixed race as an identity is then vulnerable to becoming yet another group with its own set of boundaries and limitations and becoming the new ideal, against which others will be degraded and oppressed (Nakashima, 1996, p. 93).

Nakashima saw these three positions—mixed-race identity, monoracial identity, and citizen of the world identity—not as separate positions but as ideological dimensions that overlap each other. Mixed-race people, then, can identify with all three positions simultaneously. Nakashima admits that to occupy this position requires "an exercise in cognitive flexibility and tolerance". Also, it is essential to keep in mind that each of these voices is valid and "normal" (Nakashima, 1996, p. 96).

To conclude, the present-day experience of those who blur the boundaries of blackness and whiteness are shaped within the shadow of the many and varied mixed-race positions through time and place. The landscape that Nakashima and others have articulated reveals an ever-shifting and ambiguous terrain in which to navigate race identity. In the future, the mixed-race identity position will continue to change with the varying shifts of power. In the U.S. the census of 2000 allowed, for the first time, the option for mixed-race individuals to self-define their identity. The England and Wales census of 2001 was the first that offered individuals a mixed-race option. These inclusions into census data have been important markers for those of mixed-race identity and have greatly accelerated the research into the mixed-race experience.[8]

› › › PAUSE . . . *and breathe* ‹ ‹ ‹

THE RACE CONSTRUCT

As pointed out previously, race is not a biological reality, but it is a social reality and one that is kept alive by the whole of society. The race construct, then, forms the basis for society's shared assumptions and assigns to us our racial identity. In this section, I want to outline aspects of race identity narratives and introduce the idea of body identity. I will then sum up the various aspects of the race construct to produce a definition.

Kwame Anthony, political philosopher and cultural theorist, would say that a defining feature of collective identities like race is the presence of scripts (Appiah et al., 1996/1998). He says that scripts are "narratives that people can use in shaping their life plans and in telling their life stories" (p. 97).

Appiah warns, however, that

> there is a danger in making racial identities too central to our conceptions of ourselves; while there is a place for racial identities in a world shaped by racism, I shall argue, if we are to move beyond racism we shall have, in the end, to move beyond current racial identities. (Appiah et al., 1998, p. 32)

The notion that we have a choice in how we relate to our racial identity, which Appiah is implying, is not necessarily just about someone's commitment to its centrality. The fact that society forces a commitment to a racial identity also needs to be taken into account. There are, however, aspects of racial identity, namely the scripts that inform how people of particular races should conduct themselves, that are open to challenge, change, and influence.

Traditional models of identity development often begin with a primitive nonthinking body that, over time, grows into a clear-thinking cognitive mind that somehow leaves the primitive body behind. These models give us a roadmap of narratives about ourselves and about others that become progressively more sophisticated and developed. A narrative understanding, however, is not the only thing at work in identity development. The body's development—the nonverbal experience of inner sensation, the use of posture and gesture, sound and movement—is also essential. These types of nonverbal communication most significantly mark our progress in identity development, more than the development of our understanding of our scripts.

Christine Caldwell, a somatic movement therapist, has proposed the term "body identity" to describe this nonverbal landscape. She notes that

> body identity is our core identity, out of which other identities are built. It is generated, preserved and enacted by the body, via our explicit and implicit relationship to sensation, movement, physiological processes, relationships, interactions and bodily awareness of emotion. (Caldwell, 2016, p. 9)

The concept of body identity and the importance of this area of experience places the nonverbal aspects of identity development on an equal, and possibly more important, footing with cognitive or script development. I will say more about body identity in Chapter 7 "Becoming Race-Construct Aware."

Putting together everything that's been said up to this point, I am defining the race construct as something that organizes society along racial lines, through collective narratives of identity, and through an embodiment of identity. Functionally, the race construct ensures that internal discomfort is kept out of the minds and hearts of white people, or at least does not reach levels of intensity such that there is a movement toward collective behavior change. This includes ensuring that social and political structures are kept in place that perpetuate white people's privileges. By design, the race construct also dials down empathy toward people of color, and the darker you are, the more empathy is dialed down. Within the race construct, there is also the notion that people of color bring with them values and qualities that undermine the wholesomeness and goodness of whiteness. At the liberal edges of the construct, some people of color are allowed to attain the status of whites, but if the balance shifts too far, whites will flee to new areas to create the notion of wholesomeness and goodness somewhere else. The race construct is a self-perpetuating system which, at its heart, equates whiteness with purity and innocence and sees blackness as a stain on that purity and innocence. The "race construct," then, is something we are all swimming with, or swimming against. Holding the race construct in mind also leads us away from the tendency to move toward blame, self-focus, and defensiveness and toward what is most important and what really needs to be paid attention to in the race conversation. Using the term "race construct" also brings with it the everyday reality that race shapes the lives of every one of us.

THE RACE CONSTRUCT

- a social construct that organizes society across racial lines
- collective narratives, identity scripts, and body identities that keep the discomfort of race oppression out of the minds and bodies of white people
- the behaviors, thoughts, and feelings that ensure that the social and political structures that perpetuate white privilege are kept in place
- the dialing down of empathy toward people of color
- the notion that people of color bring with them values and qualities that undermine the wholesomeness and goodness of whiteness

RACE CONSTRUCT SHAME AND BLACK RAGE

Before we look at the emotion of shame in the race conversation, it is important to distinguish between shame and guilt, as they are often thought of as a continuum of the same emotion, where one is a stronger version of the other. In some ways, this is true, but in other ways, they are distinctly different. Shame and guilt are both socializing emotions, and both involve self-evaluation. Both also guide personal choices and behaviors. Shame is a negative evaluation of the *self* and is tied to self-identity, whereas guilt is a negative evaluation of past *actions* and is tied to something you have done. Shame is the feeling of being exposed as a fundamentally defective or worthless being; in contrast, the emotion of guilt is a sense that you are a worthwhile person who has made a mistake or made a harmful error in judgment. If you are defending your self-identity, you are most likely in shame. Shame has destructive implications for interpersonal relationships, whereas the capacity for guilt is a relational strength.

For instance, when a caregiver scolds a baby for touching an electric socket, the baby experiences shame throughout its entire body and a nonverbal sense of "I'm bad." Typically, the baby will cry at this point. If the baby is then immediately soothed with loving care, there is a warm experience of reconnection. Repeated experiences such as this create the conditions where the whole self as bad is replaced by "I'm okay (but my behavior could have hurt someone)." The capacity to be motivated to change our behavior so that we can stay in relationship is the emotion of guilt.

When shame is the overwhelming experience in a child's early life, chronic shame can develop. Chronic shame during childhood creates individuals who become consumed with blame toward themselves (as well as others) when things go wrong. Chronic shame also harbors seething hostility and resentment that curtails empathy for themselves and others when shame is activated. By contrast, people who feel guilt seem to be less self-focused in general and more able to empathize with others and to accept responsibility for their part in relationships going wrong. They are less likely to get angry, but when angry, they are more likely to express their anger in fairly direct and constructive ways.

In the race conversation, shame is the emotion that permeates people's experience. That disapproving gaze toward the child who innocently attempts to have a race conversation quickly and very powerfully lets the child know that the race conversation is out of bounds. This unspoken experience is then linked with a hyperactive physiological state that the child integrates as a taboo. For a child, curiosity about skin color is wholly valid, but the taboo is clear; it is a bad thing to bring interest to this aspect of life. The disapproving gaze remains visceral and unprocessed as if something dangerous has happened. All of these physical feelings of shame then resurface in subsequent race conversations.

A function of the race construct, as previously noted, is to hide the benefits of white privilege from white people and to coerce people of color into protecting white privilege. For people of color, it is a profound source of shame to discover that you have played an unwitting part in the reciprocal drama of the race construct that is not for your benefit. Shame is ever present and easily activated in people of color, even when they are not consciously aware of it. Bowing the head and averting the gaze, along with many other cues, point toward a body in shame.

To highlight the importance of shame as an organizer of experience within the race conversation, I am proposing the term "race construct shame" as a particular type of shame that lives within the race construct and gets activated in the race conversation.

There are five aspects to race construct shame that I want to highlight. First, it is a situation-specific shame that emerges out of the race conversation and does not necessarily link back to a specific remembered experience in a particular person's life. Instead, shame is passed on intergenerationally. It is passed on through the descendants of the victims, perpetrators, and witnesses in nonverbal and implicit ways. The race conversation then triggers this shame even without there being an explicit memory to contextualize this particular shame experience. Within the race conversation, this lack of an explicit memory on which to hang the activation of shame is an inherent part of this aspect of race construct shame.

The second aspect of race construct shame, like with shame in general, is a physiological, all-encompassing bodily experience. Patricia Deyoung, in her book *Understanding and Treating Chronic Shame: A Relational/Neurobiological Approach,* uses the word *disintegrating* to capture the essence of a person's experience of shame (Deyoung, 2015) The feeling of disintegrating can be described as feeling blank, vaporized, or incoherent. It is an experience without words or thought. Along with these inner sensations, the body is activated into the submission response, where the head goes down and the body shrinks away. This overall disintegration experience of shame also feels profoundly solitary.

The third aspect of race construct shame has to do with its infectious nature. Deyoung defines shame as "the experience of one's felt sense of self-disintegration in relation to a dysregulating other" (Deyoung, 2015, p. 58). Deyoung uses the word *dysregulating* to describe someone who fails to provide the emotional connection, responsiveness, and understanding that another person needs to be well and whole. There is an assumption here that a person's wellness is dependent on an integrated sense of self and that relationships are what hold that integrated sense of self together. The dysregulation Deyoung refers to is very similar to Porges's theory of how the nervous system perceives safety and danger, which I described earlier. As you might remember, the nervous system can be hijacked through neuroception of nonverbal cues of danger and threat to life, even when actual threats are not present. It is easy to see that within a group conversation about race, an individual would probably pick up a cue of danger. They would then cue others into the same state and, before long, most of the group would be activated.

The fourth aspect of race construct shame is more cognitive in nature and happens after the initial physiological activation of the body. This aspect is experienced as an unraveling of our currently constructed identity and a profound in-the-moment questioning of who we are as an individual—are we racist, are we good enough for this moment, are we basically a good person, is our curiosity valid?

The fifth aspect of race construct shame concerns attempts to protect identity wounding. Artie Wu is a meditation teacher who helps people manage their critical inner voices. Wu has proposed a matrix of four kinds of self-negativity, one of which he calls identity self-negativity. Identity self-negativity is the feeling that you are the "wrong" kind of person, and you then want to shield your identity wound by over-proving yourself or by becoming angry. As Wu puts it, there is "a deep, simmering anger that an inherent, unchangeable part of who you are has been brutally forced into exile and hiding" (Wu, 2015, para. 7).

Wu's idea of identity self-negativity brings to life an essential aspect of race construct shame. This is where someone's identity, be it white identity, black identity, mixed identity, or simply an identity as a good person, is held up for inspection and found wanting. This identity wound can trigger a minimizing of others, an overproving of competence or an angry defense of your position.

Within the race conversation, the above aspects of race construct shame point us toward healing as a relational act. Unresponsiveness, emotional disconnection, and an unwillingness to stay with race hurt are then central to the continuation of race construct shame.

Race construct shame is a universal experience that may have anger and rage as possible elements within it. There is, however, a particular kind of rage that people of color experience that has been called "black rage," which can be directed both inward and outward. In their book *Black Rage,*[9] published in 1968 after the assassination of Martin Luther King Jr., William Grier and Price Cobbs pointed toward the history of slavery and the failure to integrate black people into the post-slavery social and political fabric. Grier and Cobbs (1968) then go on to say that this has led to a real and lasting rage in black people, especially in light of the "equality of access for all" narrative that society endorses. What happens around black rage and how it is to be relationally met, are fundamental questions that need urgent attention. One approach is to see black rage for what it is, a symptom of living life within the race construct, and treating it for what it is, a desperate cry of the ancestors.

RACE CONSTRUCT SHAME

- is experienced by people of color and white individuals,
- emerges out of the race conversation and does not necessarily link back to specific remembered experiences,
- is an all-encompassing bodily experience of disintegration that feels profoundly solitary,
- is infectious by nature,
- results in a cognitive preoccupation with "what I am" or "what you are,"
- and seeks to protect identity wounding through minimizing others, overproving yourself or angrily defending your position.

› 4 ‹

INSIDE THE RACE CONSTRUCT

Uncovering the Reality Distortion Field

The Cry of the Ancestors

The Past and the Present

Race and the Law

Race, Class, and Gender

History: The Facts

The Transmission of Fear: Intergenerational Trauma

UNCOVERING THE REALITY DISTORTION FIELD

The race construct is complex and multilayered and creates what amounts to a reality distortion field around the white individual. When that distortion field is disrupted for any reason, reality floods in with a resulting sense of horror that stops the race conversation in its tracks. To have fruitful conversations about race, there needs to be some understanding of the race construct, including why it came into being, how it operates, and why it still persists today despite many centuries of struggle.

I am going to be looking at the race construct as if it were a client in therapy, sitting in a chair in front of me. If I am to be successful in creating a dialogue with this client, I am going to need to know something about the context of this client's life. Why is the client the way they are? What history does this client bring with them? How does this client's history merge with my own? How does this client experience the world? How do I experience this client, both positively and negatively? What do I bring that bias me toward certain unconscious responses? There is much to be curious about with this client.

As the therapist, you are aware that clients like this do not present themselves for therapy that often. You have sought support and supervision to help you out, but these sources are also confused about how to proceed. Adding to this complexity, the race construct is not just speaking from the chair opposite you but is also whispering in your ear.

What you might be feeling right now is what I would call race-construct arousal. This is that particular moment where thought, feeling, and behavior become vague and incoherent. The heart beats faster and you feel it in the gut as you unconsciously organize yourself around the construct of race, despite your intentions.

As any therapist will tell you, it is taken as gospel that the past shapes the present. Therapists understand that exploring the horrors of the past and, at the same time, meeting them with compassion can transform an individual's perception of the present moment. It is the same with the race construct, which has its own history. Where we start this history, however, is important. Legal scholar and columnist Patricia Williams makes the point that we could begin with the civil rights movement in the U.S. or the Notting Hill riots in the U.K. Beginning our exploration of history at these moments, Williams points out, does focus our attention on the genuinely inspiring ideals that brought these movements together. It also allows us to be optimistic about the possibility of progress. However, this frame brings with it limitations. It is the prehistory of these movements, namely slavery (and the subsequent European colonial projects), that explains the lingering effects of racism. Williams notes that there can be no adequate explanation without reference to this history (Williams, 1997).

Taking on this prehistory is not an easy task. There are, however, some broad landing points that I believe need to be conveyed to give an overall historical picture of the race-constructed client before us. I will lay out a broad history of racism and, in particular, the internalization of this legacy into our bodies and into our minds. After this, I will discuss the genetic inheritance component to this legacy.

As you read through the history, it's almost impossible to access the states of mind that would lead individuals to inflict such brutality and harm. Was there some choice within these acts of terror? Were people coerced into being oppressors, or was it predetermined conditioning? For me, there is either the love paradigm or the fear paradigm. The love paradigm consists of connectedness, compassion, mutuality, and fearlessness; the fear paradigm includes denial, silence, rage, and greed.

Before we embark on the history of race, there are a few other points to make. The first is that making contact with the ancestral and present hurts associated with racism is difficult. It is difficult not just because of the acts committed but because so much unconscious and conscious effort has gone into setting up the conditions whereby we are desensitized from the hurt that has been inflicted. The second point is that race oppression has its own coded signals that need to be tuned into. It does not necessarily follow that because you suffer another oppression, such as homophobia, you can generalize that experience to the experience of race oppression. Lastly, as we embark on the history of racism, I want you to focus on your body experience and prioritize this experience over the experience of your cognitive mind. Remember, race is a dance partner designed to trip us up. It is the mind trying to work things out where the race construct's reality distortion field is at its most potent.

"It is the mind trying to work things out where the race construct's reality distortion field is at its most potent."

THE CRY OF THE ANCESTORS

In 2018, I went on a week-long meditation retreat. Just before the retreat, I spent time looking at information about my ancestors that my sister had put together. My heritage is from the Caribbean island of Jamaica. My mother's maiden name is Sharpe, and buried in the information my sister sent me was someone called Sam Sharpe. The Sam Sharpe I knew was an enslaved Jamaican, Baptist minister and the organizer of a rebellion that, in 1831, mobilized 60,000 of the 300,000 slaves on the island. The rebellion lasted 10 days and, afterward, the retribution from the British slaveowners took 500 black lives. Sharpe was hanged in Montego Bay square saying "I would rather die upon yonder gallows than live in slavery."[1] Sam Sharpe's biographer, Rev. C. S. Ried, says:

> I don't think it's claiming too much to say that Sam Sharpe's rebellion was the trigger that brought things to a head. There was already disquiet in British society, and there were many in England who had been agitating against it, but this rebellion, and the kind of brutality with which it was put down, I think it stirred the conscience of people of conscience. (Timeline, 2017, 44:30)

A buried memory sprung to mind of an uncle telling me that Sam Sharpe was one of our ancestors. Could this be him? The dates of birth seemed to be about the same. The meditation retreat was about to begin, so I knew that I would have to wait until after the retreat to find out more.

With Sam Sharpe in my mind as an ancestor, I became more and more aware of my body. I experienced my body taking up space and holding its own. I had a powerful feeling of my black body being face-to-face with white bodies and nonverbally communicating something that was less cautious, less deferential. In this retreat, the invitation was to bring your oppressed self and for others to bear witness. I told the retreatants about Sam Sharpe being a possible ancestor and how important that was for me. The meditation leaders attentively printed off a picture of Sam Sharpe and placed this image on a shrine among the other retreat images. This image came to represent the ancestors, and over the course of the week, retreatants ritually paid their respects. I became very powerfully infused with my ancestors' oppression and how their bodies had been domesticated through torture, beatings, and the threat of incarceration and death. My thoughts then went to my father and how he also sought to shape my body through beatings. In addition to being a means of expelling frustration, my father's beatings were a generations-old strategy to ensure that I kept my body out of harm's way and away from the real danger. "If you can't hear, you must feel" was my father's mantra. I felt compelled to communicate my inner thoughts and feelings about my father to the other retreatants, but I also knew that talking about my father without reference to the ancestors would have robbed him and me of the history and context of what shaped us. Without reference to the ancestors, I felt it would not be possible to both communicate the hurt and bring compassion, forgiveness, and understanding to the moment of ancestral time that my father and I found ourselves in when I was a child. I put the following words together, which seemed to simply flow out of me, and I read them out loud to those present. It was a powerful moment for the group and for me.

The Cry of the Ancestors

Black, naked, bound and beaten.
A crushed heart; inside a broken soul.
Sons and daughters bear witness; this was once a man.

Black, naked fearful and fertile.
White faces bright, with eyes of lust; for a mixing of the blood.

Sons and daughters bear witness; this was once a woman.
Hardy limbs, black and plentiful; claim unspeakable
horrors—more beast, than human.
Sons and daughters bear witness; this was once a people.

Daddy, this is our legacy.
But what of us; playing our part in this dance from the past.
With no balm to soothe the corners of the mind,
which lock away that loveless dread.
That, which is our inheritance.

With your muscle and sinew, giving up a little of the mind's
secret; as they smash and grind, and silently scream.
With only my small child's cry of fear and bewildered confusion,
as a mirror into a time, one should have long forgot.
But it's enough.
It's enough to ensure that this corner of the world's
suffering, does not, go unnoticed.

After many years, of unlocking the unsayable.
I want you to know that I have heard you, I have heard your plea.
I know that you have journeyed through this system they call
race; that chisels away at your bigness, and brings with it
large and small humiliations; that stir the depths of shame.
With sons and daughters bearing witness; to what was once a man.

I heard the cry of the ancestors; through your fists and gritted teeth.
Fight and perish; cower and survive.
Daddy, I hear your plea.
There is no place for vulnerability in this world, for you, or for me.

How I wish we could have looked at each other with kindly
eyes; that we could have shared a moment without fear.
That we could have been vulnerable together;
like I now know, it's possible to be.

Daddy, you followed the ancestral call, and for that I am grateful.
Willingly I step forward, with my personal sacrifice in hand.
To bring words to the wordless, and feeling to the hurt.

When the retreat ended, I was very conscious of not wanting to burst the bubble I had created around the Jamaican hero, Sam Sharpe, being a direct ancestor. It was only when I was in a group of other black and Asian heritage psychotherapists and counselors that I felt able to do the necessary checks to find out one way or the other. I was grateful for the support I received when I found out that the organizer of the rebellion in 1831 was not a direct ancestor of mine. This news was not as disappointing as I had first thought it would be. In many respects, I had already appropriated Sam Sharpe into me as if he were a direct ancestor. The process I had been on during the retreat had shifted how my body relates to the other bodies in the world. That positive gain hadn't changed even after this disappointing discovery.

There had always been a part of me that felt lacking in some way because of this disconnection from my grandparents' and great-grandparents' stories. Having been born in England, with parents and ancestors from the Caribbean, I have come to realize that this feeling of lack is very common among children born in the U.K. to Caribbean parents. By chance I had evoked the ancestors, and this had led me down a particular path of connection and release. Although I imagine I would hold a different type of embodied presence if Sam Sharpe was my direct descendant, there was still an inner journey, which was just as valuable without that direct connection. For me, the imagination and the evoking of the ancestors was enough for me to feel the presence of something that changed my relationship to self and others and spoke to the power of ritual to find inherent truths.

› › › PAUSE . . . *and breathe* ‹ ‹ ‹

THE PAST AND THE PRESENT

During my process of engaging in the history of race many years ago, the brutality of it all was hard to grasp. I was horrified by the fact that a group of people could sit around a room and coordinate such hate based on race alone. My imagination conjured up images of evil, which scared me. I therefore dismissed the idea of race as being coordinated as "conspiracy talk" and not a valid way to describe how race hate came about. The dismissal of such a possibility did, however, leave a problem. How did race hate come about? Without an orchestrated effort on the part of an elite few, this only left the idea that the history of race and race differences was somehow genetic. The idea of unchangeable human differences also seemed just as implausible. This point of stuckness led me to many cognitive somersaults before finally settling on the cold hardness of the truth.

Equiano's Narrative

In 1789, Olaudah Equiano published his autobiography, *The Interesting Narrative of the Life of Olaudah Equiano*. Equiano was a formerly enslaved African who lobbied Parliament for abolition. In his book, he records his kidnapping into slavery from what is now known as Nigeria and the journey he endured across the middle passage on a slave ship bound for the New World.

> The first object which saluted my eyes when I arrived on the coast was the sea, and a slave ship, . . . These filled me with astonishment which was soon converted to terror when I was carried on board.
>
> . . . I was soon put down under the decks, and there I received such a salutation in my nostrils as I had never experienced in my life: . . . I became so sick and low that I was not able to eat. I now wished for the last friend, death, to relieve me; but soon, to my grief, two of the white men offered me eatables; and on my refusing to eat, one of them held me fast by the hands, . . . and tied my feet, while the other flogged me severely.
>
> . . . In a little time after, amongst the poor chained men, I found some of my own nation, which in a small degree gave ease to my mind.
>
> . . . the white people looked and acted, as I thought, in so savage a manner; for I had never seen among any people such

> instances of brutal cruelty; and this not only shown towards us blacks, but also to some of the whites themselves. One white man in particular I saw flogged so unmercifully with a large rope, . . . that he died in consequence of it; and they tossed him over the side as they would have done a brute.
>
> The stench of the hold while we were on the coast was so intolerably loathsome, that it was dangerous to remain there for any length of time . . . the air soon became unfit for respiration from a variety of loathsome smells, and brought on a sickness amongst the slaves, of which many died
>
> . . . shrieks of the women, and the groans of the dying, rendered the whole scene of horror almost inconceivable. (Equiano, 1789/2017, pp. 18–19)

Equiano's narrative of his journey to the New World is horrific in its depiction of the conditions on board a slave ship and also brings to life the brutality that was metered out. We can only imagine what traumas awaited them on the plantations and how those traumas were held in those bodies.

There have been many writers who have articulated the profound impact of the African slave trade on the world economy and on the psychology between black and white people. The first thing that needs to be said, however, is that racist ideology and the race construct sprang from slavery and, in the words of Peter Fryer, author of *Aspects of British Black History*, there was "an unprecedented level of violence" which therefore "required a violent racism not merely as an ideological rationale but as a psychological imperative" (Fryer, 1993, p. 27).

The psychological imperative that Fryer names relates to the need to resolve the cognitive dissonance between the espoused humanitarian ideals of individual freedom and the scramble for and maintenance of economic power and profits. Fryer put it like this: "The rising capitalist class profoundly inscribed freedom of the individual on its banner; yet it . . . conquered, absorbed and reinforced servile labor systems throughout the world" (Fryer, 1993, p. 27).

The plantocracy and the ancillary mechanisms for maintaining and supporting the system of slavery are also important to note here. The plantocracy was the population of planters regarded as the dominant class, especially in the British West Indies. Fryer describes the period of plantocracy in the British West Indies as:

> a single crop economy and that crop was sugar, the "white gold" of the New World. . . . In order to grow sugar, British planters needed two things . . . they needed virtually unlimited long-term credit . . . Such credit was their lifeblood, and it was provided by commission agents, or "factors," in the City of London . . . This credit system primed the pump, and did so very profitably indeed . . . in the second place, the planters needed cheap labour [sic] . . . After a brief unsuccessful experiment with indentured English convicts, they found the labour [sic] they needed in Africa . . . goods were bartered for human beings on what was then known as the Guinea coast, which we now call the West African coast. (Fryer, 1993, p. 12)

At this point in the slavery narrative, someone typically brings up the idea that traders on the African coast also had a slave trade, and it was this slave trade that the British and others joined. The following is certainly not the final word on the often-imagined complicity of African traders in the slave trade, but it is important to keep in mind what the esteemed Ghanaian poet Professor Kofi Awoonor notes:

> Slavery existed in societies that had no prison systems. It was part of the punitive measures against criminal conduct. . . . It was not a long-term loss of liberty, and the children of the slaves were never slaves. . . . With the transatlantic slave trade . . . people went away, and they never came back. (YouTube, 2017, 18:21)[2]

In her book *Mental Slavery*, Barbara Fletchermen-Smith notes: "The British Empire was by no means the only empire built upon slavery, but it was the first from which there was no hope of gaining freedom with the passage of time. There was no way out except resistance" (Fletchermen-Smith, 2003, p. 21).

This point about resistance is important to stay with for a while. Throughout slavery in the Caribbean, resistance was the norm and not the exception. As a form of resistance, the slaves did as little work as possible, and the avoidance of work was considered the ultimate sign of freedom. Within the frame of the race construct, this was interpreted as laziness. The slaves would feign illness, inflict injuries on themselves, and sometimes kill themselves, either individually or in groups. This, again, was not a cry of despair but defiance and resistance.

Fletchermen-Smith (2003) also noted that

> slavery severely traumatised [*sic*] people—to such an extent that it affected people's capacity to procreate. Terror, perpetual fear, cruel abuse and gruelling [*sic*] work were the order of the day. Slave women frequently took control of their own fertility by killing their children, in order to prevent them from becoming slaves themselves. (p. 21)

In revenge for acts of cruelty, slaves sometimes beat plantation overseers to death. The ever-present threat of rebellion kept the plantocracy in a state of perpetual fear, and serious uprisings were more frequent than historians have generally acknowledged.

In his book *Testing the Chains*, Michael Craton (1982) chronicles slave trade rebellions in the British West Indies and describes no fewer than 75 such rebellions between the years 1638 and 1837—that is roughly one every two and a half years. All but 17 of these rebellions involve at least hundreds of slaves, and 22 involved thousands or many thousands.

Fletchermen-Smith tellingly reminds us that by damaging others, people also damage themselves, and I suspect that if I were to focus on the children of former slave owners, then I would discover traumas there too. In the making of empires, it is inevitable that crimes will be committed (Fletchermen-Smith, 2003, p. 15).

I imagine that you might be noticing the similarity between the past and the present here. You might be noticing the avoidance of work as a natural consequence of oppression and the race construct view that black people are lazy. You might also be seeing that the perpetual state of fear and threat between black people and white people during slavery continues to be a pattern today. It appears that, without conscious knowledge or recall of the generational past, history plays itself out anyway.

Na'im Akbar is considered a pioneer in the development of African-centered psychology. In his book *Breaking the Chains of Psychological Slavery*, he gives many examples of the profound influence the institution of slavery had on African heritage communities. Akbar looks at issues such as leadership, community division, family, color discrimination, and strategies for moving forward. His book offers valuable insights into the patterns of survival behaviors, which were a functional necessity during the centuries of slavery and which have become the dysfunctional behaviors of today for both black and white people.[3]

India and Slavery Reinvented

The wealth of the British Empire was built primarily through slavery. The wealth generated provided the capital that propelled the industrial revolution and colonialism. The moment the slave trade ended, colonialism began, and the jewel in the imperial crown was India. Starting with the East India Company's trading settlements in the seventeenth century, Britain's influence gradually extended over the whole continent until, by 1914, one half of India was ruled directly from Westminster. Several decisive events led to British rule in India: In 1612, the British East India Company was granted a trade monopoly by Elizabeth I to break the Dutch monopoly of the spice trade. In 1757, the forces of the British East India Company defeated the ruler of Bengal during the Battle of Plassey. This gave the British East India Company a base from which to fight other powerful rulers in India. Before this point, India's share of the world economy was as large as Europe's. The British capitalist class amassed great wealth from

India, while at least two-thirds of India's people, who were directly or indirectly connected with agriculture, lived in a state of poverty. This wealth further ignited Britain's Industrial Revolution, and soon after colonialism began, there was a rapid series of critical inventions. Increasing wealth afforded a certain group in society abundant resources to make technological advances that broke the dependence on old hand techniques. Some of these advances were Hargreaves's spinning Jenny (1764), Arkwright's water frame (1769), and Crompton's mule (1779). In 1785 came the adaptation of Watt's steam engine to increase the potency of these inventions so that they could further drive the relentlessness of the Industrial Revolution.

After a hundred years of Company rule in India, which left millions impoverished, there was an uprising in 1857, referred to as the Indian Rebellion. This uprising drastically changed the impression the British had of Indians from simple-minded to bloodthirsty and capable of killing the British who ruled them. In 1858, the British government passed the Government of India Act, which dissolved the British East India Company and transferred rule to Westminster. To ensure the safety of the British in India, several recommendations and acts were passed. These decisions could be summarized under the heading "divide and rule" and included increasing the number of British soldiers in India and passing a law preventing the the Indian population from carrying firearms. Also, British inhabitants were moved to all-white suburbs. Direct rule from Westminster was known as the period of the British Raj (*raj* is a word from the Indian subcontinent that means "rule"). The British Raj ended in 1947, with the partition of India into the independent domains of India and Pakistan. A period of 187 years of British rule ended, but the legacy of divide-and-rule policies is still felt today.

In 1838, during the period of Company rule in India, enslaved people in the British Caribbean were given their freedom. Five years had passed since the Slave Emancipation Act of 1833, which abolished slavery in parts of the British Empire, and in the intervening years, plantation owners were compensated for the loss of their slaves in the form of government grants. In 1834, a year after the act was passed, the British began a period of what was called indentured labor that brought Indians to the former slave colonies in the Caribbean to replace the enslaved Africans on the plantations and then later into Africa as indentured laborers during the British colonization of Africa.

James Walvin, author of *Britain's Slave Empire*, notes that after the Slave Emancipation Act and after much disquiet from slavery abolitionists:

> they decide they don't need it, which leaves them with a problem because the great economic system, which they have put in place on the back of slavery, which was primarily sugar—there were other commodities as well—had to be produced by someone. Indians seemed to fit the bill, India might be a replacement for Africa. India and Indians might produce an answer to the Labour void that had opened up in the old slave colonies. (Girmitunitedorg, 2012, 3:43)[4]

Dr. Mahin Gosine, an anthropologist at the University of Guyana, notes that Indians were brought initially to Mauritius and then to Guyana, Suriname, Jamaica, Trinidad, Granada, St. Vincent, St. Lucia, Martinique, and Guadeloupe. Just like the journey for Africans on the ships to the Caribbean, similar horrors also awaited Indians. Gosine argues that something like 12% of the indentured Indian immigrants who were brought to the Caribbean died on the way over (CaribNation TV, 2015).

In his book *Sugar Without Slaves*, Alan H. Adamson uses British Colonial Office records to reconstruct nineteenth-century Guyanese society before and after indentured immigration. What he concludes is that East Indian indentureship was a new form of slavery in that the laws and the brutalities were the same (Adamson, 1972).

DhanPaul Narine, of the Board of Education in New York, notes:

> The whole idea under the plantation system after emancipation was to divide and rule the East Indians and the Negroes . . . There were separate villages created for East Indians and

> blacks to prevent intermixing and hence solidarity. (Carib Nation TV, 2015, 5:39)

In terms of the focus of this book, the impact of slavery and colonialism was profound on two levels. The first was on a bodily level: The direct experience of trauma on individuals and family systems became embodied and was passed on through the generations. Fathers were separated from mothers, children from parents. During slavery, the affectional bonds of family were seen as dangerous to the plantocracy; because they increased the likelihood of rebellion, these bonds had to be broken down. For Africans taken to the New World, there were brutal daily traumas, and on top of these traumas were broken attachments on a systematic scale. Family, culture, and language were not so systematically broken for the indentured Indian laborers in the Caribbean as they were for Africans. This difference might suggest that the plantocracy had more respect for Indians. Or maybe the Indians had some power that the Africans did not possess to keep their family systems more or less intact. The simple fact, however, is that to maintain control and prevent uprisings, there needed to be something that differentiated the Africans from the Indians. One group needed to be favored over another to, again, divide and rule.

The second level of impact was the equally pervasive psychological level. As has already been noted, a harsh ideology was needed for slavery and colonialism to take place, especially at a time when the values of liberty and individual freedom were beginning taking root in the European imagination. Embedded in the race construct is a fundamental fear of uprising and meeting the cumulative ancestral rage passed on from generations of enslaved and colonized people. Ancestral rage continues to demand expression. Even though this generates fear, its expression will ultimately lead to healing if met with understanding and compassion. It has been some 180 years since the Slave Emancipation Act. Given the amount of time that has

"Ancestral rage continues to demand expression. Even though this generates fear, its expression will ultimately lead to healing if met with understanding and compassion."

passed, how can it be that similar dynamics between people of color and white people can still be present today, even though six or seven generations have passed? This question will be explored later in the section on intergenerational trauma.

› › › PAUSE . . . *and breathe* ‹ ‹ ‹

RACE AND THE LAW

A seminal moment in the coming together of a coordinated group of men to orchestrate race discrimination in law happened in Barbados. Barbados' profitable economy, based on violence toward African slaves and on the export of sugar, set the scene where some human beings were legislated to be less than human.

As an essential part of establishing and expanding on the slave economy, the Barbados House of Assembly, in 1661, enacted labor codes that aimed to control slave resistance along racial lines. There were two separate codes, one that governed Christian slaves—that is, England's poor and oppressed—and one that governed Negro slaves. The Barbados Act: An Act for the Better Ordering and Governing of Negroes (1661; retrieved from Huntingdon Library) of 1661 revealed, in legal terms, a brutal institution with a sugar industry at its heart.

The Act was written in the English of its time, so I have taken the liberty of translating some of it into more modern phrasing for ease of understanding. The clauses I cite will give you a sense of the brutality of the act. Also of note is that masters, mistresses, and overseers were also subject to punishments, although nowhere near as harsh, for failure to comply (Engerman et al., 2001).

The preamble to the Act refers to previous laws for governing Negroes that had not had the desired effect. It also states that these laws are being enacted for public safety and to protect Negroes as one would protect goods and chattels. To highlight the nonhuman in the Negro, there is explicit reference to them as a "heathenish, brutish and an uncertain dangerous pride of people" (Engerman et al., 2001, p. 105).

Here are some of the clauses in modern phrasing; please be warned, these excerpts are likely to be disturbing:

CLAUSE 1 No master, mistress, commander, or overseer shall give their negroes leave on sabbath days, holidays, or at any other time to go out of their plantation without a ticket specifying the time of his or her coming and going from the plantation. Any master, mistress, commander, or overseer who does not apprehend negroes who leave the plantation without a ticket and does not punish them by a moderate whipping shall forfeit 500 pounds of sugar.

CLAUSE 2 If any negro is violent to any Christian, the first offence will be punished by a severe whipping by the constable. For a negro's second offence toward any Christian, he shall be severely whipped, his nose split, and his face burnt. For a third offence, the negro will receive a greater corporal punishment as the governor and council see fit to inflict.

CLAUSE 4 Any authority that possesses runaway negroes will need to bring them to their proper owners. Failure to do so will be punishable by 9 and 30 lashes upon his naked back.

CLAUSE 5 All overseers need to do twice weekly searches in their negro houses for runaway negroes. Neglecting this duty will result in 100 pounds of sugar for every default.

CLAUSE 17 If any negro shall make insurrection, or rise in rebellion, or make preparation of arms or offensive weapons, or hold conspiracies for raising mutinies or rebellion as has been formally attempted, martial law against the actors and concealers of such mutiny or rebellion will be punished by death or other pain as their crimes shall deserve.

CLAUSE 19 If information is obtained of any runaway negro hiding place, the constable or captain of a company will raise a number of men, not exceeding 20, to apprehend or take them, either alive or dead. [There are a series of rewards of sugar for every negro found.]

CLAUSE 20 If a negro being punished by his master for running away or any other crimes shall suffer, no person whatsoever shall be accountable to any law. If any man whatsoever, through cruel intention, willfully kills any negro of his own, he shall pay into the public treasury 3000 pounds of sugar. If he kills another man's Negro, he shall pay double that.

CLAUSE 21 Any authority needs to send an account to the secretary noting which negroes have fled and run away and the time that they have been gone within 10 days or be penalized 1,000 pounds of sugar.

[There is a statement about the increase in the number of negroes on the island in recent years suggesting these cannot be safely or easily governed unless there is a considerable number of Christians to balance and equal their strength.]

CLAUSE 22 Every freeholder should provide one Christian servant for every 20 acres of land that he enjoys or possesses. The penalty for forfeiting is 3000 pounds of sugar for every three months of forfeiture.

CLAUSE 23 This Act is to be read and published in all respective parish churches the first Sunday in February and the first Sunday in August every year.

The link between racial brutality and commerce is clear to see in these codes. What is also clear is the legalized coercion of Christians (whites) and Negros (blacks) to behave in specific ways toward each other as a matter of law. Given the continuation of the trade in sugar and the other commodities that were to follow, this code, also called "slave codes," was evidently successful. It was taken up by Jamaica in 1664 and later, in 1684, the Jamaica House of Assembly passed a new

Slave Act with significant additions. This updated slave act was copied in the North American colonies of South Carolina in 1691, and then served as a model that was adopted by Virginia, Maryland, Florida, and other North American colonies.

› › › PAUSE . . . *and breathe* ‹ ‹ ‹

RACE, CLASS, AND GENDER

Race is often looked at in isolation, but when we incorporate the oppressions of class and gender, the picture of race starts to become a little clearer. To demonstrate how these oppressions link closely with each other, I want to give an overview of the foundational laws that were passed in colonial North America in the mid-1600s, which had race, class, and gender very much at their heart. The implementation of these laws gives us an important insight into the significance of patriarchy and class as pivotal social forces that shaped the making of law and their enforcement. This period of history was also the first time "white" came into use as a legal term.

Even though the dynamics of racism in North America are different from how they are in Europe and the U.K., North America has been hugely influential in shaping the dialogue of race for the world as a whole. I can remember very clearly as a child seeing the television images of the civil rights movement of the 1950s and 1960s and the narratives around the iconic figures who rose to prominence during that time, along with their assassinations. This period of history has imprinted itself on the world's psyche and is of considerable importance to how race relationships have been narrated and shaped. While watching the civil rights struggle as a child and absorbing the powerful narratives of struggle and pride, as well as the narratives of fear and violence, I had no real awareness of the history behind the laws that the civil rights movement was fighting against. The historical context to any social struggle is an integral part of the whole, and without this history, it is easy for the cognitive mind to be confused or swayed by the negatively biased racial imagination.

White antiracist writer and educator Jacqueline Battalora has a passionate interest in the social forces that make deep connections across race so difficult to sustain. Battalora (2013) gives a full account of early law making in colonial North America in her book *Birth of a White Nation: The Invention of White People and Its Relevance Today*. What Battalora wants to highlight, more than anything, in her writing and teaching is the symbolic and economic value of whiteness. The "invention of whiteness," as Battalora puts it, allowed for a disengagement from basic morality, specifically when it came to people of African descent.

I am going to give an overview of Battalora's research, but before I do, I want to bring to the fore a fundamental question that unconsciously diverts us from attending to the hurts of racism and that gets us stuck. It is a question that speaks to the genesis of racism itself and that needs clarification, or at least consideration. The question is: Did racism precede slavery, or was racism required in the "colonial context" to maintain economic wealth for a specific social group?

Some historians view the English language itself as loading negative meaning onto the color black and on blackness. Within this view, the English language, along with early observations of Africans by Europeans, provided the conditions for an entrenched position toward blackness that later resulted in brutality toward African people. Winthrop Jordan, in the historical text *White over Black*, notes: "Long before they found that some men were black, Englishmen found in the idea of blackness, a way of expressing some of their most ingrained values. No other color except white conveyed so much emotional impact" (Jordan, 1968, p. 7).

Jordan describes the meaning of *black* before the sixteenth century, as detailed in the *Oxford English Dictionary*, as

> deeply stained with dirt; soiled, dirty, foul . . . having dark or deadly purpose, malignant; pertaining to or involving death, deadly; painful, disastrous, sinister . . . foul, iniquitous, atrocious, horrible, wicked . . . indicating disgrace, censure, liability to punishment. (Jordan, 1968, p. 7)

Other historians have also taken the view that the English, along with other Europeans, were predisposed to have an emotional animosity toward the color black and, consequently, black Africans. These arguments, however, once again provide a narrative that allows us to neatly sidestep culpability and discomfort for unethical acts. Many historians have an alternative view of what drove European hostility toward black Africans. These historians firmly contest the theory of preconditioning, certainly concerning the North American context in the early 1600s.

According to historian David R. Roediger, "In certain places and at certain times between 1607 and [the] 1800s, the 'lower sorts' of whites appear to have been pleasantly lacking in racial consciousness" (Roediger, 1991, p. 24).

As we will begin to sense, there is a significant body of evidence that racism and American apartheid emerged out of a specific context—an economic context—rather than the idea of an emotionally loaded and racially hostile imagination. Let us now go through some of this history.

The British colonies of Maryland and Virginia in North America in the early 1600s were rooted in the production of tobacco. The vast majority of workers on the tobacco plantations were British men. At that time, there was a population boom in England, and poor British workers were traded as indentured laborers along with enslaved peoples. At this time, the population of the colonies was predominantly English, followed by enslaved Africans, other Europeans, and Native Americans.

An eminent authority on early American history, Edmund Morgan, notes that for the British colonies of North America in the 1600s, significant historical records reveal that both African and European men "serving the same master worked, ate, and slept together, and together shared in escapades, escapes, and punishments" (Morgan, 1975, p. 155).

The "critical measure of access to rights and privileges in law and, therefore, persons of African descent who held this status had access to all such rights, including the right to vote. In fact, there is evidence that free Africans held bond labourer's" (Jordan, 1968, pp. 74–75).

I am now going to outline a series of laws that, over time, became progressively coercive toward relationships between white women and men of African descent. It is important to start by laying out the social context of the time. We are very good at understanding the social relations that existed in the early 1700s, but generally have difficulty taking in the picture of social relations in the early 1600s. At the time, British free women could marry enslaved Africans. Take your time to let that sink in. A series of laws gave progressively more meaning to the terms "black" and "white" and created a form of patriarchal power that sat squarely within white men. The laws started with a focus on enslaved African men and progressed to simply Africans. I will also outline how the concept of whiteness within law was, in effect, another version of divide-and-rule within the context of a particular type of capitalism.

Battalora lets us know that "there is plenty of ethnographic material revealing that at least some persons of African descent were not treated as degraded beings, and behaved in manners consistent with Englishmen of a similar class. That persons of African descent were treated in a disparate manner by some Europeans at some moments in time cannot be disputed, . . . however, the entire body of available documents weighs much heavier with evidence of Europeans and Africans interacting in ways that suggest cooperation and a degree of mutuality." There is also evidence which shows that "many African men married European servants, and these marriages appear to have been accepted" (Battalora, 2013, p. 6). "In one county, one half of the free men of African descent were married to a European woman. There was a challenge to these marriages, but it did not come from the masses, it came from elites" (Battalora, 2014, pp. 8–43).

In 1664, the British colony of Maryland sought to challenge marriages between English women and African slaves, which were becoming more common. "This law punished English or other freeborn women who married enslaved Negro men. For the English or freeborn woman who entered into a marriage with an African slave, the punishment was that she too served the master of the slave for the duration of the slave's life. Also, any children that the marriage created would be enslaved until their twenties. Even though the express intent was to deter these marriages, what happened instead was that plantation owners saw these types of unions as a good thing in terms of increasing the value of the property they owned.

The 1664 act governed the state of affairs concerning marriage law until 1681, when the Maryland assembly changed the wording of the 1664 enactment from prohibiting English and other freeborn women from marrying enslaved Negro men to prohibiting English or other *white* women from marrying enslaved Negro men. So, what prompted this change in wording from "freeborn women" to "white women" and this need to invent a new category of people called "white," which was the first time this human category had ever appeared in law?

You might remember that I previously spoke about the Barbados Act of 1661, which was a series of slave codes designed to brutally restrict the behavior and movement of black bodies, and that it, too, included restrictions on the behavior of some white bodies. These codes of law were principally driven by a commitment to a particular type of commerce and by the fear of rebellion. Versions of these codes were then taken up by other Caribbean islands before being adopted in the British colonies of North America.

The fear of rebellion was also very much on the minds of the various North American colony governors, following a year-long insurrection in 1676 in the state of Virginia. The insurrection was led by a member of the British planter class called Nathaniel Bacon. Bacon's rebellion, as it was called, united slaves of African descent, indentured laborers of European descent, and free European and African laborers against the ruling elite. African slaves and European laborers were handed increasingly harsh punishments and extensions to their years of indentureship due to economic pressures that put a squeeze on plantation profits. Free European and African laborers were also finding the ability to make a future for themselves tough due to the short supply of land and opportunities.

British troops eventually quashed the rebellion, but not before it made a significant impression on the Virginia governors. To prevent future resistance, the Virginia governors sought to pursue a divide and conquer strategy (Allen, 1997). The Barbados Act and its application in various Caribbean islands then formed the ideal template for the North American colonial governors. As mentioned previously, the wording of the Marriage Act of 1664 in Maryland was changed in 1681 from "English and other freeborn women" to "English and other white women." The invention of whiteness, as Battalora (2013) puts it, was an important concept at this time. This concept had the effect of dividing African laborers from British and European laborers. At the same time, the idea of whiteness erased the divisions within the British and other European laborers so that English, Irish, German, Scottish, Dutch, French, and other European laborers all became one. Whiteness then represented a commitment to a particularly brutal and hostile type of capitalism.

In 1691, the Virginian assembly pushed for marriage legislation that went beyond the Maryland Act and would further set apart British and other Europeans that were classed as white from those of native tribes, mulattos (persons of mixed black and white heritage), and those of African descent. Even thought the Virginian law prohibited both white men and white women from marrying someone of African descent or a member of a native tribe, according to professor emeritus of history Victoria Bynum's research into this period, "magistrates prosecuted primarily white women and black men rather than white men and black women. This uneven application of the law reflected the structure of gender and racial relationships. White males claimed the right to govern all women, regardless of race. The sole sexual possession of white women by white men assured perpetuation of the dominant 'pure' white race" (Bynum, 1992, p. 96).

In addition to harsh changes to marriage laws after Bacon's rebellion, a slew of other laws were enacted that removed the rights and privileges of people of African heritage, who were, before that time, free and had the rights and privileges of free people. These laws removed the rights of people of African heritage to, for example, hold public office, possess a weapon, take part in lawmaking, and testify against whites in a court of law. The invention of whiteness could both keep alive the idea of rights and privileges in law for the free and at the same time remove these rights and privileges from those of African descent and those of native tribes. The laws enacted in colonial North America once again emphasize that race and race hostility are a social construct that benefits the few rather than a biological reality or, as some would like us to believe, a preconditioned hostility toward the color black and blackness.

Three years after the term "white" was first used in law, the first concepts of race, where mental attributes were ascribed to observable physical differences, began to emerge. I will say more about these conceptualizations of race in Chapter 5, "Nonrelational Being." What is important to say at this point is that conceptions of race and the division of the human species into distinct groups provided a soothing cognitive balm for the minds of those interested in forwarding a brutal and unforgiving form of wealth accumulation.

Working our way through the laws enacted by the colonial North American legislating assemblies and considering the intentions of these assemblies to pursue a particular type of capitalism, we can then see the need for the concept of whiteness. Whiteness, as an organizing principle, was needed to keep intact the divisions between groups of laborers and to maintain the status quo. Before Bacon's rebellion, European and African laborers lived the same lives and had the same opportunities. After Bacon's rebellion, whiteness appears. Whiteness functioned as a type of divide-and-rule, whereby the group of laborers labeled white were bestowed a shared status with the white elite, along with its embedded assumptions of superiority. Whiteness, however, didn't lift the economic status of white laborers closer to that of the white elites; instead, it created a new underclass, a new bottom. Whiteness also represented the center of patriarchal power by controlling white women through the enactment of marriage laws that prohibited, primarily white women, from marrying nonwhite men. White patriarchal power was also asserted by removing nonwhite men's ability to protect themselves and their families through laws that prohibited them from carrying firearms and testifying against whites.

In the southern states of the U.S. in the late 19th and early 20th century, the system of laws and cultural customs around race was called "Jim Crow." The Jim Crow laws made clear the boundaries of the racial order. During tough economic times, the white working class would not just value the separation of races, but militantly try to police the boundary. To stress the importance of gender and race, the most stringent policing of the color line almost always occurred around black men and white women. For whites who crossed the racial boundary and rejected Jim Crow laws, the consequences were unrestrained violence and rejection from the white community.

Dr. Martin Luther King summed up this divide-and-rule strategy in a speech, "Our God is Marching On!" [5] given on March 25, 1965, at the conclusion of three marches from Selma to Alabama. In his address, King echoes Bacon's rebellion and speaks of harsh segregation laws following the Negros and Europeans in the South threatening to unite for a just society. Through metaphor, King also tells the story of the poor white man, who, while starving and crying out in hunger, has learned to feed upon Jim Crow, for at least he is a white man—better than a black man. [5]

› › › PAUSE . . . *and breathe* ‹ ‹ ‹

HISTORY: THE FACTS

The period of slavery, colonialism, and other forms of large-scale oppression based on race is vast. Below are timelines for the European slave trade, covering indentured labor from India to the Caribbean and Africa; British rule in India; the American slave trade, including the period of segregation; and apartheid in South Africa. I have included apartheid here as it represents the tragic outcome of minds totally inhabited by the social constructs of blackness and whiteness in more modern times. A simplified graphical representation of these timelines can be found in the appendix.

THE EUROPEAN SLAVE TRADE[6]

1562 Sir John Hawkins makes the first English slaving expedition.

1625 Barbados becomes the first British settlement in the Caribbean.

1661 The Barbados Act, the first law based on race, is passed.

1672 The Royal Africa Company is granted a royal charter to carry Africans to the Americas, which formalizes the slave trade.

1791 A slave rebellion on the Caribbean island of St. Domingue, controlled by the French, is successful. After this rebellion, the first independent black state outside Africa—Haiti—is established.

1794 France abolishes slavery in all its territories.

1807 On March 25, the British Parliament abolished the transatlantic slave trade (245 years after Hawkins' first voyage).

1833 British Parliament passes the Abolition of Slavery Act, abolishing the practice of slavery in all British territories (176 years after the formalization of the slave trade). In practice, this act took many years of continued agitation to be fully realized.

1872 The last of the transatlantic slave trade is generally assumed to be a Spanish ship in 1867, but historians have recently unearthed evidence of two slave ships, one Portuguese and one from the US, landing in Cuba in 1872 (The transatlantic slave trade lasted 253 years.) (Alberge, 2024, para. 2).

The exact number of British ships that took part in the slave trade will probably never be known. In the 245 years between Hawkins's first voyage and the abolition of the transatlantic slave trade in 1807, merchants in Britain dispatched about 10,000 voyages to Africa for slaves.

Between 1750 and 1780, about 70% of the British government's total income came from taxes on goods from its colonies.

BRITISH RULE IN INDIA

Chattel slavery of Africans financed British rule in India. It fueled, for Britain at least, the most significant expansion of wealth and the emergence of the capitalist system we know today.

1612 The British East India Company is granted a trade monopoly by Elizabeth I, and then begins to establish trading posts in several cities in India. The British East India Company increasingly takes on governmental powers, with its own army and judiciary, and takes more and more control over vast swathes of India until 1757.

1757 The first war of independence is fought between the forces of the British East India Company and the Nawab of Bengal and Sirajuddaulah, who surrender their domains to the company. This establishes a period of what is called Company rule, which gives the British East India Company a base from which to fight other powerful rulers of India.

1858 Company rule ends when, following the Indian Rebellion of 1857, the British government dissolves the British East India Company and takes over administration of the colonies. The Government of India Act leads to the British Crown assuming direct control of the Indian subcontinent and Queen Victoria becoming empress of India. This period is known as the British Raj and lasts from 1858 to 1947.

During the British Raj, a series of acts were passed by the British government to ensure the safety of the British following the Indian Rebellion; for example, the passing of an act in 1859 to disarm the local population so that those found with firearms without a licence would be fined, sentenced, or given corporal punishment. To further ensure safety, the British moved to all-white suburbs on the outskirts of towns and cities, having minimal contact with native Indians whom they increasingly viewed with suspicion.

THE AMERICAN SLAVE TRADE AND SEGREGATION

1619 The first African slave arrives in Virginia.

1636 North America's slave trade begins when the first American slave carrier, *Desire*, is built and launched in Massachusetts.

1643 Massachusetts is the first colony to legalize slavery.

1681 The term "white" appears as a human category in law for the first time in Maryland.

1775 The first abolition society is founded in Philadelphia, Pennsylvania.

1865 The 13th Amendment to the U.S. Constitution is made, abolishing slavery throughout the country. Four states reject ratification of the 13th Amendment at the time (New Jersey ratified in 1866; Delaware ratified in 1901; Kentucky ratified in 1976; and Mississippi lawmakers finally ratified in 1995.)

(Chattel slavery ends 246 years after the first slaves arrive in Virginia.)

1866 The Ku Klux Klan is founded in Tennessee, a year after the 13th Amendment to the U.S. Constitution is made.

1871 The Ku Klux Klan Act is passed, giving the federal government the right to mete out punishment where civil rights laws are not upheld and to use military force against anticivil rights conspiracies.

1896 The Supreme Court sanctions legal separation of the races by its ruling in *Plessy v. Ferguson*. It is held that separate but equal facilities did not violate the U.S. Constitution's 14th Amendment that grants citizenship to "all persons born or naturalized in the United States."

1909 A small group of activists organize and found the National Association for the Advancement of Colored People (NAACP). The NAACP wages a long struggle to eliminate race segregation.

1954 The Supreme Court orders desegregation after a court case fought by the NAACP, leading to the decision that school segregation violates the "Equal Protection" and "Due Process" clauses of the 14th Amendment.

1965 The period of segregation, or what were called "Jim Crow Laws," come to an end, almost 70 years after the *Plessy v. Ferguson* ruling in 1896.

A HISTORY OF SOUTH AFRICAN COLONIZATION AND APARTHEID

1652 The Dutch East India Company establish a colony in Cape Town to use as a base for Dutch trade with Asia. Within four years of their arrival, the first war between the Khoikhoi and the Dutch broke out, as the Khoi clans tried to drive away the Dutch who had appropriated their land. This began the colonization of Southern Africa.

1795 The Dutch in South Africa reached 16,000 from only 90 in 1652. The same year, the number of South Africans enslaved in the country by the Dutch rose to 16,839. Two-thirds of Cape Town's population consisted of enslaved people. The land, its people, and the natural resources were exploited. The Dutch referred to themselves as the Afrikaners or the Boers.

EARLY 1900s The Boer War leads to the British Empire gaining control over several colonies as well as the largest goldmine complexes in the world. These colonies are incorporated into the British Empire. After the war, the British place Afrikaners in concentration camps, killing 26,000 of them.

1910 The South Africa Act is passed by the British. This act, along with the negotiated cooperation of the Afrikaners, lays the foundations for white majority rule over native African, Asian, colored, and other mixed race people.

1924 Hertzog's National Party wins the election and begins to put in place legislation to protect the privileged position of the white South African minority. During the next 15 years, laws are passed to prevent Africans and Asians from taking up skilled trades, to limit Africans' access to towns, and to enforce various degrees of segregation upon the white and black communities.

1934 Daniel Malan forms a purified National Party, as he feels Hertzog's measures are too mild.

1948 Malan's party, now the Reunited National Party, wins the election and initiates the era of strict apartheid (apartheid is another word for segregation of the races), which continues through successive governments.

1948–1954 Prime Minister F. Malan in office.

1954–1958 Prime Minister J. G. Strijdom in office.

1958–1966 Prime Minister H. Verwoerd in office.

1966–1978 Prime Minister J. Vorster in office.

1978–1989 Prime Minister P. W. Botha in office. Botha allowed Asians and people of mixed race to be represented in a white-controlled Parliament but continued to exclude the nation's black majority.

1989–1994 During F. W. de Klerk's term in office, he legalized opposition parties and made the agreements that eventually brought down apartheid.

1990 Nelson Mandela, leader of the movement to end South African apartheid, is released from prison.

1991 Apartheid comes to an end after negotiations between the governing de Klerk National Party, the African National Congress, and a wide variety of other political organizations.

1994–1999 Nelson Mandela is president of South Africa.

THE TRANSMISSION OF FEAR: INTERGENERATIONAL TRAUMA

The basic idea of intergenerational trauma is that fear, even if not named or spoken about, is passed on and inherited from one generation to another. The current literature on trauma points toward both nurture and nature as playing essential roles in this transmission, both of which I will outline in this section. Before looking at the transmission of fear, however, I want to illustrate the idea of intergenerational consequences from a financial perspective.

On February 9, 2018, Her Majesty's Treasury tweeted the following:

> Here is today's surprising #FridayFact. Millions of you helped end the slave trade through your taxes. Did you know? In 1833, Britain used £20 million, 40% of its national budget, to buy freedom for all slaves in the Empire. The amount of money borrowed for the Slavery Abolition Act was so large that it wasn't paid off until 2015. Which means that living British citizens helped pay to end the slave trade. (HM Treasury [@hmtreasury], 2018, February 9)

There is a lot to unpack in this tweet, but let's start with what the Slavery Abolition Act was about in a practical sense, and then we'll look at this tweet through the lens of the race construct.

The long title for the Slavery Abolition Act of 1833 reads as follows:

> An act for the abolition of slavery throughout the British colonies; for promoting the industry of the manumitted [liberated/freed] slaves; and for compensating the persons hitherto entitled to the services of such slaves. (Slavery Abolition Act, 1833)

The act provided the registered owners of slaves to be freed compensation for the loss of these slaves as if they were business assets. The 40% of the Treasury's annual income, quoted in the tweet above, was approximately 5% of the British GDP (*note*: 5% of the British

GDP in 2016 was around £100 billion). The British government took out a bank loan for £15 million on August 3, 1835 to finance the compensation.

Academics from University College London spent some three years drawing together 46,000 records of compensation given not just to wealthy British slave-owners but also to ordinary men and women from all levels of society for whom it was simply a financial transaction. Prominent individuals whose families benefited from the compensation afforded by the Slavery Abolition Act include former prime minister David Cameron, authors Graham Greene and George Orwell, and poet Elizabeth Barrett Browning. One less well-known but equally influential group to benefit was the descendants of one of the nation's oldest banking families, the Bearings. The money this family and others received was invested in aspects of the Industrial Revolution. Some used the money for philanthropic enterprises. The biggest single payout went to James Blair, a Member of Parliament who had homes in Marylebone, central London, and Scotland. He was awarded £83,530, the equivalent of £65 million today, for the 1598 slaves he owned on a British Guyana plantation he had inherited . The most significant payout of all went to John Gladstone, the father of the nineteenth-century prime minister William Gladstone. He received £106,769, the equivalent of £83 million today, for the 2508 slaves he owned across 9 plantations. The database that contains the payouts for slave-owners is available to view at the University College London website and is called Legacies of British Slave Ownership.

What I was first struck by after reading the tweet above was the fact that the loan repayments were taking place under the radar for over 180 years. Also, the descendants, whose ancestry could be traced back to the beneficiaries of these loans, seemed to be unaware that this was happening. As you might imagine, following the Treasury's tweet there was intense backlash, which prompted the rapid deletion of the tweet and an acknowledgment of the concerns raised about the sensitivity of the subject.

Bringing the social construct of race into the picture, the tweet makes sense. The tone of the tweet suggests that those reading it should have some measure of pride in their tax contributions going toward the ending of slavery. Given that the race construct is designed to orient us toward preventing the activation of shame in white individuals, it probably felt natural for the tweeter to focus on the fact that these repayments were no longer payable. However, the reality distortion field created by the race construct was abruptly disrupted following a flurry of reactions on social media. The shame was out of the bag, prompting the tweet to be removed. The acknowledgment from the Treasury that the subject was sensitive, hence the removal of the tweet, implied that the onus of the problem was people's hurt sensitivities. Here again is the playing out of the race construct and the avoidance of naming the real consequences of slavery on black people's lives.

The impact of slavery left a financial legacy that generations of taxpayers have had to service. This financial legacy was hidden yet continued to perpetuate toxic patterns of economic exploitation laid down by the planter classes. This financial legacy also carried with it an emotional legacy that had exacted a further toll on generations of white, black, and brown people, which has also been operating under the radar, mostly unnoticed. This emotional legacy is equally, if not more, destructive than the financial legacy, as it keeps the old patterns of the race construct, with the benefits and privileges it affords, feeling like the natural order of things—the way things are supposed to be.

Nurture and Attachment

Coming back to the intergenerational transmission of fear, I previously pointed toward the theory of implicit memories and that difficulties in the race conversation are a result of nonverbally transmitted traumas from the past. These implicit memories then trigger negative behaviors in the present. I also highlighted that it is not just the connections we make with those who care for us but also the connections we make with the broader community that are vital. These connections allow us to develop and sustain a capacity to feel physiologically safe—the kind of safe that goes beyond simply removing what others might see as threats in the environment.

Psychotherapist Dr. Aileen Alleyne, who explores themes on black/white dynamics and the emotion of shame present in black identity, argues that when we think of the Jewish experience today, it is hard to separate it from the Holocaust. In the same way, Alleyne notes that the black experience today cannot be separated from the systematic dehumanization of African slaves. She also argues that, with all kinds of trauma, we have a dysfunctional relationship with the traumatizing other, which gets passed on through the generations. However, she suggests this intergenerational trauma can be transcended (Ellis, 2012).[7]

Psychologist John Bowlby coined the term "attachment theory" in the late 1960s as a result of his studies on child development. Attachment theory proposes that there are some basic elements that are required for infant development, and one of these is developing attachments with responsible caretakers. Also in the 1960s, Mary Ainsworth (1967) conducted cross-cultural observations of attachment in Uganda and America. In these studies, she found that attachment patterns, which are strategies that children develop to feel safe and to maximize their opportunities for receiving care and protection from close adults, were applicable to both of these diverse groups. The study allowed for the fact that infants in these two groups behave differently but in ways that reflect the norms within their respective cultures.

Although attachment theory provides an important context for human psychological development, the way it is presented in mainstream psychology and psychotherapy is through a western, middle-class cultural frame, where the attachment to a single caregiver is the focus. Using this cultural frame, if attachment to this single carer does not occur, there will be negative consequences. Also within this single attachment relationship frame, the infant develops a sense of self that is a reflection of the individual caregiver's representation of the infant. This presentation of attachment does mirror what we see in real life, but there are other important aspects of attachment that generally do not get much attention. There is, for instance, the fact that the single carer is typically situated in a social and physical context. The typical representation of attachment theory also does not take into account the fact that most children in the world grow up in multiple social arrangements with varying compositions, hierarchies, and meanings—even in the West. In a culturally informed conception of attachment theory, the question is less about how secure the attachment is with a single carer and more about the child's development of trust in others as well as trust in their own agency. Professor of anthropology Thomas Weisner puts it like this:

> The universal socialization task for cultures regarding attachment concerns the learning of trust, not ensuring the "secure" attachment of an individual child to a single caregiver. . . . The question that is important for many, if not most, parents and communities is not, "Is [this individual] child 'securely attached?' " but rather, "How can I ensure that my child knows whom [sic] to trust and how to share appropriate social connections to others? How can I be sure my child is with others and in situations where he or she will be safe?" (Weisner, 2018, p. 263)

Concern over the safety of their children while they go about their daily lives is an important issue for people of color. How can the child's responsible carers ensure that their child is with others and in situations where he or she will feel internally safe? It is clear that for children, the internal feeling of safety along with the development of trust in others and the self is influenced by more than just the primary attachment. Attachment theory, like many other western psychological theories, does not acknowledge the race construct's impact nor take into account the potentially hostile world—an outside world that imposes itself on communities of color, influencing the socialization of children and child development.

Despite these points against attachment theory, much about the theory is sound and applicable to all cultural environments. In this next section, I will be using an attachment theory lens to further explore the experience of safety and trust. Attachment theory says that we are hardwired to behave in ways that promote closeness with responsible caretakers within our social group to secure protection from environmental danger. Protection is not the only aspect of attachment that is important, however. Another aspect relates to the importance of having positive experiences within a social group as well as receiving a respectful gaze from the wider world. Positive experiences with your social group and the wider world promote an internal sense of safety and the experience of a regulated emotional state. How, then, does all of this work in practice?

Going back to childhood, infants have three ways to soothe themselves: the first is the sucking reflex, which instantly soothes; the second is to avert the gaze to avoid contact; and the third is to dissociate or move away from the present moment to go "somewhere else," even if only in the mind. All other ways of emotional soothing come from our social environment. The first thing the social world does when a baby cries, is pick them up and soothe them nonverbally through movement, facial gesture, and a calming tone of voice. The baby then internalizes these experiences. The idea that something outside of me is regulating me is called interregulation. If there is enough interregulation, these experiences become imprinted neurologically and become autoregulation; autoregulation being the ability to manage and soothe our own emotional states.

From the historical legacy of slavery, I am proposing that interregulation between people of color and white people easily becomes compromised through nonverbal and unconscious processes that have been and continue to be passed on from one generation to the next. Let me outline several studies that look into these processes within and between particular populations. It should be noted that many of these types of studies assume the mother is the primary influence on a child's development across all cultural environments. Even with this being so, most studies say something important about the intergenerational transmission of internal states.

A study that explored attachment across three generations suggested that the states of mind of grandmothers tended to correspond not only to those of their adult daughters but also to those of their daughter's children (Benoit & Parker, 1994, as cited in Hesse, 1999).

Studies have also found that children respond to their primary carers in ways that preserve their carers' psychological states of mind. These states of mind then become shared between the carers and child and passed on to the next generation.

Although attachment patterns appear to play a role in passing on internal security, or insecurity, from one generation to the next, this only partly explains what is happening. Researchers have found that other processes are influencing this transmission. Beginning in childhood, we develop a theory in our minds as we attempt to make sense of others' behaviors and then predict what they will do in the light of what we think is going on in their minds. Psychologist David Premack first coined the term "theory of mind" to describe this process (Premack & Woodruff, 1978, pp. 515–526). Within the sphere of theory of mind is the idea of self-monitoring your thoughts and states of mind. Psychologist Mary Main called this *metacognition* (Main, 1991). With metacognition ability, we can think about our thinking and reflect on our state of mind. Lacking metacognition, however, we simply become our state of mind. There is also the idea of having a capacity for what psychoanalysts Peter Fonagy and Mary Target called a *reflective function* (Fonagy & Target, 1997). An example of reflective function is bearing in mind that someone's rejection of you may have occurred because they were stressed rather than because they were hostile. Author of *Attachment in Psychotherapy*, David J. Wallin, points out that:

> Reflective function lets us see ourselves and others as beings with psychological depth. It enables us to respond to our experience on the basis not only of observed behavior, but also of the underlying mental states—desires, feelings, beliefs—that make behavior understandable and give it meaning. As such, reflective function is intimately related to our capacities for insight and empathy. (Wallin, 2007, p. 44)

Metacognition and reflective function are largely implicit abilities to reflect on your own state of mind and on the state of mind of others.

These abilities are also an important protective factor in minimizing the probability of intergenerationally transmitting insecurity.

During the hundreds of years of slavery, Africans were treated as property. Their children and their children's children were also treated as property. For hundreds of years, the focus from one generation of African slaves to the next was on organizing life around danger and threat to life. In addition to ongoing threats to their bodies, there were also never-ending threats to the continuation of their important interpersonal relationships. They had little control over the fates of their family members; for instance, any one of them could be auctioned or paired off for reproduction, breaking the bonds of attachment. Although intimacy and love still flourished in these conditions, feelings of affection were severely constrained by a generationally instilled pragmatism when it came to relationships and a stoic resilience around separation and loss. Breaking the relational bonds of the family and relational bonds in general was not just practical in a financial sense; it was also an essential strategy for the planter class to maintain control. Religious and cultural practices were also broken for the same effect. Without secure relational, spiritual, and cultural bonds, enslaved Africans learned to suppress their reflective function and connection to sources of safety and, in doing so, lived with little emotional grounding, making them easier to master. Breaking relational bonds also dampened curiosity and mutuality and increased hypervigilance and distrust—the latter being much more functional in protecting their lives. With conditions remaining the same for generations, relational insecurity, hypervigilance, and distrust were inevitably passed on from generation to generation. The transmission was twofold: through the children's and caretakers' insecure relational bonds and the humiliating gaze of white slavers. After slavery ceased, these generational traits have become part of a cultural norm held in place by the race construct.

What about white people and their reflective function? For white people closely involved with the slave trade, taking part in the horrors needed a suppression of reflective function that was specific to Africans and all non-white people. Financial gain, racial ideology, and harsh punishments for crossing the racial line themselves had the effect of conditioning and organizing this group of white people to act in unspeakable ways. For the witnesses who had no direct connection with the slave colonies, the race construct, with its sense of superiority along with the racial imagination, also had the effect of suppressing reflective function, specifically around Africans and other non-white people. With conditions remaining the same for generations, this suppression of reflective function in relation to Africans inevitably got passed on from generation to generation. Once again, the transmission was twofold: through caretakers' racial conditioning being passed to their children and through the separation of whites from non-whites to keep the status quo. After slavery ceased, these generational traits have become part of a cultural norm held in place by the race construct.

All of this plays out in the present through institutional racism within political, economic, and legal institutions and systems, and individually through white fragility and racial micro/macro-aggressions.

Dr. Joy DeGruy, an educator and author, has explored the continuing legacy of slavery in her research of 200 black teenagers between the ages of 14 and 18, all from the same neighborhood, half of whom were incarcerated. From her research in 2005, she coined the term "Posttraumatic Slave Syndrome" (PTSS).

> Posttraumatic Slave Syndrome is a condition that exists when a population has experienced multigenerational trauma resulting from centuries of slavery and continues to experience oppression and institutionalized racism today. Added to this condition is a belief (real or imagined) that the benefits of society in which they live are not accessible to them. This, then, is Post Traumatic Slave Syndrome. (DeGruy, 2005, p. 121)

DeGruy points out that people of African descent post slavery most likely have posttraumatic stress disorder (PTSD). PTSD is an anxiety disorder, first recognized after the Vietnam War, caused by very stressful, frightening, or distressing events. From a clinical perspective, PTSS is similar to PTSD but would be attributed to the multigenerational transmission of stress as a result of the trauma inflicted on individuals during the period of the slave trade. The symptoms of PTSS are adaptive behavior (for instance, being silent and not activating white guilt), learned helplessness (the sense of powerlessness arising from a persistent failure to succeed), internalized oppression (or self-hate), and horizontal oppression (acting toward others in the same group or other oppressed groups in ways that reinforce the status quo). DeGruy also points to other key patterns of behavior of PTSS, like a marked propensity for anger and violence, extreme feelings of suspicion, and perceived negative motivations of others. Naming PTSS, as for any condition, can be a useful step toward developing reflective function about an individual's past and a step toward healing. DeGruy (2015) believes that:

> Understanding the role our past plays in our present attitudes, outlooks, mindsets and circumstances is important if we are to free ourselves from the spiritual, mental and emotional shackles that bind us today, shackles that limit what we believe we can be, do and have. Understanding the part Post Traumatic Slave Syndrome plays in our evolution may be the key that helps to set us on the path to well-being. (p. 176)

As noted earlier, intergenerational passing down of compromised reflective function is not limited to people of color. White people also experience, very powerfully, compromised reflective function when the focus is on race, which also has been passed down through their ancestral line.

› › › PAUSE . . . *and breathe* ‹ ‹ ‹

Nature and Epigenetics

Let us turn our attention to the other potential process of transmission of trauma across generations: epigenetics. Epigenetics is an area of research that studies how the environment communicates with our genes and suggests how fear and other emotional traits are transmitted through generations. It is known that each cell within an individual, with a few exceptions, has precisely the same DNA sequence. For instance, a liver cell and a neuron from the same person have the same DNA sequence, yet these two cells do entirely different things. Epigenetics proposes that there is a mechanism above the level of genes that determines the function of a cell. There is a well-established, evidence-based theory explaining the stability of cell division and function across a person's lifespan and a less scientifically established process where cell division and function are influenced by a person's experiences throughout their life. While the stability of cell division and function is the general rule, there are exceptions, such as in the nervous system, where epigenetics appear to drive experience-dependent modifications to cognition and behavior. Neuro epigeneticists believe that our biology may be altered by trauma and then carried on, through reproduction, to future generations (Sweatt, 2012). In a 2015 study (Tang et al., 2015)[8] of Holocaust survivors, there was the first demonstration of an association of preconception parental trauma with epigenetic alterations in both parent and offspring (Yehuda et al., 2016).[9]

For the witnesses of slavery and those directly involved in bringing slavery about, there was an ever-present fear of an uprising. This fear drove the need to have tight control of, and distance from, the slave population, to minimize the risk of being exposed to their rage. Although scientifically untested, I propose that this fear has been passed on through epigenetic transmission from the victims, witnesses, and perpetrators of slavery and is therefore still present today.

A study published in 1998 by psychologists Scott Vrana and David Rollock examined physiological responses to encounters with unfamiliar people (Vrana & Rollock, 1998). The study was conducted with 54 black and 51 white undergraduate males and females. Each subject was left alone in a room after being hooked up to equipment that monitored their heart rate, perspiration, and facial movements. A stranger would walk into the room, introduce themselves and then proceed to take the participant's pulse. After a minute, the person would leave the room. Sometimes the interaction was with someone of the same race as the participant, sometimes not. All interactions were between people of the same sex.

A change in heart rate is expected to accompany an interaction with any stranger. The researchers found, however, that when the stranger is racially different, heart rates go up more than if they were of the same race and that changes in heart rate were more pronounced in men. For white men, heart rates went up almost ten beats per minute when a black man entered the room. For black men, heart rates went up two beats per minute when another black man entered the room and decreased by about two beats per minute when a white man entered the room. The researchers could not explain the reasons for these effects, but I will offer my speculations shortly.

For white men in the study, I believe the transmission of fear is partly at work here. Ancestrally, there have been generations of white men who have maintained a state of readiness for rebellion from black men, or at least readiness within the racial imagination. It would make sense that this anxiety is passed on genetically, in part, almost as an evolutionary survival strategy.

To explain what the researchers could not, we should note that this study occurred in a medical facility with white men as the experts in this particular setting. I speculate that the environment explains the heart rate changes for the study's black men. When another black man enters the room, unconsciously, there is a misfit. When a white man enters the room, unconsciously, this is how it's meant to be.

Given that there are no definitive studies in epigenetic inheritance of fear in humans, it is perhaps right that there is some skepticism as to its validity within the scientific community. Whether you believe in epigenetic transmission of fear or not, these ideas are part of the conversation of race and part of the dialogue about how the fears, present during slavery for millions of people, still exist today.

› 5 ‹

BEING WITH RACE

The Problem of Internal Discomfort

Nonrelational Being

THE PROBLEM OF INTERNAL DISCOMFORT

After the abolition of slavery, postraumatic symptoms in survivors and witnesses were left largely unaddressed. Ex-slaves continued to be preoccupied with physical and psychological survival, leaving little room for reflection or contemplation. Post slavery, people of color had to work out how to be in a world that actively disengaged from their inner distress. At the same time, they had to hold onto their distress and keep it locked down because there were dangers, both real and imagined, in verbalizing these concerns. Even though people exposed to trauma may try to "hold-down" their distress and it might appear outwardly that they have succeeded, there is still a lot going on inside the body. For white people, being in relationship with this hidden distress was problematic and needed resolving.

The race construct was a way to guard against connecting with this "held-down" distress and a way to sidestep the experience of internal dysregulation. How can we communicate with one another about race with all of this going on? Where do we start?

"Even though people exposed to trauma may try to 'hold-down' their distress and it might appear outwardly that they have succeeded, there is still a lot going on inside the body."

In the field of psychotherapy and body therapy, it is clear that human-made traumas that are created in relationship need to be resolved in relationship. In this chapter and the next, I am going to lay out a series of ideas rooted in trauma theory that together leads us to a paradigm shift. This paradigm shift involves recognizing that our nervous systems and minds are hypervigilant to implicit, nonverbal racial cues that prime the body to respond as if there was actual danger or threat to life. This paradigm shift also recognizes that when we become aware of race, these implicit, nonverbal racial cues are triggered, which inevitably brings inner distress and discomfort along with feeling physiologically unsafe. From this base of understanding, I will lay out what I call The Race Construct Awareness Model and then explore ways of working with this model individually, with a psychological practitioner, and with peers. All of this will inevitably involve consistent and conscious processing, which requires intention, attention, and time (Phelps & Thomas, 2003). Seeing these processes for what they are, without the need to wade through the many distractions that the race construct throws up, naturally leads us to respond to race hurt in the same way we would respond to any other hurt.

Resolving Internal Discomfort

In everyday one-on-one relationships, problems can be resolved in one of two ways: One side of the relationship can accept that they have done something that triggered hurt in the other and then respond in ways that connect with the hurt experienced in the other. This relational mode of resolving difficulties has a high likelihood of leading to repairing, and even healing, relationships. There is also what could be called a nonrelational mode of resolving difficulties. This mode involves one side of the relationship not acknowledging that they had a part to play in the distress felt by the other, and this side then tries to hold the other wholly responsible for the distress between them, and then attempts to either force the other to shut down by silencing them or attacks them in some way. Within the nonrelational mode, reflective functioning and empathy and compassion shut down. Inner narratives might be, "If only their behavior were like mine, the discomfort would go away, and we could just get along," or "Someone has to pay for making me feel this way!" In the field of trauma, this nonrelational mode employs what is called "top-down regulation." In top-down regulation, there is a reliance on cognitive abilities to self-soothe and move away from difficult conscious and unconscious internal feelings. Top-down regulation can be extremely functional, in that we can use it to transform feelings of self-blame and to unburden ourselves from feelings that weigh us down. In the area of interpersonal relationships, however, top-down regulation is often used to avoid uncomfortable truths and sidestep difficult internal feelings.

Moving on from this general discussion about resolving the internal discomfort inherent in relational problems, I want to turn once again to how we relate to one another around race. To date, there has been no collective response to the distress caused by slavery and colonialism that has been proportional to the energy that went into organizing those systems. The normal response to perceiving distress in another is paying attention to the other and demonstrating an intention to understand them. This way of being was, and still is, effectively short-circuited by the race construct. Instead implicit memories of the past, along with consciously remembered visual and cognitive narratives that call attention to the dividing line of race, are aroused. The past then becomes the present, as the humiliation that people of color experienced is evoked within one side, and at the same time, the fear of a historical-style "slave revolt" is evoked within the other. Responding to race hurt is made even more difficult to untangle by the often-invoked white privilege of being able to avoid feeling the uncomfortableness of race.

We cannot think of ourselves as entirely helpless, however, as it is possible to transcend the social conditioning of the race construct enough to allow for some connection and healing to take place. It is also true to say that, within the race conversation, the potential for healing does not take place only within the descendants of the enslaved and colonized. There is potential for healing for the descendants of the witnesses and perpetrators, who were coerced into accepting what was happening in their name.

Here is a broad summary of how the resolution of internal discomfort within the race conversation might look based on these nonrelational and relational modes of being. Starting with nonrelational resolution of inner discomfort, the person of color is objectified so you can disassociate from the internal discomfort that is inherent in the race construct. In this mode, the mind performs cognitive somersaults to step back from the experience. If you were to notice this experience in the moment, it might look like confusion. To move away from the evoked tension and shame, some measure of top-down regulation is activated. Nonrelational resolution of internal discomfort inevitably leads to scripts about the racial hierarchy as well as what might be seen as the more benign narrative of "We are all the same." With relational resolution of internal discomfort, there is an acceptance that, within the relationship, you are sometimes a trigger for distress in people of color (including people of color being triggers for other people of color). You are also aware that how you respond is an essential component to mutual healing.

I will say more about relational resolution of internal discomfort in Chapter 5. For now, I'm going to explore nonrelational resolution of internal discomfort from the perspective of what was called the new science of human beings, which started in the late 1600s.

› › › PAUSE . . . *and breathe* ‹ ‹ ‹

NONRELATIONAL BEING

Just as the formalizing of the slave trade began in the mid-1600s, what was called the new science of human beings began to emerge with seminal publications that theorized and formalized the race construct. These early works were examples of nonrelational resolution of internal discomfort at its most disconnected. It should be noted, again, that these narratives came about in the context of Europe's commitment to a particularly brutal form of capitalism. Within this accumulation paradigm was the systematic removal of resources and people from Africa and the Indian subcontinent for profit. For the planter class and those who provided the steady stream of capital, there needed to be a sense of cognitive consistency between personal ethical values like freedom and the pursuit of happiness, and the sanctioning of brutality for profit. Pseudoscientific narratives were then created by Europeans in the natural sciences that dehumanized whole nations of people with the express intent of maintaining a psychological and physiological sense of internal balance. Narratives were also needed that explained the behavioral and emotional symptoms that enslaved people were exhibiting as a natural consequence of being traumatized over multiple generations.

French physician and explorer Francois Bernier is often cited as the first to promote a conceptualization of race. He ascribed mental attributes to observable physical differences and divided human diversity into distinct groups. Bernier dedicated his major writings to Louis XIV, the king of France. Due to developments in printing, his work reached large audiences in Europe, and his ideas become influential in future European philosophy and natural sciences.

Bernier published *A New Division of the Earth, According to the Different Species or Races of Men Who Inhabit It* in 1684. This publication appeared three years after the North American colony of Maryland first used the term "white" in law.[1] Twenty years earlier, the first slave codes were passed into law in the Caribbean.[2] Bernier cites various species or races of men: People from Europe were one species; Africans were another. The third group included the Japanese, Vietnamese, Thai people, Russians, Tartans, and Turks. Those from the Arctic Circle were identified as the fourth species; and, finally, Native Americans represented the fifth.

Another publication that was very influential in dividing up the human species was by Swiss botanist Carl Linnaeus. In 1735, Linnaeus published the first of ten editions of *Systemae Naturae*, in which he formalized the concept of race and proposed four subcategories of *Homo sapiens* that laid the basis for nineteenth-century racial classifications. Linnaeus (1758) tied racial diversity to four geographical regions, four fundamental personality types, and four behavior generalizations:

1. *Homo americanus* (Indians) are red and upright; they are obstinate, contented, and regulated by custom.
2. *Homo asiaticus* are yellow and stiff; they are grave, dignified, avaricious (grasping or greedy), and ruled by opinions.
3. *Homo europaenus* are white and muscular; they are fickle (frequently changing loyalties and affections) but also keen and inventive and governed by laws.
4. *Homo africanus* are black and relaxed; they are cunning, lazy, careless, and governed by sudden and unaccountable change of mood or behavior (Linnaeus, 1758, as cited in Rice, 2009, p. 195).

Johann Friedrich Blumenbach (Blumenbach, 1795, as cited in Rice, 2009), a disciple of Linnaeus and a prominent German anatomist, believed, unlike his contemporaries, that other races could transform themselves to meet the European standard. He defined Europeans as the original and perfect form, from which humans developed into other forms. Humans, then, originated with the European form, then devolved into the American Indian form, then to the Mongolian form (East Asians or Northeast Asians), then to the Malay form (the Polynesians and Melanesians of the Pacific and the aborigines of Australia), and then into the African form. To accommodate the concept of other races transforming themselves to meet the European standard (a concept that moved beyond Linnaeus's simple descriptions of race based on geography), Blumenbach had to conceive of a fifth category, the Malay, which Linnaeus did not recognize. In 1795, Blumenbach wrote a dissertation called *On the Unity of Mankind*, which is considered the starting point for anthropology. In this dissertation, he ascribed the term "Caucasian" to the European race. He believed that the people of the Caucasus Mountains—a small mountainous region between the Black Sea and the Caspian Sea, which today comprises Georgia, Armenia, and Azerbaijan—were the most beautiful and geographically close to the supposed Middle Eastern center of human creation. Blumenbach's class of "Caucasian" included most Europeans, North Africans, and Asians as far east as the Ganges Delta in modern India.

The writings by Bernier, Linnaeus, and Blumenbach had concerned themselves with psychology and anthropology. Alongside these writings, political philosophers were contemplating the rights of the individual and ideas of liberal freedom. John Locke, an English philosopher and physician, famously stated that all men are equal as self-evident. These words might remind you of the constitution of the U.S. and indeed, Locke had a significant impact on popular eighteenth-century social and political thought that eventually led to the development of American constitutional democracy. Locke, by any measure, was a powerhouse of humanitarian thought. In 1689, Locke anonymously published *Two Treatises of Government*. The fourth edition was published many years after his death in 1821. He was concerned with the development of a just and ordered society based on reason and consent, including the idea of creating a civil society. On the issue of race, however, his ideas of reason and consent become both confusing and self-contradictory. The very prescriptions he was arguing for, of life, liberty, and the pursuit of happiness, with sleight of hand, he did not apply to all of humanity.

In book I of *Two Treatises on Government*, he opens with a sharp critique of slavery, stating that "Slavery is so vile and miserable an estate of man, and so directly opposite to our nation; that it is hardly to be conceived, that an Englishman, much less a gentleman should plead for it" (Locke, 1821/2010, Book I, Chapter I, para. 1).

In the second treatise, in the rather slender chapter on slavery, Locke paradoxically notes that the condition of slavery can exist as a "state of war continued, between a lawful conqueror and a captive" (Locke, 1821/2010, Book II, Chapter IV, para. 24).[4] There are strident arguments from many quarters about whether Locke was advocating for or against chattel slavery. It is evident that Locke was attempting to rationalize the act of slavery as a state of war, whereby slavery would fall into a category of the right and just thing to do. Along with this, Locke could, at the same time, keep intact his ideas of liberty and freedom for all men. Whatever the intention behind Locke's words, his thinking concerning race was clearly a nonrelational resolution of internal discomfort.

Another British powerhouse of philosophical thought was David Hume. His writings in the eighteenth century emerged out of the question "What is a good life?" He lived in a time known as the Age of Reason, and his writings countered the prevailing view that a good life was pursued through rationality. Hume (1758/1777) argued that humans are more influenced by feelings than by reason. For Hume, a human was just another animal. He believed that we, first of all, feel our way toward accepting or not accepting an idea and, on that basis alone, declare it true or false. Reason, Hume then argues, comes afterward, in the attempt to support the feeling attitude. Hume's involvement and interest in the colonies brought him face-to-face with the question of race and having to resolve his arguments around human reason and emotion alongside his interest in the institution of empire and slavery.

In 1748, Hume published *Essays, Moral and Political,* in which an essay entitled "Of National Characters" appeared. In the 1753 publication of this essay, he added a footnote; it reads:

> I am apt to suspect the negroes, and in general all the other species of men (for there are four or five different kinds) to be naturally inferior to the whites. There never was a civilized nation of any other complexion than white, nor even any individual eminent either in action or speculation. No ingenious manufactures amongst them, no arts, no sciences. On the other hand, the most rude and barbarous of the whites, such as the ancient GERMANS, the present TARTARS, have still something eminent about them, in their valour, form of government, or some other particular. Such a uniform and constant difference could not happen, in so many countries and ages, if nature had not made an original distinction betwixt these breeds of men. Not to mention our colonies, there are NEGROE [sic] slaves dispersed all over EUROPE, of which none ever discovered any symptom of ingenuity; tho' low people, without education, will start up amongst us, and distinguish themselves in every profession. In JAMAICA, indeed, they talk of one negro as a man of parts and learning; but 'tis likely he is admired for very slender accomplishments, like a parrot, who speaks a few words plainly. (Hume, 1753, as cited in Garrett, 2000, p. 171)

In the 1768 and 1770 editions of the same essay, minor alterations were made. The footnote was also relegated to an endnote. In the 1777 version, before Hume died and when the slave trade was in full swing, the essay was altered further, perhaps to highlight the pressing need to dehumanize African slaves further so that consciences could be cleared. The first sentence, which previously had read:

> I am apt to suspect the negroes, and in general all the other species of men (for there are four or five different kinds) to be naturally inferior to the whites. (Hume, 1753, as cited in Garrett, 2000, p. 171)

was changed to:

> I am apt to suspect the negroes to be naturally inferior to the whites. (Hume, 1777, as cited in Garrett, 2000, p. 172)

Hume's footnote sits so starkly against the image of Hume as a hero to academic philosophers. Maybe the fact that it was a footnote and then an endnote represented a wish in Hume to not have to think too much about the question at all. Hume held strong beliefs about the traits humans shared with the animal kingdom. He believed in emotion over reason. When it came to the institution of slavery, however, he reasoned things out such that white humans were less animal and endowed with more reason than black humans. Hume also had to reason his way toward resolving the behaviors of those around him who were directly involved in the slave trade including his wife's family so that they remained, in his eyes, good men.

Both Locke and Hume were eminent men and great thinkers, but their thinking capacity failed them with regard to race. They both succumbed to the type of confused thinking that ignored the impact of enslavement and edited out the brutality. When they were speaking about "men," they had in their minds a particular type of man—a white man—and possibly, but not necessarily, a white woman. There are many reflections on Locke's and Hume's writings on slavery, some of which defend them as "men of their time." This might be so, but it is very clear that Locke's and Hume's liberal thinking around the rights of individuals hit a cognitive and emotional barrier when it came to African people. Their thinking was contemporary for the time, but their espousing of great liberal values for all men at the same time as they were rationalizing how not to ascribe these same liberal values to Africans was not just an exercise in extreme nonrelational resolution of internal discomfort but also a honing of the race construct itself.

The study of human variation, in the early sciences where humans evolved separately, alongside the accompanying philosophical thinking, had resolved what must have been pressing internal discomfort, even if the "logic" of that resolution was confusing, contradictory, and nonrelational. The conceptions of race within the above publications were not born from curiosity nor a drive to seek out the truth. They were conceived, instead, out of a need to resolve the cognitive dissonance that inevitably arises when trying to reconcile being part of a group that sees themselves as moral, and at the same time continues to support brutalizing African people for profit.

The table below reveals that the concepts in these publications did not marshal racial terror, as some might believe, instead they played the crucial role of rubber-stamping what was already happening and authorizing its continued existence.

NONRELATIONAL BEING

Internal discomfort resolved through the study of human variation by the early sciences and philosophy, which asserted that humans had evolved separately

1684 A few years after the first laws based on race were passed in the Caribbean and the North American colonies, Francois Bernier wrote *A New Division of the Earth* that promoted a concept of race that provided cognitive consistency to white people while the rights and privileges of people of African heritage were being systematically removed.

1689 Soon after Bernier wrote *A New Division of the Earth*, John Locke writes *Two Treatises on Government* where he critiques slavery then attempts to rationalize slavery as a "state of war," and therefore the right and just thing to do.

1735 A few years after a North American Colony outlawed being freed from slavery, Carl Linnaeus wrote *Systemae Naturae* that was very influential in outlining and dividing up the human species and formalizing the concept of race hierarchy.

1753 David Hume wrote *Essays and Treatises on Several Subjects*, an, in 1777, wrote *Essays, Moral and Political* where he outlined his belief in emotion over reason. When it came to slavery, he reasoned that white humans were "less animal and endowed with more reason" than black humans.

1795 As various territories around the world were abolishing slavery, Johann Friedrich Blumenbach published his thesis *On the Unity of Mankind*, in which he ascribed the term "Caucasian" to the European race. He also presents the theory that other races could transform themselves to meet the European standard.

› 6 ‹

FINDING YOUR VOICE

MAKING A DECISION

If you are reading this book and you have read this far, you have become aware of the various levels of race oppression and may well be on the way to moving into action to not perpetuate it. The decision, however, is not just a cognitive one. Cognitive processing and labeling, as most of this book has, until now, been about is, of course, an essential ingredient to the decision-making process. It is important to have a cognitive narrative that makes sense so that we can begin this work with confidence. Despite having acquired all of this information, the driving force in decision-making is essentially a body decision: feeling it in your bones or feeling it in your gut. A decision to not perpetuate racism is, more often than not, a nonverbal sense of "getting it." This is akin to lifting a veil to reveal a previously explored aspect of the world as if seen for the first time. Temporarily set aside is the daunting weight of racism, with its unforgiving history, to be replaced by an internal sense of something more compelling, more purposeful. This crucial part of the process then allows other aspects of you to become more fully energized. With coherent narratives "in the mind" alongside what is essentially a body/heart decision not to perpetuate racism, the journey toward a sense of healing can begin. Healing not just for personal gain but also for the communities we live in, and especially for our young people.

Unfortunately, we are coerced, cajoled, and enticed into retreating from the people we need to be with and the states of mind we need to inhabit, which makes it difficult to get to a place where we can engage with our racial identity without playing out our racial identity—where we "feel it" without "being it." The easily triggered race construct, both within ourselves and in the people around us, robs us of that hope of healing. It is almost impossible to attend to race harm as an individual. Race trauma is formed through relationship and must be healed in relationship. Within the backdrop of the race construct, healing takes place through the coming together of like-minded individuals; together they can orient their efforts toward attending to the hurt with positive regard, curiosity, and compassion.

Here is an imagined story that illustrates a lifting of the veil and the shift that I feel is possible when we are relationally resourced.

> You have shares in a multinational company. These shares have been handed down to you, and, though you don't give it much thought, this is part of your inheritance. The income from these shares is small, but it allows you to work four days a week instead of five, which gives you time to gather your thoughts and enjoy the finer things in life and allows you space to think about things other than what is directly in front of you.
>
> Every once in a while, you think about the company you own shares in and what the company does. Occasionally the company is highlighted in the news, and you don't like what you hear—but the shares are so much a part of your life that it's difficult to give them up. You feel a bit embarrassed at times, and maybe even ashamed, but the feelings soon pass, and it's business as usual.
>
> You meet someone in your travels, and they start talking to you about the company you are associated with. They don't know you own shares; but you do. You feel uncomfortable, but what can you do? You would much rather talk about another subject and tactfully move the conversation to safer ground. In a candid moment, you might speak to someone about the position you are in and about how, when you think about the company, you feel bad and you don't know what to do. You think perhaps you can give up the shares; but then you hear, through a shareholder's letter, that the company is really trying hard to be a good company, an ethical company, although you are doubtful. You say to yourself that if unethical companies around the world were to lose their shareholders, the whole economic system would collapse and then where would we be? You hear from an economic analyst on the news that the capitalist economy is not a perfect system, but what are the alternatives? The company itself says that they want to do better but are beholden to their shareholders, who expect the

same profits this year as last. Those arguments make you feel a little bit better, but you are still a little uncomfortable. After a while, that uncomfortable feeling goes away, but you know that at some point it's going to come back, unannounced and unwelcome, out of the blue.

To avoid these unwelcome intrusions into your mind, you place yourself in spaces that give you the comfortable arguments you are used to about why things should remain the same, how you are only one person and you couldn't possibly make a difference. You wonder, even if you did take your shares out of this unethical company and put them in a more ethical one, this wouldn't change anything on the big scale would it?

You wake up one morning to find that the company you own shares in is on the news again for grossly unethical behavior. The uncomfortable feelings that you were grappling with before come back to the fore and take over your world as the news story plays out. You start to read about other companies that do the same things as the company that you have investments with. Your horror at what you find brings up the type of fear that leads you to feel that the world is somehow infected by evil, and you despair. As you continue to explore and speak to other people, you discover that rather than there being evil in the world, there are only decisions that look evil. You decide to put yourself into the types of arenas that allow those uncomfortable, complicit feelings to be seen and responded to because you feel in your bones that there's something, other than denial, that can be done. It's a massive leap of faith, but you're on a journey now. The genie is out of its bottle, and there is no putting it back.

Below are extracts from two race conversations that I hope will bring to life what the process of making a decision in your gut looks like and feels like, at least as it does for these two individuals. The first conversation is with a white male psychotherapist, and the second a Sikh male psychotherapist.

ANDY

Andy is a white psychotherapist who is passionate about psychotherapy and politics. Prior to this part of our conversation, I guided Andy through a mindfulness exercise that encouraged him to explore his cognition, emotions, and sensations at the thought of having a conversation about race. I was interested in bringing to his awareness the initial moments of discomfort, which are usually the optimal place to catch ourselves, in the moments before we become dysregulated. (FYI: The forum Andy refers to is a forum for therapists that invites a deepening of the race conversation.)

EUGENE What was uppermost [in your mind during the mindfulness exercise], and what were you aware of?

ANDY I have been sitting on something from the Forum that has happened around the race conversation which took me by surprise. It was a moment where I changed. Someone mentioned something to me, and it changed my worldview, it was just a comment. . . . I don't really know where I am with it yet; I haven't settled . . . and since then, other little things have happened that I might have noticed but not "felt." . . . I'm left with some unknowns that impact how I see the world and myself in it.

EUGENE It feels important, perhaps we need to just get straight to it . . .

ANDY Well, I might go a bit red and rouge . . . . I thought and felt that I really was quite comfortable with that [the race conversation]. At times in therapy, I could bring up the topic; I might often introduce it. I might ask what it's like working with a middle-class white guy from Surrey for somebody who's from Africa who's got a very different world outlook and probably comes from a country that my ancestors might have colonized. I could encapsulate that. . . . I had some kind of minimal awareness of these issues, but I've been wondering for some years now. It's not a bad reaction I get, or a nonreaction. The conversation quite often doesn't go anywhere. So that has been sitting in the background.

EUGENE So, you bring it up, you're curious, but it doesn't take you into places where you might want to go.

ANDY Ahh, well, I thought I did! So here's the rub; here is the body thing, I can feel it, the little hairs on the back of my neck; be careful what you wish for . . .

EUGENE So, what was the overall experience about the comment that was made to you in the Forum?

ANDY I was speaking to one of the facilitators. I mentioned the race conversation, or somehow that was in the room, and he said something along the lines of, "But if someone really brought that topic to you, their experience, could you cope?"

EUGENE Hmmm.

ANDY And I think not. I think not. Because actually until that moment I thought "yes," I believed yes, I mean I really believed. And in that moment, it started to dawn on me. . . . Could I?

The moment that Andy describes of the world suddenly changing is something that I have heard on many occasions. It often comes after an initial, sometimes extensive, process of curiosity and exploration. This exploration is typically driven by a particular personal hurt and through communion with other hurt souls. This journey then transforms into a decision to work toward no longer perpetuating race hurt.

RAJ

Raj is a psychotherapist of Sikh heritage. Prior to this section of the conversation, Raj had been talking about his explorations of his culture and his culture's relationship to him as a Sikh man in the U.K.

(FYI: The conference Raj refers to is the Black, African, and Asian Therapy Network conference.)

RAJ I think there's something, I want to call it special or different about Sikhs. I've gone back in my family history. We were branded the Marshall Race by the British. We were recruited to fight; a big proportion of the Indian army were Sikhs. So, we were special, or maybe more aggressive I'm not sure. . . . It's all been put into me, at some level. I'm supposed to be a certain way. Now I feel like . . .

EUGENE Now you're a counselor!

RAJ I'm vulnerable . . . someone called me a traitor, someone in my family. Being a Sikh and Sikhism is very important to me, so I felt disappointed by that. If I go anywhere or challenge anything in my culture, it will be seen as . . . anarchic rather than adding something. It's a sadness when I speak about that as well . . .

EUGENE It's like many journeys of healing . . . it sounds like you've done a lot of reading, a lot of research, a lot of thinking, a lot of trying to process and trying to make sense . . .

RAJ Healing is a good word.

EUGENE What was it like to have done all of that?

RAJ [*exhalation of breath*] Like I said, I was doing something different, away from the culture, it's threatening—for me internally, and I guess for others. People still say "You're an Asian male counselor"! What? It's like, what!

EUGENE Oh right, yeah.

RAJ They wanna know what you're about, what are you doing. "Do you still deal with Asians?" There's presumptions and assumptions, I find. The healing journey has been difficult.

EUGENE How did you come to this healing journey? I know you're a counselor, so that might have given you a little professional impetus . . .

RAJ I think it was more than that; it was a redirection. I didn't have therapy until I started my training [as a counselor], so there was something else going on; maybe it was personal—history, family, collective culture . . . it felt enlightening actually while I was doing it; and still there's never an end, I don't think. Still learning things about myself all the time . . . but the cultural part I think needed to be addressed first. One of the first layers I think.

EUGENE Say more about that?

RAJ Yeah, the caste thing, Sikhism and where we stand, where we're supposed to stand.

EUGENE You were trying to work out your place in relation to where you were supposed to be?

RAJ In the family business—arranged marriage, it was all for somebody else. I never realized why. It's almost for an ideal that didn't exist, the norm. Break the mold comes to mind. The actual process, I will be honest with you, has been very difficult at times. I almost felt like I was giving up and conforming, but no, I didn't think that was useful. . . . I feel I've been honest culturally . . . I feel I'm near the end of the cultural stuff. Not at the end of it, but I understand a lot of it . . .

EUGENE And what did you gain from this painful process of exploration?

RAJ I feel much more solid. . . . I went to conferences, I found a few Asian guys that could talk to me about this; it was really important actually. I can empathize with it and be willing to talk about this stuff. I needed to be understood, and I needed to understand myself. The rational part is understanding the history. The "actual" part is understanding how this all affects me on a basic level, what bits do I need to keep . . .

I will mention my daughters. They had a huge impact when they were born. And some of the practices toward them were quite . . . I found quite oppressive. So, there is that gender thing as well that goes on.

EUGENE Hmmm.

RAJ One word I'm looking for is liberation; that's what comes up.

EUGENE It's a word that often comes up for people.

RAJ Yeah, it makes me emotional, that makes me feel something when I say that.

EUGENE Yeah.

RAJ It's an ongoing process, me feeling stuff. I name it now—in safe places. There is a bit of me thinking; I hope this helps.

EUGENE Oh no, it all helps, absolutely.

For Raj, it seems, making a decision not to perpetuate racism and other oppressions was very much tied up with being a victim within his own culture. Trying to live a more authentic and ethical life can often make people within your own race and culture experience a sense of betrayal for "crossing over to the white side," as it is sometimes seen. The rejection for that betrayal is extremely painful. Raj also demonstrates having the kind of support that is needed, from like-minded individuals, in order to go through a journey of "being yourself" and "being your culture" at the same time.

RACE-CONSTRUCT AROUSAL

Putting together everything we have looked at so far, we can say that the race construct has trained generations of us, throughout our lives, to respond less energetically—or not at all—to the hurt and pain that people of color experience through racism. The race construct also orients us to attend to white people's hurt and pain before the hurt and pain in people of color. Also, when race is the focus, dissociation, confusion, anger, and blame are the central experiences, regardless of racial identity, along with dysregulation (not providing the emotional connection, responsiveness, and understanding that another person needs to be well and whole) and the feeling of being physiologically unsafe. All of this is the essence of what I, as previously mentioned, am going to call "race-construct arousal" or "race-construct hijacking."

I see the concept of race-construct arousal as having both a historical-legacy element and an in-the-moment-trigger element. For the historical aspect of race-construct arousal, I will use the term *generational loading*. I will say more about this concept in a moment, but for now, I want to expand on the in-the-moment-trigger elements. Generally, for people of color the triggers come about through what have been termed *racial micro/macroaggressions*. For white people, the trigger typically arises from temporarily stepping outside the area of safety afforded by the construct of whiteness. It should be noted that white bystanders can be triggered by racial micro/macroaggressions and people of color who have not explored their blackness can be triggered by stepping out of an imagined bubble of whiteness.

AROUSAL TRIGGERS

Racial Micro/Macroaggressions

The term "racial microaggression" was first coined by Chester Pierce in 1970 (Pierce, 1970). Professor Dereld Wing Sue expanded the term to refer to "brief and commonplace daily verbal, behavioral, or environmental indignities, whether intentional or unintentional, that communicate hostile, derogatory, or negative racial slights and insults toward people of color" (Sue et al., 2007, p. 271). Racial microaggressions are not limited to human encounters; they may also be environmental in nature, as when a person of color is exposed to an office setting that unintentionally assails their racial identity.

Stepping Out of Whiteness

The concepts of whiteness and white privilege bring with them unearned insulation from race-based stress. The experience of stepping out of whiteness, more often than not, creates feelings of insecurity, defensiveness, a sense of danger, and even an experience of threat to life.

Robin DiAngelo, author of *White Fragility*, says the following about white race insulation:

> Although white racial insulation is somewhat mediated by social class (with poor and working class urban whites being generally less racially insulated than suburban or rural whites), the larger social environment protects whites as a group through institutions, cultural representations, media, school textbooks, movies, advertising, dominant discourses, and the like. . . . White people seldom find themselves without this protection. Or if they do, it is because they have chosen to temporarily step outside this area of safety. (DiAngelo, 2018, pp. 99–100)

Stepping outside of the protective cradle of whiteness during the race conversation is generally experienced as if something is "wrong." The spectrum of responses to this sense of wrongness ranges from mild discomfort up to a feeling of annihilation and a pressing demand, from within and from others, to protect what whiteness stands for, all of which overrides logic or reason.

Generational Loading

Generational loading is the passing on of nonverbal racial cues of danger and threat to life through the generations, which primes current generations' bodies and nervous systems to hypervigilantly neurocept nonverbal racial cues of danger or threat to life by the slightest of racialized triggers from outside or within the body.

External triggers are neurocepted[1] from other bodies and from the physical environment and are unconscious and nonverbal. A nonverbal racial cue could trigger generational loading if, for instance, you find yourself the only one of a particular race in a railway carriage full of people.

The internal triggers of generational loading come from racial conditioning within the mind that sits on the edges of our consciousness. The race construct carries with it ideas of blackness and whiteness, of white superiority and race hierarchy. These imprinted narratives and racial biases wait patiently in the wings, ready to clash discordantly with our more conscious beliefs about ourselves as capable, good, and honest people.

Neurologically, the amygdala evaluates a threat to our identity just as it does a threat to our physical body. The amygdala then stays on guard for a trigger that would then activate a threat state in the rest of the body.[2]

Generational loading is similar to Dr. Isha Mckenzie-Mavinga's concept of ancestral baggage. Mckenzie-Mavinga is a transcultural counselor and, in her book *Black Issues in the Therapeutic Process,* she outlines ancestral baggage as

> . . . a way of understanding how the dynamics of former generations' relationships get passed on and affect black issues in the present. I am therefore suggesting that a black client's emotional situation may be affected by his or her upbringing and also by his or her ancestors' modes of response. This is a proposition about intergenerational patterns of relating that date back to ancient African kings and queens and to the slaughter and genesis of slavery. (Mckenzie-Mavinga, 2009, p. 78)

Summary

With the brain and nervous system having been primed by generational loading, the triggers then move us into race-construct arousal; these triggers being here-and-now everyday racial aggressions, from the almost imperceptible to out-and-out old-style racism and also from perceived threats to the social construct of the wholesomeness and goodness of whiteness.

In line with trauma theory, I see the two aspects of race-construct arousal—generational loading and the arousal triggers—as acting initially on the limbic system of the brain. The limbic system is the part of the brain responsible for regulating states of arousal, attachment relationships, motivation, memory, emotion, and survival reflexes. With the limbic system triggered, there is a dampening of the social engagement system and an activation of the active and passive defense systems. A dampening of empathy, curiosity, and compassion is the inevitable outcome, along with confused thoughts, feelings of being unsafe, and physiological discomfort.

Below is a breakdown of the various elements of race-construct arousal.

GENERATIONAL LOADING: AN EMBODIED INTERGENERATIONAL HISTORY

- The passing on of nonverbal racial cues of danger and threat to life through the generations primes current generations' bodies and nervous systems to hypervigilantly neurocept nonverbal racial cues from the environment
- Epigenetic alterations to DNA and the transmission of fear
- Nervous system primed and hypervigilant for implicit, nonverbal racial cues that signal danger and threat to life
- Amygdala primed to trigger threat state in the body when racial biases clash with personal values and beliefs
- Priming of the cognitive brain to assign race identity scripts of blackness and whiteness

AROUSAL TRIGGERS

Racial Micro/Macroaggressions

- Microaggressions—the commonplace verbal and nonverbal indignities communicated toward people of color
- Macroaggressions—old-style racism and acts of racial terrorism

Stepping Out of Whiteness

- The experience of wrongness when stepping out of the protection afforded by white privilege
- A pressing demand, from within and from others, to correct the feeling of wrongness

GENERATIONAL LOADING + AROUSAL TRIGGERS = RACE-CONSTRUCT AROUSAL

- An inner feeling of danger and of being unsafe
- Triggering of the defense system and dampening of the social engagement system
- Limbic activation and physiological discomfort
- Race-specific loss of curiosity, compassion, and reflective function
- Activation and reinforcement of race identity scripts
- Confused thoughts or thought paralysis
- An internal sense of wrongness
- A pressing demand, from within and from others, to embody whiteness

› › › PAUSE . . . *and breathe* ‹ ‹ ‹

TOWARD A RACE-AWARE PARADIGM

At times, I have found myself wanting to detach from the concept of race, as if being untethered from race would somehow minimize its potential to do harm. At other times, I have found myself ducking and diving within the race construct as if in a boxing ring, throwing lefts and rights to get what I want. Sometimes this has meant playing on the fear generated by race for my own ends or playing the "poor me" script to get a particular position I thought I wouldn't get otherwise. After all of my positionings and repositionings, I have come to realize that decisions made on the thinking and problem-solving levels do little to loosen the race construct's grip.

For those ascribed with a white identity, stepping out of the comfort blanket of whiteness means stepping into the harsher end of the race construct and the discomfort that comes with it. Again, for white people, staying at the level of thinking does little to foster an integrated sense of understanding and flexibility and often leads to further confusion and shame.

In previous chapters, I talked about the race construct as a series of implicit triggers that are the legacy of slavery and colonization. In addition to carrying implicit triggers, the race construct carries with it an array of nonrelational cognitions that, in a disconnected way, serve to resolve inner discomfort around race. This nonrelational, or problem-solving, mode in the mind is doing one of two things: it is either trying to improve on past strategies that previously worked to avoid discomfort or it is continually replaying past experiences that didn't work to find a more successful way to prevent the discomfort next time around. With this latter strategy, however, the replaying of the uncomfortable event to problem-solve it away seems only to intensify the discomfort.

Along with the mind, the body is impacted by race. The impact on the body can occur through experiencing or witnessing overt racism or racial microaggressions in everyday life or through the intergenerational transmission of anxiety from our ancestors. The impact of race on the body results in generations of people of color and white people who embody an implicit understanding of blackness and whiteness, which plays itself out unconsciously and maintains the status quo.

Incorporating the ideas above, I propose that it is possible to shift from being stuck in race-construct arousal into a new paradigm. This shift does not remove the discomfort but seeks to update our relationship to it. The shift occurs both conceptually and in the gut. I have witnessed this shift on many occasions and know that it is possible to move from a position of triggered defenses into a more flexible and situation-specific engagement with the issues of race. Together with this inner flexibility, there is a greater capacity to stay connected in social engagements when the race construct is evoked. I share with others the belief that there can be a "staying with" the impact of race trauma on people's lives while retaining some measure of inner freedom to respond with more flexibility in the moment.

This paradigm shift involves recognizing that, through generational loading, our nervous systems and minds are hypervigilant to implicit, nonverbal racial cues that prime the body to respond as if there was an actual danger or threat to life. The shift also involves the recognition that, when we become aware of race, this generational loading triggers race-construct arousal: inner distress, discomfort, and a feeling of being physiologically unsafe. A constant awareness of these processes within our bodies and attending to their effects will allow us to engage more consciously and consistently with the required intention, attention, and time (Phelps & Thomas, 2003). This processing leads us to become what I will call "race-construct aware." Being race-construct aware primarily involves a willingness to develop a more flexible relationship with our discomfort. We can increase our flexibility around race issues by gradually becoming aware of our patterns of arousal and defense. Through this process, we can become better able to stay with what is most important in the race conversation, which is to remain curious and reflective to the hurt and distress experienced by racism. This paradigm shift would then lead to the response we would naturally bring, without being encumbered by the distortion field of the race construct, to any hurt we witnessed in another human being.

This paradigm shift has at its heart the relational mode of being. In line with this paradigm shift, I am proposing a model I will call the "race-construct awareness model," that aims to disentangle us from race-construct arousal. The model outlines what prevents meaningful engagement in the race conversation as well as where it is most useful to place our attention. The race conversation, in this context, includes both the verbal and the nonverbal interactions we have with others as well as the inner dialogues we have with ourselves.

"We can increase our flexibility around race issues through a gradual process of becoming aware of our patterns of arousal and defense."

The essence of this model involves connecting to the body-memories of the above concepts; staying connected to our embodied experience of the breath, sensations, and movement; and staying relationally open. Just like we might allow the verbal story of our experience to be narrated, we also allow the story of the body to be told. This undertaking of intention, attention, and time then moves us to being race-construct aware. Our awareness is primarily of the body, but attention is also paid to the many associations that might emerge, such as past memories or felt impulses to move. The essential quality of this awareness is one of compassion and a sense of shared suffering.

THE RACE-CONSTRUCT AWARENESS MODEL

1. To recognize that the **race construct** serves to keep the distress associated with the violence and brutality committed in the name of race out of the minds and bodies of white people. Racial micro/macroaggressions can then continue unnoticed and unacknowledged, which maintains the status quo.
2. To recognize that **generational loading** primes the

nervous system to receive nonverbal racial cues of danger or threat to life.

3. To understand that when race is the focus, generational loading is triggered, leading to **race-construct arousal**.
4. To become **race-construct aware** through an active and compassionate exploration of how the race construct impacts our body identity and racial identity.
5. To actively find resources that honestly and compassionately support us to stay at the contact boundary[3] of our experience when race is the focus.

The first three parts of the race-construct awareness model—recognizing how the race construct maintains the status quo, the importance of nonverbal race triggers in communicating safety or danger, and race-construct arousal—have been covered in previous chapters. We are now ready to move to the fourth and fifth parts of the model, which are about sensitizing us to the race construct's effect on our body identity (i.e., the nonverbal aspects of identity) and its impact on the cognitive landscape of our racial identity. This awareness cannot be fully realized outside of relationship. To get to where we want to go, we will need to share our experiences with other people. The race construct was created through relationship, so the harm done needs to be healed through relationship. Finding the right people and resources that honestly and compassionately support us to maintain our connection to our experience, which is most likely discomfort, can assist the shackled parts of us to move in new ways and into new positions. This process can have profound implications for society's mental health and can be our small contribution to the eradication of the broader system of racial oppression.

› 7 ‹

BECOMING RACE-CONSTRUCT AWARE

Mind, Body, and Heart

Mindfulness

Bodyfulness

Compassion

Getting Ourselves Resourced

MIND, BODY, AND HEART

Coming back to the comment from Jay Smooth that the race construct is a dance partner designed to trip us up, being race-construct aware also means not giving up when you get things wrong, which you inevitably will. We need to be willing to stay on the boundary of the hurt that race has inflicted on both sides of the black/white divide. Race-construct arousal is a challenging landscape to navigate. Within this landscape, the bodily, emotional, and cognitive aspects of our experience can be very powerful. They can very quickly move us into experiencing a sense of danger or even threat to life. To stay with these types of experiences, we need to have a map to guide us and to give us a sense of the territory we will be stepping into. A map is no substitute for the terrain itself, but it can bring some measure of felt safety.

Typically, when we try to stay with the race construct and our part in it, we tend to focus on our behaviors—on what we do. From a trauma perspective, the more we focus on our behaviors to the exclusion of anything else, the more those negative behaviors can increase. The more we analyze and reanalyze our behavior, the worse we feel. What, then, do we focus on?

There are three elements to this process that can be described simply as mind, body, and heart. There is also a particular quality of attention that we will need to bring to our experience. This attention, which is primarily directed to our inner-body sensations but might also include emotional and cognitive aspects of our present experience, needs to be compassionate, forgiving, and from the heart.

I am going to outline these three elements, beginning with an approach that fosters an awareness of right here, right now experience called "mindfulness." In particular, I will be looking at a model of mindfulness that I feel is useful for addressing race-construct arousal. I will then outline an approach called "bodyfulness," coined by body practitioner Christine Caldwell, that focuses on developing an appreciation of the body's wisdom. Finally, I will outline the neurological and practical aspects of compassion.

MINDFULNESS

Mindfulness is a practice that has been adopted from Buddhism, which can assist us in staying connected to our senses and our bodies' sensations and movements. It is one of many practices that can be used to explore the connection between what is happening in the body and what is happening in the mind. Bringing mindful awareness to our present experience during race conversations is an essential antidote to the mind's tendency to become preoccupied with negative past events or an imagined negative future, which then triggers the active and passive defense systems. Mindfulness also sustains coherent thinking as our bodies play out the dance of finding ways to escape cognitive and bodily discomfort.

Developing a mindfulness practice that helps us cope with the stresses of everyday life can also be used as part of a program of self-care when under race construct stress or in becoming more race-construct aware. Developing race-construct awareness involves bringing mindful awareness to the various aspects of our present-moment experience as we face race-construct arousal. The very act of noticing and becoming aware of the present moment, without trying to do anything else, is often enough to bring a different perspective to our experience.

Allowing the mind to be present to what is, however, is not straightforward when it comes to race. If you already have a mindfulness practice, you have a substantial head start with in-the-moment mindfulness; otherwise, you will need to develop a routine of sustained practice, preferably with support, so that you feel a measure of competency. The phrase "the race construct is a dance partner designed to trip us up" is a useful one to carry with us through this process. It is important to keep in mind that whatever your social context, the race construct will have an effect. How different people will be affected, however, is difficult to predict. A seemingly small oppression that is easily shrugged off by one person can have a devastating effect on another. Also, what to you might be considered an unforgivable act of oppression can have a minor impact on a different person. We need to prepare ourselves to expect the unexpected and to bring an attitude of compassion for ourselves and for others along the way.

As mentioned in Chapter 1, we all have a particular window of stress tolerance (Siegel, 1999), and for many of us, our race-related arousal window is very narrow indeed. To widen our bandwidth for race stress, we can develop a practice of mindfulness, which effectively expands our window of tolerance, and by doing so, we become better equipped to handle race stress without becoming dysregulated. The simple act of bringing mindful awareness to what is happening in the present moment can have a significant impact on our sense of safety. An expanded window of tolerance allows us to remain coherent in our thinking, responsive to our experiences, and compassionate toward ourselves and others.

Mindfulness can be developed and practiced as a daily meditation on your own or alongside others. For myself, I have practiced mindfulness meditation in a Buddhist context for many years, as a solitary practice and in groups. These practices remain a vital part of maintaining my overall well-being. I also practice mindfulness meditation with other people of color, which I personally find very supportive as another powerful context in which to practice.

For the rest of this section, I am going to explore how mindfulness can be practiced along with some blocks to developing mindfulness. I will also be exploring mindfulness, people of color; and whiteness; the challenge of being with yourself; where to place your attention; relational mindfulness; and what to do if you do not feel sensations in your body. To further illuminate these areas, I will present four extracts from race conversations I have had, with a black male therapist, with a white female therapist, with a black female ordained Buddhist, and with a Sikh male therapist.

Mindfulness, People of Color, and Whiteness

The mindfulness approach (and the bodyfulness approach I will be outlining later), just like psychotherapy and psychology, carries with it unexamined beliefs, attitudes, and practices that, in themselves, marginalize certain groups of people. The practice of mindfulness, as we know it, came from Buddhism in India. However, in the West, it is often presented to us filtered through the construct of "whiteness," with its particular sense of wholesomeness and goodness, which can have the effect of making people of color feel excluded.

PATRICK

Patrick is a black male therapist who uses mindfulness in his work. In the following extract, Patrick reflects on the cultural aspects of how mindfulness is taught and how this impacts his therapeutic practice.

EUGENE Are you familiar with mindfulness as a practice?

PATRICK I have certain judgments [about] the terminology of mindfulness. I'll just tell you that from the off [start].

EUGENE Okay, do you want to say a bit about that before we start [the rest of the conversation]?

PATRICK In my work, mindfulness is very much considered a central part of what I do. I just find that there's a separation between the terminology and what "it" actually is. In my mind, you could use anything to help with your mindfulness practice—anything whatsoever—but there tends to be certain exercises that, through my experience, have been used to practice mindfulness. I just think . . . Come on!

EUGENE So, what are the norms you see?

PATRICK Things like, "just focus on a leaf," or there are certain types of music. I am of Jamaican background, and I like reggae music—I don't think I ever experienced it where, I'll go somewhere, whether it be at work or when practicing mindfulness in a workshop, and they'll say, "Right, respond mindfully to this piece of music" and it's a piece of reggae music. That's where my head goes. If the idea is about encouraging and engendering mindfulness, and it needs to be done in that way . . .

EUGENE It's culturally loaded?

PATRICK Absolutely, a lot of it. And for me, how it relates to race is [that the] dominant group and dominant perspectives seem to have gotten hold of mindfulness and how you do it—and the language around it. Everything around it just seems to reflect that. For me. I'm saying these are my judgments. The other side of it for me is that the actual thing is so important—what "it" actually is.

EUGENE How would you put it into words?

PATRICK For me, it's about being so much more aware of "your" existence, of "your" life. For me, in essence, that's what it is; and then the whole idea of the skills and structures—for you to be aware of that.

EUGENE However that comes about?

PATRICK Yeah. It's so important. It's fundamental.

EUGENE Certainly mindfulness practice and the mindfulness industry don't really attract black people that much.

PATRICK And I personally think that's sad, because as I said, what the actual thing is, black people could benefit so much from. From my experience of it, it's how it's delivered, how it's been packaged; it excludes. For example, in my work, I work with quite a few young people, predominantly female. My stance comes from what they have said. Things like "Patrick, mindfulness! What is this shit?"

I'm thinking, "Well, where's that coming from—that it's a load of shit."

Then I say, "That's awareness, it's a facet of mindfulness."

[They say] "No it ain't."

[I say] "What makes you say 'no it ain't'?"

[They say] "Well because we're supposed to stop, we're supposed to breathe in a particular way."

To me, they feel excluded from this thing. How much is it about them and where they're at, and how much of it is how this thing has been presented and delivered to them? For what it actually is—when they get it—what a difference it begins to make in their lives.

Patrick is highlighting the sense of disconnection that people can experience when mindfulness is presented in a certain way or where the practices are presented as just the way things are done or as a one size fits all. Mindfulness teachers need to be aware of the impact that the construct of whiteness has on western mindfulness practice and custom. Adjustments then need to be made so that people of color, and many other marginalized groups, feel they can more fully connect to the practice and engage. With all this being said, within the context of working toward developing race-construct awareness, mindfulness can offer powerful avenues for healing.

The Challenge of Being With Yourself

Another aspect of mindfulness, as it is packaged and practiced in the West, is that it will take your problems away or make you feel good. This way of thinking about mindfulness then raises the question: With there being real internal and external problems, isn't "making" yourself feel good a side-stepping of these problems? This question does not even need to be asked, however, once you begin to understand that the focus of mindfulness is not making you feel good, although this might be a by-product of the process. Mindfulness is about being with yourself, and this is not always easy.

LAURA

This extract of a race conversation with Laura, who is a white female therapist, is an example of someone initially struggling with connecting to mindfulness.

EUGENE You said you had a mindfulness practice, and I'm curious about what brought you to that.

LAURA I did an MBCT [Mindfulness Based Cognitive Therapy] thing. I hated it! I really didn't like it at all.

EUGENE What was going on?

LAURA It was something that the person who was leading it said to me after the first or second session that I didn't feel included. I didn't touch it with a barge pole. I was then going through something very stressful. I just thought, what can I do? I went back—I then just got fascinated by just doing it as a practice. I dip in and out, but I know that when times are tough, I get back to it. I've had a fairly regular practice for about eight years, something like that.

EUGENE I'm curious about your experience of not taking to it initially? Was it about the person leading? Or was it something about doing it? Not getting it perhaps?

LAURA It was something about what the person said that made me feel not included and rejected—and maybe it's the fear. It's like walking through the counseling door [for the first time]. Am I really going to make this a part of my life?

EUGENE Hmmm.

LAURA I'm not fearful of it now. I wish I could do it more.

EUGENE There is a stepping into the unknown element, isn't there? There is the idea that it's supposed to make you feel calm, but sometimes that's not how it pans out.

LAURA Yeah, to try to get that across to people. Can you be with yourself? There's a part of me that loves that.

EUGENE What about that sense of danger and even threat that people say they experience when they're having the race conversation. I guess that's something you experience as well?

LAURA Yeah, yeah. As soon as you said in your email [that you wanted to have the race conversation], I was [sharp intake of breath] I want to do this, and I believe in this stuff, and even today I was thinking, "I don't really know what 'this' is?" Why is that? Is it a basic survival thing? Is it as simple as that? It still saddens me that we can have lots of conversations about lots of other things a lot of the time. Why does it have that sort of [sharp intake of breath]?

EUGENE This is what I'm trying to get to and trying to explain.

LAURA I just read *Different Drummer* by William Melvyn Kelly. He was around the same time as James Baldwin. It's really powerful and made me think about so many different things. Just that thing of, in America, [at one point] most black people were slaves; and you just think, of course, that has an impact. Obviously, that has an impact.

For Laura, not feeling excluded was important. There was also something for her about fear of the unknown. After the initial pushing away, she came back to the practice, and the part of her that needed to be with itself was engaged. This idea of being with yourself is an important one in mindfulness. Being with yourself means being with the positive and negative, cognitive and nonverbal experiences that arise within us without trying to work "it" out.

During the race conversation with Laura, the nonverbal, sharp intake of breath emerged as the most prominent communication. Alongside this appeared a clash between her ethical beliefs of wanting engagement and her gut feeling of danger. With race-construct arousal, strong feelings of confusion, despair, numbness, rage or feeling overwhelmed are likely to arise for many people. People also make contact with deep wells of badness, either in themselves or in the world. These are very challenging feelings to stay with, so you must take care to look after yourself and proceed only when you are ready. The invitation is to come back to the practice of mindfulness if you

"Being with yourself means being with the positive and negative, cognitive, and nonverbal experiences that arise within us without trying to work 'it' out."

feel you have to push it away for a time. Part of that readiness will be finding the right people to support you in this process, at least initially.

Where to Place Our Attention

If your mindfulness practice is quite advanced, you will be more able to stay with *what is* in the present moment when experiencing race-construct arousal. If staying with what is, feels overwhelming, what do we do? For us to stay within our window of tolerance, we need to be able to place our attention on aspects of experience that bring a sense of inner cohesion before turning toward aspects that bring about disintegration. Pioneer in somatic psychology Dr. Pat Ogden has developed a useful mindfulness model for addressing the types of overwhelm we are concerned with regarding race-construct arousal. Instead of mindfully attending to what might potentially be overwhelmingly strong emotions or persecutory thoughts, Ogden says that we can direct our mindful awareness to sensorimotor processing when our arousal is on the edge of becoming too much. Ogden suggests that we bring "directed mindfulness" to the "building blocks of present moment experience" (Ogden & Fisher, 2015, p. 162). In doing so, individuals are guided toward various aspects of their experience, noticing which aspects bring a sense of inner cohesion and which aspects bring a sense of disintegration. Ogden names the five building blocks of experience she uses as:

- cognition: what is going on in our thinking mind—thoughts, beliefs, and interpretations
- emotion: feeling, mood, motivation
- five-sense perception: smell, taste, sight, touch, and hearing, including internal images in the mind's eye and remembered tastes and smells
- movement: large movements, gestures, and posture changes as well as small movements, like the heartbeat and small involuntary movements

- body sensation: tingling, tension, relaxation, warmth, coldness, tightness

These five building blocks make up our experiences. Although they are all happening at once, we usually focus our attention on one or two of them. In the West, the two are commonly cognition or emotion—to the exclusion of the others. Bringing directed mindfulness to movement, sensation, and five-sense perception gives us a higher capacity to remain in our window of tolerance. Being in our window of tolerance means that our arousal is not too high nor too low, which allows us to stay reflective and compassionate toward ourselves and others. We are then open to a fuller experience of ourselves. Ogden says that "Noticing and changing somatic tendencies in the present to the exclusion of emotions and content limits the information to be addressed to a tolerable amount and intensity that can be integrated" (Ogden, 2009, p. 226).

Ogden is saying here that bringing attention to our movements and body sensations creates the conditions whereby we can integrate what we experience rather than be overwhelmed by it. This opens up the opportunity for the gradual integration of strong experience within race-construct arousal and an opportunity to begin organizing these experiences differently. Observing our experience in the race conversation as we bring our attention to the building blocks of experience, we can start to create a space for aspects of the implicit[1] history of our bodies to be known. Attending to these aspects without judgment and without getting caught up in creating meaning allows us to attend to what had previously been too threatening even to acknowledge.

"Beringing attention to our movements and body sensations creates the conditions whereby we can integrate what we experience rather than be overwhelmed by it."

Relational Mindfulness

To support the process of directed mindfulness, that one person can guide another in following their body's impulses and in being more present in the body. Ogden describes this approach as "relational mindfulness," and involves exploring implicit processes within a relationship. This is an advanced practice, however, and only someone who is experienced in this approach should guide another in this process.

The following extract from a race conversation presents an example of directed mindfulness.

MAITRINITA

Maitrinita is a black female member of the Triratna Buddhist Order. Prior to this extract of our conversation, I had asked her to reflect on the thought of having a conversation about race and to be present with her thoughts, emotions, and physical sensations. We join the conversation as I direct Maitrinita to be mindful of the aspects of her experience that keep her regulated and those that destabilize her. Maitrinita is quite developed in her practice of mindfulness, so I was confident that she would remain grounded while she went through what was, for her, an emotional conversation.

EUGENE What was foremost in your experience [during her reflections on thinking about having a race conversation]?

MAITRINITA A sense of just being scattered, not quite focused on anything, fragmented. Yeah.

EUGENE What aspect of your awareness was the most destabilizing? What was the most uncomfortable?

MAITRINITA I think cognition, the thoughts. The apprehension of bringing it up as a subject. What to say. How to say it. How not to hurt anyone. That sort of thing.

EUGENE Did you have an experience, in your awareness, of hanging onto something that was more stabilizing?

MAITRINITA Well the fact that I was aware of my body and the breath—that felt stabilizing.

EUGENE Okay, I'm going to take you through the organizers of experience. In terms of your cognition, what meanings were you making of your experience?

MAITRINITA The thoughts were around "Oh no, not this again!" Wanting to push away—some aversion to bringing it up and having that kind of conversation.

EUGENE What thoughts were you having around the aversion?

MAITRINITA "I don't want to do this." "Someone else could do it better." "What do I say?" Those kinds of things. And the sense of discomfort and the idea of not being liked because I'm bringing it up. It kind of rocks the boat—that idea of rocking the boat.

EUGENE You're going to rock the boat, and no one likes that?

MAITRINITA Yes, and also doubt. Am I really seeing this clearly? Is it really racist? Who can I check that out with?

EUGENE Okay, in terms of the emotional realm, what were the key emotions?

MAITRINITA Mostly unpleasant or neutral. I guess there was fear, as an emotion; that would be the strongest part of it, but mostly it's a bit more low key than outright fear; but it's in that trajectory of experience. It feels like I want to push it away, so it's quite aversive. Also a bit flat [sigh], it's like, again, "Why should it be me who has to bring it up? Why doesn't someone else notice it? Why is it not broader than just my experience?" It feels like a burden, really, that I have to carry.

EUGENE You're the one who is responsible for bringing it up?

MAITRINITA Yes; and is my experience valid? If it's not reflected in anybody else, then is it true?

EUGENE What about the organizer of five-sense perception: sound, smell, touch, taste, and also any inner images or memories? Did any of that come up for you?

MAITRINITA What passed through my mind is what comes up frequently when I think back. When I was three or four, watching the civil rights movement on the television. Watching all the water cannons and the dogs attacking these black people who were marching for equality. It was such a shocking image to see. In the 1960s the TV wasn't doctored, you just watched whatever—there was no filter or anything.

But I do remember saying to my mum, "Why is this happening? Why are they hurting these people?" She couldn't really give me a response. So, for me, I've always associated people who protest or who go and march for their rights—I always associate it with the chance that you might be killed—yeah, you can be killed. You saw them with their truncheons, and really laying into them. So for me, I've always been a bit scared. When bringing the question of race as a subject, that's always there—as the catastrophe part. That's in there as a kind of fearful response or a view that I could be killed if I express [myself].

EUGENE So, even though you may be in a group of well-meaning people, they're okay, and you feel safe in some ways, that feeling is still there, just in the background, just lurking somewhere.

MAITRINITA Yeah, yeah.

When Maitrinita replayed in her mind's eye her childhood memory, she connected to a sense of fear that is typical for many people. What is also typical, as with Maitrinita, is that directing our attention to cognition and emotion is potentially more dysregulating, and that focusing on the body is more stabilizing. This is not always true, however, as some people experience focusing on the body as more dysregulating. In fact, sometimes, a focus on the body can be very uncomfortable. Not everyone is the same and, for these individuals, a mindfulness practice that involves physical movement, like a walking meditation or communing with nature, rather than sitting still offers an alternative approach to mindfulness.

Not Feeling It in the Body

In this extract, Sikh male therapist Raj sees value in the mindfulness practice but struggles to make a connection with the feelings in his body.

EUGENE Mindfulness, is that something you have a familiarity with?

RAJ Yeah. I struggled with meditation and mindfulness programs because it doesn't relax me. I'm always thinking it through. I've got the headspace app.[2] I've used that quite regularly. I've tried meditation teaching. That was a few years ago. A bit of me wanted . . . the only way to describe it is "stillness." I know there's a block somewhere.

It's about living in the present. You don't think about what's in front of you or behind you, that's how I've been taught. But I can't find the stillness—yet. I can't feel it in my body . . . at the moment.

EUGENE So you've spent time circling it, trying to find a way in.

RAJ Knowing the theories.

EUGENE Yes, knowing the theories—giving it a good go.

> **"Attention can be given to the numb parts of the body with the understanding that an attitude of patience and tolerance during the mindfulness practice translates to the same attitude when not practicing."**

Raj knows where he would like to get to with mindfulness in a cognitive sense and has undertaken to stick with it even though there are aspects of his body's communication he is desensitized from. Not feeling sensation when mindfully attending to the body is also the experience of many others. For these individuals, it is necessary to accept that this is the case and trust that this will change. Attention can be given to the numb parts of the body with the understanding that an attitude of patience and tolerance during the mindfulness practice translates to the same attitude when not practicing mindfulness. It is said that the brain used for practicing mindfulness meditation is the brain used for daily life (Cayoun et al., 2018, p. 134).

BODYFULNESS

Just as the race construct imposes racial identities and racial scripts for the mind, race oppression also imposes a body identity and, in effect, body scripts that, like racial scripts, play themselves out implicitly.

Body Listening and Body Talking

Alongside the well-established idea of developing a social identity, body practitioner Christine Caldwell is interested in helping people to turn the spotlight onto their bodies and to develop a body identity. To facilitate body identity development, Caldwell arrived at the concept of bodyfulness. In this approach, there is a conscious staying awake to our senses, our breathing, and our movements. If we consciously move the body as we listen to its sensory signals, we connect the inside of the body with the outside rather than reinforce the body's domestication. Achieving this kind of connectedness involves developing body listening skills and expanding our ability to sense the body's signals in complex and nonjudgmental ways. Caldwell notes that these body signals are similar to those of crying babies—there are no words. Developing a body identity involves spending more time simply experiencing the embodied self directly, including bodily actions and bodily speaking, and allowing the body to tell the story (Caldwell, 2018).

The Body as Wrong

People of color, and other people who experience discrimination and marginalization, have their physical culture inseparably linked to their identity and therefore marked as wrong. Caldwell puts it like this:

> In this act of oppression, specific body parts, ways of posturing and gesturing, ways of moving, how space is used, eye contact, voice tone, body size and shape, and other markers of the body are singled out as evidence that a person is a member of a nondominant group, and that evidence is used to lower their status, lessen their physical safety, diminish their rights, and exclude them from resources. (Caldwell & Leighton, 2018, p. 36)

Just as certain bodies are evidence of low status, other bodies are evidence of high status. Higher status bodies receive higher degrees of safety, more rights, and more access to resources. Within the race construct, the body of a person of color will have a lifetime of exclusion and coercion when comparing it with the white body. The pain of this cultural pressure forces an abandonment of the body's wisdom in favor of objectifying the body, ignoring the body, or seeing specific parts of the body as the problem. Abandoning the body's wisdom results in self-criticism, attempts to control the body's appearance, chronic health issues, and exhaustive attempts to either fit in or to resist the dominant white body narrative (Caldwell, 2018).

True Harm Versus Rattled Feelings

Developing bodyfulness involves, among other things, an appreciation of the body, listening to pain, and becoming aware of true harm versus rattled feelings. Caldwell sees the process of judging, misinterpreting, or trying to ignore body signals as a form of internalizing body oppression. She invites an appreciation of the body instead of evaluating it. Additionally, she encourages changing our relationship towards pain and pleasure. Pain is a signal that something is amiss, but when we don't like the body's form of communication, we often force the body to adapt. Concerning becoming aware of true harm versus rattled feelings, Caldwell says

> any abuse of power will sooner or later land on the body and seek to incarcerate it in some way. . . . In this context, we can

> see the abuse of power as involving an assumption that certain people threaten or harm us by their very existence, by their "uppity" actions, or even their different form and appearance. . . . The argument here is that developing one's body identity might be one of the essential methods of investigating the difference between true harm and the rattled feelings we get when our comfortable positions are challenged. (Caldwell, 2018, pp. 44–45)

Listening to the Body

In Chapter 8, I will give examples of mindfulness and bodyfulness that can help us stay in contact with our experience. For now, I want to explore the idea of listening to bodily pain and changing our relationship to it. This practice can be applied to developing race-construct awareness as well as to developing oppression awareness in general—both external and internal oppression.

The following is an extract from a race conversation with Nandaraja, a black male member of the Triratna Buddhist Order, who has an advanced meditation practice that also involves bodyful awareness. The dialogue follows a reflection on the pain inherent in the race conversation. Bold sections of text highlight important themes throughout the discussion.

EUGENE There's something about hurt that sits just underneath all of these conversations, and I'm wondering how you work with it?

NANDARAJA For me, if I'm hurting, I'm not going to be receptive. That's about me and my feelings. If, in my communication, I sense that others are getting emotionally agitated, then I back off and postpone it rather than go for the jugular.

It's like, pain is pain, but a lot of pain has to do with a mental construction of ourselves, of our identity. My ego doesn't want to think of itself as the bad guy. So when it does anything unskillful, it will find a justification, however irrational. I do the same kind of thing when I feel threatened or attacked.

I do not want to stimulate any kind of threat, but at the same time there is a challenge there, because there is something hidden that I'm not aware of, and the more defensive I am, the more I will remain ignorant. The problem then is willful ignorance. By willful ignorance, I mean I'm defending myself against being hurt and only seeing the discomfort.

So I have to start with myself. I just notice in what ways I ignore uncomfortable information. That comes from my meditation practice. How then do I work with that? It's like delicate surgery, you probe; if it's too painful, you stop, back off. But then, next time, you have to be very gentle and very acute in your perceptions, so, just noticing my body, how it feels. When you focus on other people, it's about noticing all the little movements, their gestures, what it is that's indicating discomfort. The slight raising of the voice, the changing of the pupils, the facial expression—all that; there's a lot of information which I don't notice if I'm angry or upset.

My experience is that **physical pain has a different sensation to psychic pain,** but unless you can stay with physical pain, what tends to happen is that psychic pain creates the illusion of a physical pain. You experience physical pain, whereas all that's happening is that people are just talking. As far as you're concerned, the words are hurtful, and the expression is rejecting. So, it's about working backwards—teasing out what it is in this psychic experience that is real physical pain and what of it is a recording of trauma stored in the body that replays itself when certain words or expressions trigger it into autopilot.

So what I do in meditation is literally to go through my memories and find an uncomfortable one. Then [I] sort of open the box and then explore it. Physically what is happening is that I'm just sitting. Psychically those memories trip all kinds of emotions and thoughts, and then I have to untangle them. What is it about this six-year-old experience that I'm having now, sitting on the cushion? And do I want to let that six-year-old "run" my life? I have more information now, and I'm not as weak as I used to be, I'm much more powerful. So just noticing—all right, this is how the condition occurs, this was the imprint, this is how it's stored in the body as a memory, and these are the associated feelings and sensations that get replayed. I replay it, and if I can replay it often enough, I can see, "Ah yes, actually what I thought had happened, didn't happen," or even if it did happen, I'm not the same person, so I don't have to react, I can now respond. But in order to respond, I have to be mindful. I can't get lost in the memory. I can't get identified with my past. So, it's about acknowledging the past, but not holding onto it.

It is a difficult process, and in order to stay with that pain, you have to **start when you are in a good mental state**. So, I do it when I feel really on top of my meditation practice. Then I can go to the roots of what's been traumatic rather than just going over the edges of them. Behind quite a lot of them [the past memories], there's either deep fear or deep rejection or feelings of being abandoned. Those tend to be the roots. If I can go there when I'm in a positive mental state, it might bring me down, but at least I understand, and if it gets too much, I can say okay, that's enough.

EUGENE What you're saying is that, in exploring discomfort for yourself, you see other people as having the same kinds of patterns, probably the same kinds of discomfort around the [race] issue. The way you work with it for yourself is the way you work with it with others.

NANDARAJA Yeah.

EUGENE And you found some success working in that way?

NANDARAJA It's hard enough working with myself; so, if I'm working with other people, I have to be even more sensitive. The nature of a blind spot is that you don't notice it unless you're looking for it. Even if you are looking for it, however, there's a part of you that doesn't want to look, because it means you have to change, and change is usually painful. When you see that changing is going to be less painful than not changing, that's the motivation to end the cycle of pain.

EUGENE There is a certain kind of fear, hurt, or discomfort that gets activated in the race conversation, which other people might feel, even if you don't. The ordinary way of thinking about this is that **if "they" can't feel it, then "they're" not going to change**, and to push and keep pushing. The other side of that is people who don't want to be the cause of discomfort in another person, so the [race] conversation doesn't then happen. Where are you on this idea of you being the cause of discomfort?

NANDARAJA I don't think like that.

EUGENE OK.

NANDARAJA I don't accept that I create feelings in other people or that other people create feelings in me. It's more that I take responsibility for my feelings. I self-examine the whole process—the sensations in the body, the feelings, and the thoughts are all interconnected. If I can stay in the pain and still maintain a rational perspective, I can untangle all the various bits and then see more clearly. Seeing events more clearly, the pain becomes bearable and, because the pain is bearable, I then see through the illusion of the pain and see that, actually, it's my mind that's causing the pain. Just thinking "Am I causing the pain?" doesn't work. I have to experience the interconnection between my thoughts, my feelings, [and] the sensations that I'm feeling and disentangling them.

EUGENE Whatever you discover through this practice, then, you naturally apply to another person, with an understanding that they'll be going through a similar process, although less aware of it.

NANDARAJA Yeah, I'm experimenting with myself and applying that to others.

EUGENE **There is a real challenge in unraveling race associations though, isn't there?** I feel like I "lose hold of my mind" far more easily in conversations about race than in conversations about other oppressions. This experience seems to be a universal one. People who are ordinarily very eloquent and organized in their thinking around all kinds of political and global issues of oppression, when nudged toward the race conversation something happens and they lose that flexibility. There is pain in oppression, but with race, there appears to be something else.

NANDARAJA To my mind, it's about what is associated with the body as pain. The only reason you are not able to keep your mind clear on a certain subject is that when you're in pain, your mind gets clouded. There is the Buddhist notion of the second arrow. There is first a raw physical sensation [the first arrow], and then there are the thoughts that come with it [the second arrow]. The thoughts and words in themselves are just words, but it's the meaning that then triggers certain feelings.

EUGENE OK, so you are saying that there is a snowballing of associations around race from which it's hard to disentangle. Each association then resonates in the body and then creates something that is very hard to unravel.

NANDARAJA It creates a physical agitation, which then creates a mental agitation, which then feeds back on itself. It creates a resonance, and that's what interferes with clear thinking.

EUGENE From a person of color's point of view, there is pain there. For a person who is not a person of color, there is pain there too. I'm curious about your view on where that comes from, how that pain got there.

NANDARAJA **Guilt is a form of pain.** Guilt, for me, is a much more subtle kind of pain. People don't like to feel guilty, especially when they feel guilty about something they have no control over but nonetheless identify with. In the [race] conversation, it's very important to recognize that feeling guilty is not helpful, however well-meaning. A lot of people think that because they feel guilty, that makes them more ethical. Guilt kind of blinds you. The body doesn't want to feel pain and, if guilt feels painful, the easiest way is to ignore anything that reminds you of things that make you feel guilty. Why would somebody deny the Holocaust when there are so many facts pointing to the truth? It's because they don't want to feel guilty, and they want to feel proud of their parents and grandparents. It's all driven by what I call the pain/pleasure circuitry of the body, with an intellectual layer on top that keeps us stuck. The body cannot tell the difference between a thought and an actual event. So, when particular thoughts happen, the body reacts as if it's a reality. Just because you feel physical discomfort doesn't mean you have to feel the mental discomfort.

EUGENE So even labeling thoughts is an act of creating a kind of reality.

NANDARAJA Yes, but if you know that you're labeling, then you can have a bit more perspective. You know that you're part of the process, it's not something that is happening to you and that you have no control over.

EUGENE Everyone's process is different, but if you were able to put it into words, you could say something to yourself like, "Here is this sensation, it feels like guilt, and it creates particular sensations in various parts of my body." Is it this process of mindfully naming and labeling that breaks the spell?

NANDARAJA Yeah, and that's painful. You can also be aware that you're creating pain for yourself with guilty thoughts and then justifying those thoughts because you think that, somehow, guilt will make you into a better person.

EUGENE **Is there an antidote to guilt?**

NANDARAJA For both guilt and shame, the antidote is compassion. Guilt and shame are things that need to be examined and dissolved in order to see more clearly. To do that, you have to recognize guilt and shame in yourself and notice your patterns around it.

If in your meditation practice you know how it arises and how you dissolve it, including what you say to yourself or what you do that stops it from happening, you can then extend the same to other people and see if that is helpful to them.

The way of working that Nandaraja outlines above takes years of practice and guidance from experienced practitioners. What he offers however, is a glimpse into the potential for working with painful mental states and moving beyond them to create less suffering. His perspective is very much of the body and an exploration of the embodied self. He advocates a mindful and compassionate investigation of the uncomfortable, including shame and guilt and how these emotions can manifest as physical pain. It is important to have a sense that this type of change is possible so, at some level, we can walk out into the world with more of an mindful and bodyful understanding that both resources and empowers us.

COMPASSION

Responding to Suffering

Developing mindfulness and bodyfulness brings us not just positive and life-affirming experiences but also an awareness of our suffering and the suffering of others. Developing race-construct awareness brings with it the bodily distress of external oppression alongside the bodily distress generated by the internal threat to our identity.

Developing a capacity within to not just make contact with suffering and distress but also dissolve it is going to be important in this work. Generating mental states that both diminish suffering and release energy tied up in negative mental states provides us with the potency and motivation that we will need. We must first generate this capacity for ourselves, and then extend this capacity to others.

There are different aspects to meeting suffering, from understanding someone cognitively—what might be called theory of mind or mentalizing—through to the capacity to share the feelings of others—which might be called empathy—through to developing a strong motivation to improve others' well-being—which might be called compassion.

I want to briefly explore mentalizing alongside empathy and empathy alongside compassion. All of these aspects of making contact with ourselves and others are important, but concerning the development of race-construct awareness, it is important we keep the focus on the development of compassionate mental states.

Mentalizing, or theory of mind, is the capacity to understand that different people may look at the same situation and draw vastly different conclusions based on their beliefs, emotions, and desires. It is an implicit knowledge of how minds work, making sense of behavior and predicting what others might do based on what we think might be going on in their minds. Mentalizing might also be seen as the experience of "feeling clearly" (Deyoung, 2015, p. 38) rather than thinking clearly, even though thinking might be involved. Mentalizing is fundamental to maintaining regulated states while in relationship with the self and with others.

"Mentalizing is fundamental to maintaining regulated states while in relationship with the self and with others."

Empathy, on the other hand, is the capacity to share the feelings of others. When you are empathic, you feel what another person feels but at the same time know the emotion you are resonating with is not yours. With empathy, we can resonate with the positive feelings of others and feel good. We can, however, also resonate with the distressing feelings in others and not feel so good. If we have the capacity, empathy can keep us connected to another's distress, which then offers the possibility of the other person's feelings being heard and acknowledged. If we do not have this capacity, however, empathy can lead us into what might be called empathic distress. Empathic distress is the blurring of the line between you and another so that someone else's distress becomes your distress.

Along with empathic distress come strong feelings of aversion, self-focus, and a desire to withdraw from the situation (Singer & Klimecki, 2014). You might have heard the phrase "compassion fatigue." This is something that affects those in the helping professions and those who help others in distress. In extreme cases, compassion fatigue might lead to someone feeling the symptoms of trauma from spending so much of their time with people who have experienced trauma more directly. Technically, compassion fatigue is not possible; it is more correct to describe what people call compassion fatigue as empathy fatigue.

Compassion and the Body

Along with empathy, there is another social emotion that responds to suffering, which is compassion. Empathy, while important in meeting suffering, also brings the potential to over-identify with suffering. Brain imaging studies have shown that the areas of the brain that light up when a person experiences empathic distress are the same areas that are activated when they experience physical pain. In contrast, imaging studies have shown that compassion activates different brain areas from those responsible for processing pain. Compared to empathy, compassion does not mean sharing the suffering of the other; instead, it is characterized by feelings of warmth, concern, and care for the other as well as a strong motivation to improve the other's well-being. Compassion is feeling *for* and not feeling *with* the other (Singer & Klimecki, 2014). When it comes to race-construct arousal, or indeed any distress, the social emotion of compassion needs first to be developed for the self before turning it outward and focusing it on others.

From a neurological perspective, compassion is incompatible with emotional states like judgment and evaluation. You might be a very caring person, but if you approach someone in a caring way out of a sense of duty, that person will perceive, biologically, that you are acting out of duty and not out of compassion. Your physiology—the muscles around the eyes and the upper face—and your tone of voice will reflect which space you are coming from (CCARE at Stanford University, 2012).

Compassion is not a cognitive function; it is an implicit level of acknowledging and witnessing without reacting.[3] Biological systems that promote compassion can only come online when our active and passive defenses are not in the driving seat.

Developing Compassion

How, then, can we promote compassion? It turns out that we can train ourselves to develop compassion. The key to developing compassion is to make it a daily practice. There are a whole range of self-directed resources available online and through phone or tablet apps that can suggest various compassion practices. Some invite you to recite something that brings your awareness to what you are grateful for. Some compassion practices help us focus more on our commonalities rather than on what differentiates us. Performing random acts of kindness toward others is yet another compassion practice. There are also forgiveness practices, where the focus is on those who have hurt us and mentalizing what their state of mind might have been or on empathizing with what they might be feeling. The important thing is to practice regularly. I recommend you find someone to teach you a compassion practice along with a mindfulness practice. Being with others, at least initially, is a powerful way to stay connected with the practices as well as to get support in navigating the mind's tendency to become distracted and disengaged. For people of color who wish to learn these practices in a person-of-color space, there are resources out there; not that many, admittedly, but they are there.

In certain Buddhist communities, the mindfulness practice would be paired with what is known as a loving-kindness practice called the *mettā bhāvanā*: *mettā*, meaning kindness or something you feel in your heart; *bhāvanā*, meaning development or cultivation. When you practice being mindful, unpleasant feelings arise as you allow yourself to feel them. This is where a compassion or loving-kindness practice comes in. Cultivating compassion effectively cultivates a body that can hold stressful experiences. Compassionate mind–body states then promote more of a sense of mindfulness. Both practices are important, and it is recommended that both practices be explored. You can learn about the stages of the mindfulness and loving-kindness practices easily online or, better still, find a physical space where they are taught and where you can practice them with others.

MICKEY

The following is an extract of a race conversation with Mickey, a female psychotherapist of multi-ethnic heritage. She talks very powerfully about her experience of being a child in her home country, South Africa, as someone who visibly appears to be of South Asian heritage and the journey of compassion she made toward her persecutors, her family, and herself.

EUGENE What impact can race conversations have on you?

MICKEY More often than not, I have quite a visceral reaction. My body changes, I start to scan the conversation in my head—I kind of stiffen up, I also feel quite ready for a fight. I never fight, but literally my body shifts as if preparing for something.

EUGENE These tensions sound familiar to you.

MICKEY It takes me back to being a child in South Africa and of the way African people were spoken to—being called a girl or boy. I find, in my everyday life, those are words that still affect me. I cannot bear for a woman to be called a girl. I know where that takes me back to. I also have quite a visceral, I mean, unbelievable knee-jerk reaction to being confronted by an Afrikaner. There's no other ethnicity that makes me feel quite like that—it's just there.

EUGENE You feel kind of hijacked.

MICKEY You're absolutely right, thinking goes out the window, and it's a struggle.

EUGENE How do you make sense of those sensations in the body?

MICKEY In a way, I see it as a product of everything in my family—I think of what my family dealt with, how they had to swallow down their pride or show that they weren't hurt. I see that in me, and I am mindful of how much of it is still there and what it takes to evoke those things.

EUGENE So what is the race conversation like for you now?

MICKEY I think I'm quite a feeling person, so I pick up on people's moods and people's reactions quite quickly, so several things can happen. It can be a conversation or an exploration and be a real learning process for me, for them, for both of us—or it can be something where I feel quite stubborn, and I think, "I'm not going to give an inch," and it feels like a battle. I suppose I also feel slightly on the back foot [feeling threatened], "Who am I going to upset with all my ideology or my feelings? What's going to happen if I say something?" That's the censoring.

EUGENE You can do harm just by speaking your truth.

MICKEY Yes.

EUGENE I suspect you have gone through a process that has led you to struggle less with the race conversation. It's still not easy, but it's easier.

MICKEY Yes.

EUGENE What's allowed that to happen?

MICKEY Quite a lot of things—I was exiled along with my family, so, going back to South Africa more often, being able to listen to Afrikaners a bit more, especially those who are termed the "born frees" [has been important]—the young people born post apartheid, who now go to school together. They know about apartheid, but they've grown up differently. Going back has given me a lot of time to reflect on how people struggle with the race thing. The ignorance—it's a really hard one for me; ignorance does play its part. Children take on what we all do, what our parents [did], our socialization [of them], and if we don't know any different, that's the way they're going to think. So, having the opportunity to explore more, to meet different people, I think that's helped as well as putting things into a more therapeutic context, to think about why people are the way they are, to think about their triggers. All that has helped, along with my training—that's what we do [as psychotherapist], we think. That's of great importance—thinking therapeutically about what's going on.

EUGENE There's a process of witnessing the healing that's happening in South Africa.

MICKEY Healing is a really good word to use because that's exactly what I have felt and taken part in.

EUGENE Perhaps this process has allowed your heart to open up a little bit, maybe to even see ignorance in a slightly different way. Another part of what you're saying, though, is about studying the human condition, how they operate, how they work.

MICKEY Yes.

EUGENE And I imagine you have a bit of distance from it. I don't know if that's how you would say it.

MICKEY Yes, distance, but it hasn't distanced me from it. It has allowed me to step back and look at it more.

EUGENE Yes, and not get so . . .

MICKEY . . . caught up, yes absolutely. Caught up in that state of not being able to think—that almost fragmenting thing of wanting to react to it.

EUGENE So that feeling of fragmentation isn't quite so strong as it used to be.

MICKEY It's quite contained, yes. That's the interesting thing. At this minute, I'm thinking of a baby crying, and nobody's taking care of the baby, and the baby is really fragmenting and falling to pieces. But I think no, if I was ever aware of feeling like that, it was a long time ago. So even at the moment, when the hairs at the back of my neck are standing up, I know that nothing is going to kick off [erupt into action], and I will be able to think about it.

EUGENE There's still a strong feeling of it, but it's less; you don't feel completely overwhelmed by it.

MICKEY No.

EUGENE It's still a big experience though.

MICKEY Yes. It's always going to be there, but it doesn't have the knee-jerk reaction, it doesn't need any actions. It can still bring me to tears. Because of the age I'm at now, I think a lot more about the elders in my family and how dismissive I was [of them]. How politically motivated I was. They couldn't see themselves in any way as black. I think much more about their experiences. What they must have had to go through for the benefit of the rest of us. Here I am, as a result of everything that they went through. I can't really take a position of sitting in judgment about what they went through. That is quite a sad feeling to have because I won't be able to have those conversations with them. I am more understanding, I think a lot kinder toward them—a very important shift for me.

EUGENE There's a lot of compassion there.

MICKEY Yes, and a reparation from very unkind thoughts about them. When I think of them now, it no longer evokes anger that they never did anything, or said anything, or that they tried to be more white when they were actually black, and things like that.

EUGENE There's been healing for you too, that has allowed your heart to open up to them and where they were coming from.

MICKEY I feel less of a need to be so attacking when people just don't get it. That black people come in every shade, we all look different. And accept me when I say, "This is how I identify"—don't always try to tell me what I am.

For Mickey, there has been an almost crippling union of several aspects of the race construct: the direct witnessing of racial violence and humiliation toward black people; the entanglement in fear-driven

"It is not possible to get to a place of healing without moving toward developing a practice of compassion for yourself and others."

repression of her family's natural response to move to action; and the holding of explicit knowledge that, when the layers of the race construct are peeled away, she is black in the eyes of many white South Africans. All of this leaches into the mind and heart and becomes embodied shame, despair, and dysregulation. There are many cognitive layers to experiences like Mickey's that could and should be explored, but one thing is clear: It is not possible to get to a place of healing in situations like this without moving toward developing a practice of compassion for yourself and others.

GETTING OURSELVES RESOURCED

A study of African American college students found that students who strongly identified with their racial group noticed higher frequencies of racial discrimination but were also more protected from the negative mental health outcomes associated with racial oppression (Sellers & Shelton, 2003). The study also found that an increased sense of community belonging and a commitment to activism were linked with resiliency against oppression. With the race construct demanding distance and separation between individuals and between individuals' minds and bodies as well as turning the body's energy inward, there is an equally pressing need to get resourced to escape the harmful impact of racial oppression.

Getting Resourced

Resources and support are all around us. The race construct, however, keeps us disconnected from the resources that foster change. Resources may take the form of ideas and ways of thinking that become, in effect, a map that makes sense of our experiences. Our resources also include the people within our communities and across communities. Resources are out there, but we do need to be proactive to find them.

The Cognitive Mind as a Resource

Having a coherent narrative about the function of race as a mechanism to exclude people of color from the world's resources is an essential first step in bringing our cognitive mind to personal and interpersonal change as well as cultural and worldview change. Many of the previous chapters in this book have been about bringing clarity and coherence to the race narrative, where ordinarily the race narrative is incoherent and incomplete and, as such, creates cognitive dissonance and confusion. The cognitive mind as a resource involves labeling, demystifying limiting beliefs, understanding why you are the way you are, and developing curiosity and compassion. Cognition as a resource might also involve using the mind to direct attention away from cognitions that confuse and limit us and toward noticing the impact of these thoughts on our bodies and our behavior. It is important to focus on behavior, but without some understanding and a coherent narrative of where the behavior comes from, we will remain stuck on the level of behavior and there will be no healing. Humans are driven to find understanding, even if that understanding is fragmented and breaks down under the most superficial of challenges. Our understanding, therefore, needs to be robust enough to withstand inspection.

Thinking about our behavior is probably the most challenging aspect of race-construct awareness because, as noted previously, thinking about our behavior comes with self-evaluation, self-blame, and societal taboos. When thinking about our behaviors, we must initially make an internal decision to challenge, with compassion, our guilt and shame and to cultivate an inner sense of acceptance and responsibility.

There are several cognitive models that allow us to frame our identity development in such a way that it deepens our understanding. Some of these models give us a sense of movement through stages of development, like the person of color identity development models, mixed-race or biracial identity models, and white identity models. A good summary of these models, including an integrated model by John and Joy Hoffman (1985, as cited in Silva Parker & Willsea,

2011), is outlined in an article entitled "Summary of Stages of Racial Identity Development."[4]

Another model I feel helps us become race-construct aware is by clinical psychologist Valerie Batts, who has put forward a model that gives us a map of various behaviors within the race construct, as played out by modern exclusion (or modern racism), and their complementary behaviors, as played out by internalized exclusion (or internalized oppression). The term "modern" is used to differentiate between the subtle race construct behaviors of today with old-style, coercive and explicit exclusion behaviors from the past. Batts uses the word "exclusion" as an inclusive term to describe the impact of power imbalances on the many historically oppressed groups that includes people of color (Batts, 2017).

Batts' article gives many examples of modern exclusion behaviors that are not malicious by intent; in fact, they might initially be seen as very supportive. Nonetheless, because of personal and cultural biases and preferences, it is often hard to accept decisions that might affect the power imbalance on a personal, interpersonal, institutional, or cultural level. For instance, one modern exclusion behavior is "disabling help," or practicing a kind of "help that doesn't help." In the domain of race, this is when white people do something for people of color—"often motivated out of guilt or shame . . . in the culture of niceness and politeness" (Batts, 2017, p. 15)—based on the belief that people of color cannot assist themselves. The complementary behavior, in people of color, would be "disabling help seeking," an expression of internalized oppression and exclusion that might involve attempts to get over or around the "system" through activating guilt and playing psychological games. Another way that internalized exclusion might be expressed is to take care of whites' feelings by hiding feelings or points of view that might be reacted against or misunderstood.

> If a white person practices "disabling help," many people of color will "resort to disabling help-seeking rather than confront the behavior. . . . Such actions reinforce the dysfunctional behavior on both parts and keep the system intact. (Batts, 2017, p. 21)

Batts's (2017) model is worth further exploration and is an excellent place to identify particular behaviors that you might be falling into, unaware, that have the consequence of excluding or perpetuating the impact of race, regardless of motivation.

Community as a Resource

Another vital resource is people. Intergenerational race trauma plays itself out within families as well as between individuals and society. This type of relational trauma has a crushing impact on trust, which can then lead to a kind of resource phobia in general, and a "people as a resource" phobia in particular, especially when it comes to race. It should not be underestimated how huge a challenge resource-phobia poses for attending to unresolved race hurt. I'm talking here not just about people of color but also white people, who can more easily sidestep doing this work but who need to be part of the solution of attending to the impact of racism.

"Being with other people and having them as a resource as well as your being a resource for them are crucial parts of the process of finding your voice and becoming race-construct aware."

Being with other people and having them as a resource as well as your being a resource for them are crucial parts of the process of finding your voice and becoming race-construct aware. I would say that it is almost impossible to do this work on your own because most of what we are working with is in our bodies, which have implicit processes that are either met or not met, understood or misunderstood. For sure, there are those who have strong cognitive abilities who appear to hold the answers, but it's in the nonverbal arena where the real change happens, and the non-verbal happens during connection.

Observing the Race Conversation

It is a big jump to dive straight into a race conversation, so observing from a distance, monitoring the impact of the conversation on you while in relative safety, can be an important first step. To get yourself resourced, the initial invitation is that you intentionally seek out and attend situations where race issues are taking place—these could be movies, plays, conferences, or community discussions—to observe the race conversation without necessarily taking part in it. What connections do you make between what you observe and the themes of this book? Study your own experience at the level of bodily sensations. What associations do you make with the sensations that you experience? What thoughts and memories arise as you focus on your body? Do you even feel your body? You might want to try tracking your impulses to stay quiet and your impulses to speak. If the desire to speak is there, experiment with talking into the space if that is possible. Again, monitor what happens to you and what impact you have on others. It goes without saying that you also bring your curiosity and your compassion on this journey. Finally, monitor how long it takes to get back to a regulated place in your body and mind when the race conversation is over. Does the time it takes to recover lessen over time? If not, what do you feel you need to do?

One-to-One Therapy

You might be impacted by racial battle fatigue (Smith et al., 2011), which is when your battles for racial justice are affecting your physical and mental health. Alternatively, you might be feeling an urgent need to challenge racial injustice within your place of work or within your family but feel frozen by the prospect. In both cases, it is likely that you are not being heard. If so, finding a therapist can sometimes be useful. A therapist might help bring some clarity to your inner experience and honor your need to be heard. A therapist might also assess your inner and outer resources to ensure that your well-being remains intact. Finding a therapist who is not easily triggered into race-construct arousal, however, will not always be straightforward. The good news is that there are a growing number of therapists who can work with these dynamics, given the growing urgency within the therapy profession to consider race as relevant to healthy well-being.

People-of-Color Spaces

For people of color, I believe coming together to create a sense of belonging with those who want to heal together is the single most important thing that can be done to mitigate the detrimental effects of racism. I have been continually amazed by the simple act of coming together in community to share, support, and inspire each other. When I first attended such groups in the context of my profession as a therapist and in the context of Buddhism, it was difficult for me to identify what was happening that made the group such a powerful experience. On many occasions, I would say to the people-of-color group I was in that I found it hard to put into words what this experience was giving me. I knew, however, that it was having a beneficial effect and making a difference in relation to my racial identity. It also positively affected how I relate to other people of color and my relationship with white people.

Participating in people-of-color groups led me to become aware that I thought I would be different if white people were not around. I would somehow be freer to be the real me. Although that statement is no doubt true to a point, what I realized from spending more time in these groups was that I was the same there as I was anywhere else. In fact, my inner freedom was less related to the white-other and more related to freeing myself from the patterns that I was locked into. In these people-of-color groups, people's defenses were not completely deactivated, but they were less active. This allowed a level of vulnerability to emerge which, in the context of race, I had not really taken in or witnessed in that way. The vulnerability inherent in the social constructs of race that I saw in others matched my own vulnerability, and this was deeply connecting and healing.

Having spent time in these types of groups over many years, I feel I am now able to put words to what these groups are about for me. It is not so much the verbal interaction, but the nonverbal interaction, the implicit expression of experience, that gets met and responded to on a body-to-body level. I don't think these types of experiences are unique to these types of spaces, but the chances of this quality of attention to race experience are much more likely in people-of-color settings.

Examining Whiteness Spaces

The idea of white people coming together to think about race might initially sound strange or even horrifying. What would they be talking about, and what would prevent such a gathering from descending into tokenism?

Two white therapists from London, Bea Millar and Suzanne Keys, brought themselves, over many years, to therapeutic race conversations in mixed black and white spaces. They found these spaces useful in deconstructing the race construct and identifying their part in it, but also felt they needed a different context in which to explore white identity, in particular. They decided to create another space that specifically looked at these concerns. These spaces facilitated exploration of what it means to be white and to be ascribed a white identity and to deepen their understanding of the many complex aspects of white identity within a supportive environment. They believed that white people needed to take responsibility for working through these feelings with each other so they could bring themselves more fully into relationship with people of color. The examining-whiteness spaces that have been created are well attended by both white people and people of color, highlighting an appetite to focus on these issues. Miller and Keys have developed a rare and important space. The invitation is for others who feel motivated and integrated enough to do the same.

Creating Your Own Community

The people resources just described might not be available to you where you are, or they might not be happening at a time you are available, or you might not have the financial resources to access them. The invitation, then, is to create your own community. Find a group of like-minded people and set up a reading group, for instance, where every month you discuss a particular book or set of ideas. Alternatively, the theme of the group might be about raising children of color or being in mixed-race relationships. Reach out to those around you; you might be surprised to find that there is a lot of interest from people who are just waiting for something to be created.

› 8 ‹

FEELING IT— NOT BEING IT

A Particular State of Mind

Getting Uncomfortable

Is It Safe?

Lifting the Veil

The Call to Action and Speaking Our Truth

Staying at the Contact Boundary

Connecting Oppressions

A PARTICULAR STATE OF MIND

The development of curiosity and concern towards the other requires the recognition of the other as a fellow human being.

KEVAL, 2016, P. 13

It is a real challenge to reflect on our personal experience of the race conversation and to create the conditions that bring about our best thinking as well as our curiosity, concern, and compassion toward both our own experience and the experience of the other.

The invitation is for all of us to "be with" race-construct arousal without "being" race-construct arousal. This involves staying at the boundary of our discomfort and, at the same time, compassionately meeting our implicit responses and biases. Ultimately, we are breaking away from our race conditioning and the suffering it causes, in ourselves and in others.

Many of us are trying to navigate the tricky waters of responding to the suffering inherent in the race construct. Even though we did not ask for any of this, we nonetheless have the oppressor within us. We either buy the oppressor story and play out our assigned roles, or we feel the weight of our assigned roles and the suffering that it causes us and others.

Intention, attention, and time are needed as we go through the process of race-construct awareness (Phelps & Thomas, 2003). It is not enough to read, listen, and understand. We must set an intention or make a decision. This type of decision almost always includes being touched by the suffering that is before you. There is a cognitive element to decision-making, but there is also decision-making of the heart. You also need to attend to what or who is in front of you, but what kind of attention will it be? Will it be a wary attention or a kindly attention? The cognitive element of this decision is a kind of cool logic that pushes aside personal discomfort so that the natural human response to distress can emerge. Lastly, time is needed to make a particular type of journey. Healing takes its own time, but it's also true that no healing occurs if you do not make time for it to happen.

In this final chapter, I will explore the predictable patterns of the race conversation and the themes that generally emerge in the various forums in which the race conversation takes place. The sections that follow are based on the five parts of the race-construct awareness model (see Chapter 6, "Toward a Race-Aware Paradigm"). My aim is to bring the model alive in terms of how the race conversation can play out and to expand on the themes that underlie it. I have again included a series of conversations in which individuals tell their stories and are heard and acknowledged. You may want to bring together a group of interested people to reflect on these conversations, and then have a discussion based on them. There is something about becoming more familiar with the bodily sensations that accompany the race conversation and embodying a realization that, much of the time, the sensations you are having do not relate to a current external threat—unless there is an actual external threat. Either way, you can learn to separate the two.

"What would it be like to be fully aware of the race construct in our body, emotion, and thought and not follow the predictable patterns the race construct demands?"

What would it be like to be fully aware of the race construct in our body, emotion, and thought and not follow the predictable patterns the race construct demands? What would it be like to let go of the moorings of the race construct that, internally, tie us down? What would it be like to mindfully stay with the sensations of the body—responding rather than reacting? What would it be like to put aside the kind of judgments that take us into a negative preoccupation with the self? Can we let go of our faults, can we let go of the faults of the people around us, the people closest to us? Is it possible for our adaptations to the race construct, our strange behaviors, our internalized racism, the internalized racism we see in others, to just "be"? When we find fault in one another, do these faults mean that we can't be in relationship with each other? What would it be like to act from this nonjudgmental state of mind?

GETTING UNCOMFORTABLE

When a white body feels frightened by the presence of a black one—whether or not an actual threat exists—it may lash out at the black body in what it senses as necessary self-protection.

MENAKEM, 2017, P. 99

#1

To recognize that the **race construct** serves to keep the distress associated with the violence and brutality committed in the name of race out of the minds and bodies of white people. Racial micro/macroaggressions can then continue unnoticed and unacknowledged, which maintains the status quo.

Back in the early 1900s, there was a street that was commonly known as Black Wall Street. Black Wall Street was in a U.S. district of Tulsa, Oklahoma, called Greenwood. On Greenwood Avenue, there were African American–owned luxury shops, restaurants, and hotels. Greenwood also had its own school system, post office, savings and loan bank, hospital, and bus and taxi service. It wasn't just affluent African Americans who lived there; a significant number of African Americans worked in menial jobs, such as janitors, dishwashers, porters, and domestics. The money these people earned from outside Greenwood was spent within the district.

Following an allegation of attempted sexual assault of a young white woman by one of the young Greenwood residents, there was word of a possible lynching; 75 armed African Americans clashed with 1,500 whites outside the Oklahoma Courthouse. The African Americans retreated to Greenwood. On May 31, 1921, mobs of armed white men descended on Greenwood for two days, looting homes, burning down businesses, and shooting African Americans. Hundreds of black residents died, and thousands of homes were destroyed.

If we went looking, we could probably find hundreds of similar stories across the world. What is shocking is not so much this one event but the predictability of these types of events.

A significant challenge for people of color is that when they go about their business, they are also aware of certain realities. They are aware that when they assert their rights to equality, they also become targets. They are aware that Malcolm X, who fought for black rights, was murdered. They are aware that Martin Luther King, who was awarded the Nobel Peace Prize, was later murdered when he started to advocate for equal financial rights. They are aware of Sam Cooke, who gave messages of peace and love and unity and who, when his message included financial independence and he went about creating the conditions where this could come about, was killed in very suspicious circumstances.

There are countless stories of brutality, naked violence, and racist assassinations that took place decades ago. But what about now, in the twenty-first century? Haven't things changed? What are people of color responding to now that is making them so angry? Also, how do we meet that anger?

When there is racial unrest in the twenty-first century, what has been called "black rage" is often the media's focus. The media are not, however, interested in hearing about or listening to black rage. Instead, they desperately want to move away from it. They ask questions like "Why the looting and violence and damage to property?" Or "Why can't change come through peaceful, moral persuasion?" How we meet black rage in the race conversation is important, but before we think further about black rage, we need to name the forces within which black rage comes about. With black rage, what is very rarely implicated is white rage. White rage is an important concept that helps us understand black rage.

White Rage

Carol Anderson, author of *White Rage,* says this:

> White rage is not about visible violence, but rather it works its way through the courts, the legislatures, and a range of

> government bureaucracies. It wreaks havoc subtly, almost imperceptibly. Too imperceptibly, certainly, for a nation consistently drawn to the spectacular—to what it can see. It's not the Klan. White rage doesn't have to wear sheets, burn crosses, or take to the streets. Working the halls of power, it can achieve its ends far more effectively, far more destructively. (Anderson, 2017, p. 3)

White rage steps forward when people of color step forward to take control of their lives and their financial circumstances. It is predictable, brutal, and unforgiving. People of color understand that if they put their foot on the accelerator of their lives, they can only get so far before they run the risk of losing their reputation, their possessions, or even their lives. Some have taken to the streets to protest, and sometimes this had led to looting and violence. If we want the looting and violence to stop, there is a compelling argument to be made for white power and privilege around the world to stop the looting of and violence toward people of color.

"People of color understand that if they put their foot on the accelerator of their lives, they can only get so far before they run the risk of losing their reputation, their possessions, or even their lives."

White power and privilege have two sides. On the one side is white rage, and on the other is white fragility. Reflecting on the impact of white fragility is deeply uncomfortable for white people. White rage, however, is so imperceptible in its application that uncomfortable feelings do not usually even register for white people. People of color, however, are all too familiar with an often unnamed aggression toward them. William Henry, in his book entitled *Whiteness Made Simple*, notes that "Black folk are the best witnesses to whiteness because white folk don't seem to get what is at stake when merely trying to live, whilst being black, in their world" (Henry, 2007, p. 13).

The idea of stepping out of whiteness that I proposed earlier means white people being aware of how white rage and white fragility operate, and then taking steps to counter the effects. This process inevitably means that there is going to be discomfort. It goes without saying that the playing out of the race construct, with its racial micro- and macroaggressions as a result of white rage, is also deeply troubling and uncomfortable for people of color.

The playing out of white rage and white fragility on the larger political stage finds its way into our institutional lives, our everyday interactions, and our individual race conversations. In both significant and subtle ways, white rage—triggered by people of color who demand fairness and equality—and white fragility—triggered by being faced with the distress of people of color—makes the race conversation an uncomfortable activity at best. All of this commonly makes the race conversation a one-sided affair, with people of color doing the most and gaining the least or, at most, gaining very little.

Here is an everyday example of how all of this works. A therapy student of color came to me about her supervisor.[1] She had come to realize that her supervisor's white fragility made it impossible for her to get what she needed out of the supervisory relationship. She was advised to challenge the supervisor, but her demands for change did not make her supervisor any more competent. For the student to engage someone who could give her a service equal to what she was paying for, she had to defend her decision to leave and risk triggering white rage. There is no old-time racism here but, instead, a modern version of racism, which is more inconspicuous but still has the power to impact people of color on a systematic scale.

Black Rage

The typical response to people of color's anger and rage is fear. Anger is scary for sure, but the degree of fear that is expressed in both white people and in people of color is often quite extreme and results in an array of socially sanctioned responses that suppress its expression. What, then, is contributing to the intense fear of the anger of people of color and of black rage? If we take the example of Greenwood's Black Wall Street mentioned earlier, it is evident that the real fear here is not so much the emergence of black rage, but what might follow. I am suggesting that black rage is predictably followed by brutal and unforgiving white rage, which brings about more black rage, and on and on it goes—this is something to be genuinely fearful of. A central question for many in the race conversation is: How can we meet black rage if it emerges? More pressing than this, however, is: What can be done about the white rage that swiftly follows? Anderson tellingly warns us that white rage manages to maintain not only the upper hand but also, apparently, the moral high ground (Anderson, 2017).

"Black rage is predictably followed by brutal and unforgiving white rage, which brings about more black rage, and on and on it goes."

The countless acts of civil unrest that have been swiftly followed by white rage have, over time, become a powerful aspect of generational loading. Black rage, then, can be the trigger for embodied versions of the past that includes the fear, terror, and injustice of white rage. Is it possible, then, to respond to black rage simply for what it is: a symptom of living a life within the construct of race and an expression of distress and hurt? For those on the path of race-construct awareness, is it possible to hold onto this truth without triggering white rage and the implicit memories we carry in our bodies from the past?

› › › PAUSE . . . *and breathe* ‹ ‹ ‹

I've Hurt Someone

I will now present three conversations that further illustrate getting uncomfortable in the race conversation.

ORYAN

Oryan is a white Israeli therapist and counseling trainer. In this section of our conversation, she recalls her initial interest in bringing race issues into the training room, followed by her cognitive and bodily experience after she has done so. The therapist forum mentioned in the conversation is a space for therapists that invites a deepening of the race conversation.

ORYAN The first thing was excitement—before things went wrong. Also, I was pleased that I have something to give, that I come from a position of "that's the discussion I want to have, that's the discourse." There was then a feeling of being inadequate or the wrong person or being too white to be able to speak about anything that would resonate with anyone who has a different experience.

EUGENE Is there a particular place in all that where you tend to dwell?

ORYAN I kind of hold both of them. A little while ago I probably came too confident to the conversation, and the backlash was "you don't know what you're talking about," or "you speak from a very specific position." It wasn't what I was expecting it to be. Fear was there. I don't know if it was really mine though.

There's so much, and it just gets very complicated. Then there's what I feel in my body. I can say things very freely, I'll bring up race without thinking, without preparation. I didn't seem to have fear or need to psych myself up beforehand. Afterward, though, I feel the anxiety, the uneasiness, and I feel wrong.

EUGENE Can you describe what happens in your body during all of this?

ORYAN It would be like adrenaline, noticing that something went wrong, and my heart beating. I can feel the blood pumping and just feeling very "wrong." Either because I said something wrong or because I didn't react to something that was said.

EUGENE So there's a surge of energy?

ORYAN It's not pleasant.

EUGENE And a sense of wrongness.

ORYAN Wrongness.

EUGENE And if your body could do something in that moment?

ORYAN It'll go away. Just go away. If I could do anything, I would tell that feeling to go away. I think I shut down more than anything else. I would also speak less.

EUGENE A kind of shrinking internally. How long would that typically last before you are okay again?

ORYAN It depends on the situation. If I've instigated it, it will come in waves. It will go, and then it will come back again, say in the evening. Or it will go away and then come back the next week. Sometimes I wouldn't even notice when it's back, and I would notice it like a few days later.

EUGENE So you might have said or done something in the context of race, and then that moment comes back into your mind down the road, and the feelings come with it.

ORYAN It would be mainly physical, and then there would be the thoughts and emotions that are connected to it, yeah. I also don't seem to learn, in that I should be nervous before I go into it again.

EUGENE I suppose I assumed that you would be nervous before the race conversation, but that's not your experience. For you, the stuff comes afterward.

ORYAN Yeah.

EUGENE Do you have some reasoning behind those feelings and why they're so intense?

ORYAN Because I hurt somebody, because somebody gets hurt and that's not a good position to be in. I don't like to be in that position.

EUGENE You don't want to be that person who has hurt.

ORYAN Yeah. A while ago I was just in that position. My students wanted to say things to me anonymously because they didn't want it to affect their marks. I was thinking—really, like they feel so unsafe with me because I'm marking. That was very unpleasant. Later I started to think about it, to see what belongs to me and what doesn't belong to me, and what belongs to the group and what doesn't belong to the group; not to shirk responsibility, hence the changes that I'm doing this year, but I really had to think. I had to work very hard to get out of feeling that that's the one thing I am [to them]. That was a process that lasted a couple of months, which was still there when I came to your therapist forum. The forum wasn't easy.

EUGENE You are describing an experience that many people have.

ORYAN And they had their own experience also. I don't think their experiences were much easier.

EUGENE It becomes very personalized, doesn't it. Even though race is a global construct, your experience of it was a very personal one.

ORYAN There wasn't space for that when it started. When there was some space, I could have some distance; it stopped being just personal. It was easier to bear and then do something with it.

Getting Into Hot Water

RUTH

Ruth is a white psychotherapist who has written about her experience of race in the therapy room. In this section of our conversation, an unwelcome image comes to mind that is part of generational loading.

RUTH I was thinking about coming here, and my anxiety was that I wouldn't have anything to say. I'm very interested in conversations about race though. It's not something I want to avoid.

Usually, what I'm feeling in a race conversation is something like excitement or anticipation that, as a therapist, I might be able to help someone to have a conversation they haven't had before. There is also an interest and curiosity to see what they say or where it goes or what they do with it and what I might learn and maybe a bit of confidence. If anything, I hold myself back from having that conversation. I didn't know if you were assuming that people might be more worried than excited about a conversation like that.

EUGENE I know that people have both worry and excitement because potentially it can be very, very liberating. It also has the potential to become a disaster, and both of those potentials coexist.

Did an image come to mind [when we did the mindfulness exercise]?

RUTH Yes, an image came straight to mind. A very unwelcome image. I've grown up around racism. One of the things I recollected [from] the 1970s was there used to be cartoons in magazines like the *Reader's Digest*. They were hand-drawn cartoons, and quite often there would be an image of cannibals. Any reference to Africa would have a picture of someone in a pot—a missionary or someone like that, with people standing around with bones through their noses. The cannibals had loincloths or something like that and big pot bellies. The missionary probably had a big potbelly as well, but I can remember it quite clearly as a frequent image that would come into my vision with some sort of joke, or a one-liner underneath. The joke could be the missionary saying something to another missionary. Sometimes they'll be on a spit or hanging on a stick and being carried through the forest. Sometimes the joke would be the other way round. The two cannibals would be saying something to each other, although that was more unusual.

The generic picture of that kind of cartoon image came into my mind and then I thought, oh shit, not that; that's very unwelcome, don't like that at all. And why, why has that come in now? It must have come through for a reason, and I need to trust my unconscious. Am I feeling in hot water? Also, what are the various permutations here about who is in the pot? In the mindfulness exercise, I was registering my discomfort with the image.

EUGENE What was your immediate response to that image?

RUTH It's an image that's a representative image of racism really. It could be taken as an image in its own right to represent the roles we're both playing, that we are both in the work. The water is heating up maybe, and we're both cooking together. It needn't be a terrible image, but it is a terrible image because it's an image of completely insensitive, white mainstream culture. So my reaction is shame and more annoyance that I've come up with that image so quickly.

Pressing It Down!

Rebellions of the past, like those that took place during slavery, the civil rights movement, the various riots in London, or the Black Lives Matter marches, seem like moments spaced out in time that come around every decade or so when tensions get high. There are moments of rebellion being reenacted, however, every single day, that go mostly unnoticed.

MAITRINITA

In this section of our conversation, black female member of the Triratna Buddhist Order, Maitrinita talks about her family's long history of pressing down the injustices of racism.

MAITRINITA I'm very aware of my history of people being crushed by asserting their civil rights. During the mindfulness exercise, I was starting to become aware of the conditions that have led me to be where I am now. My family, they're great you know, but they put their heads down and get on with the work. They keep all the injustices that they suffered; they keep it down, they keep it down. If I go back to slavery, they kept it down and survived. I come from a long history of pressing it down, of pressing it down. They survived. I came from survivors. We come from survivors. What now are we going to do with this precious life?

Because I can see it now a bit more maybe, I have a choice to respond differently and take the risk of, well, not being liked. It may be a mess; probably I need mess rather than to be so controlled over it a bit more, you know what I mean?

EUGENE There's no way out of the mess sometimes is there? Someone I was speaking to today talked about the real possibility of death in asserting their rights, and then having to come to a different relationship with that image of speaking out.

MAITRINITA I saw rebellion being crushed on TV but I also saw it within my family. Rebellion [for me] was maybe not putting a thing back in the right place. Tiny little acts of rebellion that didn't need the level of violence that was there to keep you controlled. Expressing myself generally as a human being, the angry part of myself, the more fiery parts were not given the conditions to grow in my childhood. You did what you were told, and if you didn't, there was the belt; there were beatings. It was not just society and what was out there [that kept you down]. So that's more conditioning.

EUGENE Once upon a time, there was something functional

about that. It was a survival strategy. If just one of us was doing the rebelling, we were all going to get it, so we have learned to police ourselves. Even though we are living in different conditions, it's still automatic.

MAITRINITA My parents come from violence. My dad's father hated him. My mum had a step-uncle who treated her like some sort of slave. All of that is impacting on some of us.

EUGENE It seems as if these functional strategies were from a long time ago, but it's not that long, really, for it to still be living on within families. You mentioned that you have a choice of responding differently?

MAITRINITA When you talked about the moment before the race conversation, it seemed very vague, but there is a gap isn't there? Am I going to be reactive, or am I going to give myself a choice as to how I respond? I guess I didn't quite see it like that until just now. That gap between having something unpleasant come up and our response. What is our response? Do we respond? Do we even recognize the gap?

› › › PAUSE . . . *and breathe* ‹ ‹ ‹

IS IT SAFE?

We weren't post-racial in 1988 and we're not post-racial now, which begs the question: were we ever? And will we ever be?

BOAKYE, 2019, P. 143, EBOOK

#2

To recognize that **generational loading** primes the nervous system to receive nonverbal racial cues of danger or threat to life.

Primed for Danger

I previously described generational loading as the passing on of nonverbal racial cues of danger through the generations, which primes current generations' bodies and nervous systems to hypervigilantly neurocept nonverbal racial cues from the environment, others, and the self. These nonverbal racial cues then create predictable patterns of racial bias within the racialized imagination and interrupt our ability to feel safe. Without safety, the race conversation is experienced as little more than a battleground where you feel a need to be either armed and ready to fight or prepared to surrender.

Can the Race Conversation Ever Feel Safe?

In healing or therapeutic conversations, being emotionally sensitive and present to another's reality is what creates the condition of safety; this safety creates the conditions for healing. For people of color, being seen and witnessed in the context of whiteness doesn't often bring about the desired safety, instead it elicits a range of implicit memories that cue responses to danger. The supposed fertile void of silently waiting for something to emerge is instead experienced as persecutory silence.

As noted earlier, this demand to be heard and acknowledged and to have equal access and rights to the space, in itself, implicitly triggers a sense of danger for both white people and people of color. This danger then triggers the body to prepare for white rage, and to prevent this possibility, we feel a pressing demand within ourselves and from others to close down the source of race distress. Shame can also be triggered. Is it possible, then, to feel safe while having the race conversation across race lines?

It is important to note that when people say they do not feel safe, they also mean that they feel fear. It is fear that drives our behavior and our inability to respond. The question then becomes: How do we work with the fear that we feel? Fear is the feeling we try to tune out of our awareness if we can, and if we do become aware of it, we are quick to deny it. We are fear driven and, at the same time, desperate to appear that we are not. It feels instinctive to defend yourself if you feel under attack. It also feels instinctive to present outwardly that we have got it together and that we are strong and unbreakable. But does it need to be like this?

Paradoxically, by attending to the fear, shame, and confusion behind the anger there is hope and a way through. At some level, communicating and acknowledging the political and social realities of people of color and validating that, for them, the stakes are high just in being alive creates some measure of safety. Without this acknowledgment being communicated through words as well as nonverbally through the body, there is little chance of the desired safety coming about. What would it be like to park the fear and communicate that why someone would not feel safe or why they would be angry makes sense to you?

The conversation that follows is from someone talking about their experience of apartheid. While apartheid is an extreme form of the race construct, there are similar and predictable patterns of danger and of being on a battlefield when a person of color brings their experience of race into any white space. This pattern is evident, regardless of whether the historical context is South Africa, the U.S. the U.K., or any other country in the world. Whether racism is hidden or blatant, the pattern is the same.

RABIYA

Rabiya is a South Asian therapist who grew up in South Africa before coming to the U.K. as a young adult. Rabiya's reflections of being in South Africa are typical of the predictable patterns of generational loading.

RABIYA I remember being with this group of white friends having dinner, many of whom were South African. They were talking about the "black thing" in South Africa. One of them was a white South African man who was very active in politics, and he was trying to educate a non-South African woman who had just been to South Africa. She said it was a wonderful country, but she didn't really like "the black thing." The man was, like, "What do you mean? That 'black thing' you're talking about, it's all over the world." All I said to them was "What you are all talking about is white privilege." Then I left.

EUGENE You left the room.

RABIYA Yes, I went out for a cigarette. I thought I said my statement with such authority.

EUGENE Did they continue the conversation when you left?

RABIYA They grabbed onto what I said and then carried on with what they were doing. I didn't want to engage any further.

EUGENE I'm sure it was a fascinating conversation between them, but something was happening for you that they weren't aware of.

RABIYA [Long pause] It was that imbalance of power. White people defending me and my experience. They are the ones who have the voice and can be heard and listened to by this woman who had just visited South Africa.

I was the person who had grown up inside apartheid, whose parents have never voted. There was the white South African, yes, I kind of respected his position and his politics, but it was that whole dynamic. They were the ones talking to this woman, and it felt like it was on my behalf. They are the ones having the arguments about it, talking about it.

EUGENE There was something about your voice not having the same kind of validity.

RABIYA Also, when she talked about the "black thing," she didn't see me as included in that. So to her, I was probably very close to a white South African.

EUGENE You felt invisible at that point?

RABIYA I felt she wouldn't have been talking about me.

EUGENE Somehow, there wasn't a space for your experience in that conversation, or it felt like that from your perspective.

RABIYA Yes, it was probably an entertaining and enjoyable argument for the other white people to engage in. For me, to bring in my reality would just kind of bring down the jolliness.

EUGENE Your experience would dampen the mood.

RABIYA There was a determination to show how passionately they feel about this. I would have had to compete with that to own it. Oh god, there's the anger. . . . It's like, I have to compete?

EUGENE That phrase, "I have to compete to own what is mine" feels important. What would have happened if you had brought your experience into the room? How would that have played out?

RABIYA I think they would have dismissed it because they want to own this passion. Or they might have taken bits of my experience to support what they wanted to say; I wouldn't have really felt listened to.

EUGENE The energy that you might expend would be fruitless, as they wouldn't be able to receive all of it.

RABIYA I have this fantasy that I would find some amazingly concise, intellectual, and sharp thing that I could say that would encapsulate it all, and they would then have to listen because it would feel powerful to them. The discussion was passionate but still intellectual. If I could give something more powerful and intellectual, with a bit of personal in it, then that might make a difference. Just me and my experiences feel like not enough.

EUGENE If you had communicated the emotional part of your experience, what do you imagine might have happened?

RABIYA It would be like I become the poor, wounded black

person, an object everyone would feel sorry for. I should be able to contain it and not bring that stuff up when we are having a friendly dinner.

EUGENE There are a lot of forces at work here. It's hard to stay in a jolly mood with this topic. You protected yourself by leaving and came back when it was all over.

RABIYA Yeah.

EUGENE From your point of view, what would have helped you to feel valid?

RABIYA There could have been some acknowledgment that they were talking about apartheid and the impact that it still has on South African society. I grew up with that and experienced that.

EUGENE So for them to turn to your experience of that?

RABIYA Yes, we could have all talked about it. We could have talked about the white South African guy's end of it and my end of it. It could have been very educational for this woman who had just been to South Africa. I wanted more of a real conversation about experiences rather than having this political right or wrongness because it feels so complex to me.

Yes, everyone knows that it was wrong, everybody knows that the world is bloody shit in lots of ways and unequal and unjust. Let's talk about it—really. What was it like? Let's try to understand each other.

EUGENE Showing your underbelly in apartheid sometimes had the consequence of death. So you could not really show all of the human parts of you. If you push it down and only show particular emotions, then everything is fine. There has been so much conditioning over time.

RABIYA Huge conditioning.

EUGENE Conditioning to only express a certain range of feeling.

RABIYA It distorts what it means to be human. In apartheid, to be human means to be white. If you are not white, your sense of yourself is of not being fully human. I always wanted to be that. I wanted my parents to be that. I wanted everyone to be that. Why aren't we all that?

White People Can't Educate Me

PATRICK

The theme of danger and of being armed with knowledge and words is also evident in this section of conversation with Patrick, a black male therapist.

EUGENE Some people have spoken about feeling a threat, or a presence that's threatening, although they can't really describe what it is. Sometimes there is a threat, but sometimes there isn't anything particularly threatening, it's just conversation, just words, but yet that feeling of threat is there. Is that something that's present for you, or has been?

PATRICK Threat . . . I'm thinking about the conversations I would have with colleagues. How I deal with the threat is to look to place myself in the position of the knower, when in actuality I'm driven by the threat of, "Hang on a moment, someone may actually know more than me. You can't educate me or improve or increase my awareness on this issue because you're white." For me, therefore, that's a threat. How I may then deal with that is again to create the prejudice, the presumption about that person or these people, as a way of managing that threat.

There are times when I think about the threat as related to my own sense of where I believe I should be when it comes to race conversations. How I sometimes respond to that threat is to say, "Right, I need to know everything. I need to know everything about this." I've got to read this book, within this time, on this particular day because, if I don't, I'm not going to know. If I don't know, I'm not going to be equipped, I'm not going to be armed.

EUGENE Yeah, I was thinking about that word—armed.

PATRICK But against what? Whatever it may be, for me, it reflects a threat and, therefore, how I am responding to that sense of threat.

EUGENE I was relating what you are saying to a young person on the street who says, "I need a knife." His knife is in effect your words with which you can slice them up, push them aside and say "Next!" I guess that's a kind of armor as well. The way you're seeing things is that they might feel they have something to teach you, but they can't.

PATRICK No, they can't.

EUGENE Potentially, your soft underbelly might be prodded with some kind of taser. There's a risk of this in real life, isn't there?

PATRICK It's a bit like, the fear seems really there until you actually confront it and then realize, hang on a second, so that's what it is.

EUGENE Sometimes, the fear can be more fearful than the actual thing itself.

PATRICK Exactly. Absolutely, yeah.

EUGENE So there's a sort of pre-made script that this is futile so let's just load up with ammo. The white other probably has their own version of that on the other side too.

PATRICK This is what race conversations can do and does for me—it could be another person of color—it's the same thing! But that's what it does.

It's Race and Diversity Day!

The dreaded "race day" is probably familiar to many who work in mental health, the public sector or even the private sector. The organization wants to do something to address race issues, probably because there has been a significant event in the media that has put the question of race back on the agenda. There is a sense that the race day might have the potential for understanding and change, but often it is experienced very differently.

BARBARA

In this section of conversation with Barbara, a white therapist and therapy trainer, she talks about her experience of the race day when she herself was training to be a therapist.

BARBARA When I was training as a therapist, we had "the race day." They were OK, but it was when you got into group discussion that the real stuff comes. That's where you're on the edge of your seat thinking, "I thought I was in that [sorted and confident] camp. I thought I understood." It's scary because you've really got to know yourself.

EUGENE When you reflect on the fear, how do you account for it? The people in that room were not a danger to you, I imagine.

BARBARA The fear is what gets the conversation going, in a sense. It's what lights the flame so that we actually talk. If you were feeling comfortable, it means that something hasn't touched you. Could we honestly bring ourselves?

EUGENE What made it uncomfortable for you?

BARBARA For me, it's about trampling on people. To trample on someone and not even know you've done it, oh my god, that would be so humiliating and awful. It's only by having a conversation though, that you can figure out what you are and what you're not doing. Also, what do you think you are doing and what does the other person think you are doing?

EUGENE There is this general, unexpressed, internal life of the [black] other and, because it's unexpressed, you don't know where to put your foot. If you put it in the wrong place, all hell could break loose. If you hit on the right place, however, you could hit the bull's eye and have a very fruitful and healing conversation.

BARBARA Also, are you prying? You might be trying to make contact, but is it seen as prying and none of your business? This is true of just about everything in counseling, so why does race always feel a bit more loaded? That's something I'm interested in.

EUGENE Have you had any thoughts around answering that?

BARBARA [*pause*] Somebody might think you're just like that bunch of people who—and it's like, oh god, I don't want you to see me as that because honestly, I don't want to be that person [a white extremist]. How do you be authentic and be seen as authentic? So much of that depends on each person's experience, good and bad.

EUGENE It's further complicated, isn't it, by the fact that one person's authentic might be seen by another person as outrageous and "How could you possibly think that?" Authenticity itself comes under scrutiny and gets turned on its head. You might say to yourself "I'm being authentic, but I've just been told that I've been offensive." It's a mind bend, that's for sure. What you're describing here is a landscape of landmines that probably everyone experiences.

LIFTING THE VEIL

The effect of oppression by its very nature tends to be invisible to those who hold more power and privilege.

AFUAPE, 2011, P. 28

#3

To understand that, when race is the focus, generational loading is triggered, leading to **race-construct arousal.**

The White Gaze—The Black Gaze

I have used the metaphor of the veil to represent the thin yet impregnable barrier between the world seen by the white gaze and the world as it is seen by people of color. The world of the white gaze imagines that people of color see them as they want to appear. They do not imagine that the way whiteness makes its presence felt to people of color is wounding, hurtful, or torturous. The world, from the perspective of the person of color, is very different from the imagined representation of goodness (hooks, 1992).

In his book *Black Skins, White Masks,* Frantz Fanon said this of the white gaze: "I am being dissected under white eyes, the only eyes. I am fixed" (Fanon, 1952/1986, p. 31).

Fanon's experience was of a gaze that sought to discipline and objectify. Under the white gaze, deeply embedded in the race construct, is the averted black gaze. Throughout the periods of slavery, colonialism, and, more recently, racial apartheid systems in various countries, an effective strategy for maintaining amenable and less threatening black servants was centered around control of the black gaze. Over the centuries, people of color were (and still are in some parts of the world) brutally punished for looking at, or appearing to observe, white people. This effectively turned the person of color from a person with their unique thoughts, emotions, and beliefs along with the assumption of alikeness, into an object with a body that is useful for labor and disposable. In the domain of the race construct, only those like us can share a mutual gaze.

As the race conversation begins, the metaphorical veil is lifted, sometimes in unannounced and unwelcome ways. Something is said or done that is out of your control. Perhaps you are on a journey of race-construct awareness, placing yourself in a space that you feel will deepen your understanding. What lurks beneath the lifted veil is the visceral discomfort and shame, the very opposite perhaps of what you'd imagined. There is shame by association, shame because you feel you haven't been strong enough, kind enough, or capable enough. There is also troubled sleep as a result of meditating on your naivety or your lack of knowledge.

"As the race conversation begins, the metaphorical veil is lifted, sometimes in unannounced and unwelcome ways."

Another critical aspect of the white gaze on people of color is that it effectively internalizes white privilege so that the person of color then feels responsible for the imposed constraints of power. The white gaze, then, both suppresses the inner yearnings of people of color and at the same time protects white privilege.

The internalized aspect of the white gaze, when turned toward other people of color, is what makes parents gaze disappointingly at the overtly African features of their newborns or give preference to their lighter-skinned, green-eyed children. This is internalized racism or what could be called the negative black gaze. Of prime importance for people of color is the importance of developing what transcultural counselor Isha Mckenzie-Mavinga calls a positive black gaze (Mckenzie-Mavinga, 2016), which counteracts the effects of the negative black gaze. She also suggests that the positive black gaze may be something that white people can offer to people of color. Mckenzie-Mavinga does not outline what the positive black gaze in white people would look like in practice, but I see the development of the positive black gaze as a part of race-construct awareness. As race-construct awareness develops and the intensity of arousal to nonverbal racial triggers diminishes, the positive black gaze will naturally arise.

Meeting Racial Battle Fatigue

In 2011, a study examined the experiences of 661 black men in search of correlations between racial micro/macroaggressions, societal problems, and academic achievement (Smith et al., 2011). People of color, in general, believe the proverb "You've got to work twice as hard to get half as far." Alongside this widespread belief is the belief that education is the great emancipator, or the great equalizer. People of color are then faced with the probability of working harder in education than their white counterparts and also facing the racism of white educational institutions. Not surprisingly, the study found that increases in the educational attainment of people of color is associated with higher levels of stress as a result of daily, constant and random, racial micro/macroaggressions. This continuous cycle of stress is what the authors of the report call racial battle fatigue (Smith et al., 2011), as mentioned in Chapter 7.

This 2011 study also shares another important finding: As black men progress up the education ladder, they are increasingly exposed to racial ideologies that are more embedded and less subtle (Smith et al., 2011). For the vast majority of black men, education has paid off in terms of better jobs and higher income. These benefits have, however, come at an emotional, psychological, and physiological cost (Smith et al., 2011).

Racial battle fatigue is not confined to educational settings but also arises in historically white institutions, such as mental health institutions, governmental departments, sporting bodies, and political institutions. Online trolling also contributes significantly to racial battle fatigue, as it can often tip the balance of that individuals struggling to stay sane.

If you have been impacted by racial battle fatigue, finding a therapist with whom you can work to bring some clarity to your experience can sometimes be a useful option.

Following on from these points about the white gaze and racial battle fatigue, I want to illustrate how these themes play out in race conversations. The two conversation extracts that follow are from a white and black point of view.

SAMI

I received the following email from Sami, a white psychotherapist, after a colleague and I had run a trainer's forum workshop. This workshop happened during the aftermath of George Floyd's killing in the U.S. when people of color were feeling especially connected to Floyd and the subsequent disaffection.

> Dear Eugene,
> When I attend these sorts of meetings, and when I read literature on enslavement, institutionalised racism, and white privilege, I am in turmoil. I am still traumatised by witnessing the death of George Floyd. I don't perceive my turmoil and personal trauma to be a bad thing, but rather, it is necessary for me to feel this way, and I am willing to stay connected with this. I have been processing since the meeting yesterday. I am impacted by the beautiful words left by your beloved colleague. I am also impacted by one of the participant's stories of trauma, and I am still holding much of what was expressed by yourself Eugene and by the other men in the "black men on the couch" series. I went to bed at 2 a.m. this morning with a book that I wouldn't normally engage with as bedtime reading, but I was drawn to it, like a magnetic force pulling me. It is entitled *Post Traumatic Slave Syndrome: America's Legacy of Enduring Injury and Healing* by Dr. Joy Degruy. I woke up this morning with a realisation that I haven't apologised.
>
> Just as one white voice, amongst many, I want you to know that I am deeply Sorry for the harmful and devastating effects caused by those white, inhumane slave-trading/owning ancestors and current white murderers of Black People that I am ashamed to be associated with. I am also deeply Sorry for my own part in the perpetuation of institutionalized racism, by way of my own blind spots (up until recently) around white privilege and around my own previous inertia.
>
> I am Sorry, and I Care, and I will keep doing my best to raise awareness (within the field [of therapy] and institutes

that I am a part of) of institutionalized racism and the devastating effects this can have on health, well-being and on the psyche, as well as on relationships between people of all heritages.

With Respect and Sincerity,

Sami (personal communication, August, 21, 2020)

Sami is on a journey of race-construct awareness. She took herself into a space that she thought would progress her journey. She listened to individuals who, body-to-body, had communicated racial battle fatigue. What she was experiencing was the lifting of her personal veil, just a little bit more, and the discomfort and turmoil that lay underneath. Sami also navigated the central challenge of race-construct arousal, which is to stay out of the defensive mode of white rage, silence, or denial and stay with the distress.

MAITRINITA

In this next section of conversation, black female member of the Triratna Buddhist Order, Maitrinita talks about her multilayered experience of having the image of the golliwog[2] presented to her out of the blue.

EUGENE Have you had an opportunity for a race conversation across race lines, and what effect has this had on you?

MAITRINITA When I used to be in a writing group, I had a race conversation. It was over the image of the golliwog. There was a story presented where the writer included an image of a golliwog. I didn't say anything the week it was read out. I spent the week thinking about it and talking to other people. There was embarrassment and shame around it. I think the shame made me feel the outsider. Also, I wanted to rationalize it, and maybe if I talked about it with other people it might change it and make it [the shame] go away.

I can't remember what the story was, but this golliwog was in the story, and there was a lot of discomfort. I guess my sleep was affected at the time with lots of anxiety about how to approach this and what to say in the next group.

In the group, I talked about whether we carry on with the same stereotypical images as writers or do we do something fresh. I thought I was perhaps stopping people's freedom of expression, the author seemed open enough to hear what I had to say, but in the end, I just felt a bit flat. I didn't feel empowered.

EUGENE The experience was significant for you. How do you explain why things happened in that way? Your experience was met in some way but not in the way that you wanted. How do you understand where those feelings came from, and what do you think might have made it go better?

MAITRINITA I don't know what would have made it go better except that it would have led to a more general conversation. I guess when you mention race, it flattens things. People don't want to be accused of being racist, so they say nothing.

EUGENE You've had this multilayered experience where you talked about what writers could do in the future, but you are left with the emotional part to hold onto.

MAITRINITA I think another of my responses is to make it broader [than my own experience] which deflects it. It leaves me with the feeling that I haven't been seen and that I have to be the one who makes it nice so it's not sticky and painful and pushing it [my feelings] onto other people.

EUGENE I guess you're bringing up the central dilemma of a lot of people. There's something about holding pain or just throwing it out there. Do you have a right to throw it out there? And if you do throw it out there, do you know what's going to happen?

Doubt

Lifting the metaphorical veil and looking beyond the white gaze is not easy nor straightforward. Most likely, you will experience doubt that this is even possible. There is doubt in your ability to hold back distress and doubt in your capacity to hold the confusion and discomfort that might arise.

As with any process of change, resources will need to be available to you to support you through a process. You might not believe that the resources are available, but they are out there. The question is, how do you find the motivation and energy to overcome the race construct's tendency to generate inertia? There are issues of ethics on the one hand and fear of change on the other. The information covered in this book might go some way toward lifting doubt, but ultimately it will be connecting with like-minded others that energizes us to continue.

Grief and Loss

There is a profound sense of loss experienced when people of color become fully aware of how race has influenced their lives. Bringing an awareness to the damping down of countless people's humanity in order to sustain white privilege is a deep grief that profoundly connects people of color to each other.

It is, perhaps, easy to confuse the symptoms of trauma—the stoicism, the apparent toughness and the no-nonsense, getting-things-done attitude—with there being anything more. One of the outcomes of trauma is the mounting of defenses against grief and sadness. Grief is seen as a vulnerability and a threat to the integrity and protection of the individual, so it tends to get suppressed and unexpressed. People of color have a deep history of grief and loss that has not been met, or even acknowledged, by both white people especially and also by people of color in any substantive way. The American president Thomas Jefferson, who believed that slavery was against the celebrated Declaration of Independence, at the same time could not imagine the internal life of the enslaved was any different from the surface behaviors he saw as they served him. In 1781, he noted, in the only book he ever published, that for black people, "love seems with them to be more an eager desire, than a tender, delicate mixture of sentiment and sensation. Their griefs are transient" (Jefferson, 2006). Jefferson was talking about what he saw as black people's lack of ability to be tender with each other and to experience the grief that accompanies loss.

"There is a profound sense of loss experienced when people of color become fully aware of how race has influenced their lives."

Black grief, then, is yet another part of normal human expression that, over time, has been suppressed, and that suppression has become the norm and a part of the landscape of implicit memories. Given that the direct threat to life has decreased in modern racism, the suppression of grief from the white gaze no longer serves a purpose but, nonetheless, keeps people of color locked in pain and shame.

The conditions needed to make contact with this grief are a willingness to see beyond the presenting feelings of anger and strength and an understanding of the importance of connectedness. When working through trauma, grieving is a necessary part of the journey to connectedness. Connectedness is fundamental to trauma recovery and the resurrection of personhood. Looking beyond the anger and holding onto the certainty of the tenderness underneath is essential and addresses a burning question held by many people of color: Can I be angry and even confrontational, as sometimes I feel, and still be loved?

"When working through trauma, grieving is a necessary part of the journey to connectedness."

Lifting the Veil of the Mixed-Race Experience

As the race construct gets enacted inside all of us, it's a challenge, even if you identify with just one racial group. If you are mixed race, the sense of identity and belonging, which is so vital to feeling safe, can be full of doubt. Lifting the veil from the mixed-race experience often reveals feelings of alienation, a lack of identity, and a search for safe harbors of belonging, as the following two conversations bring to light.

SU

In this section of conversation, mixed-race Asian, female Buddhist Su talks about her experience of being mixed race.

They've Got My Back

SU I'm mixed race; my father is from Pakistan, and my mother is white British. For pretty much most of my childhood, and actually a great deal of my adulthood, I had to decide which I was. Asian people see me as Asian. I don't know what white people see me as: someone with a tan I guess, I don't know. That was very much the thing growing up. I always felt I had to make a choice about where I stood, and I really don't know. My [full] sister is white. Her objective experience is different to mine but her feelings—you know, it's really tricky. She very much feels her heritage as much as I do, but I guess people look at me and would say, yes, there's someone who looks Asian, but they wouldn't look at her and say that.

EUGENE Some might say she should not be part of a people-of-color space the way she looks, even though she is Asian?

SU I see both sides, and I just want to sit on the fence. I

don't know if that's just the mixed-heritage experience, you know.

EUGENE The mixed-heritage experience can often be something like that.

SU There's a lot of us about now, and we're growing. My friends who are mixed-heritage black very much identify with being black, where that's certainly not been my experience. Maybe it's because of the prejudice of the Asian community that I have experienced as well as the white British.

EUGENE The African and Caribbean experience is very different from the Indian continent experience, isn't it? The impact of the British Raj and how all that was organized.

SU There were Asian people who had status within that.

EUGENE There were lots of privileges for some weren't there, that took people very close to that white goal?

SU Yes, my dad would rather shockingly say, "Oh I've got this Indian GP now, she's very good you know, but she's Indian." And I'm like, Dad, you can't be saying stuff like that. But that's the thing between Pakistanis and Indians and Bangladeshis and Indians, and then there's the whole thing of—"You're not a Muslim so what are you?" You know?

EUGENE So where are the spaces that you feel safe?

SU Safety, yeah, yeah, that's paramount. Absolutely paramount. It's about being around people of color—that's the key for me. I just feel a sense of OK, people have got my back here, I'll be OK.

EUGENE They've got my back.

SU They've got my back, yeah!

EUGENE That's an interesting phrase, isn't it? It's like, something people might say when they're going into a war zone. You've got your mates, and they've got your back.

SU Yeah, extremely important. I think for me it's more about being seen and being accepted.

Why Can't I Be Black Like You?

In this section of conversation, Earl, a mixed-race black man, talks about his relationship with his Guyanese father as a mixed-race boy growing up in London.

EARL My dad was a black man from Guyana; he came to London in 1958. My mum was a white English woman. When I was a child, I would go and see him now and again at his flat. When I walked up the stairs of his flat, I would hear him and his mates. His mates came from all the different islands. He had no two mates from the same island. They would all sit around playing cards and drinking rum in his flat. As I walked up the stairs, I could hear all the different accents from the various islands. I could identify them, "Ahh that's Trinidad, or that's Jamaica." It was really exciting. As soon as I walked in, they would all stop talking in their island accents, and they would start talking in what they thought was standard English.

I was disappointed and felt humiliated, really humiliated, as again I thought: Why can't I be black like you? Why don't you incorporate me into your world? As they heard me coming in, I would hear my dad say, "It's my son, it's my son," and they would all say: "Hello Earl, how's school going?"

I didn't have the vocabulary at the time, but I wanted to say that I just wanted them to relax and talk to me normally. I would say "Yes, fine, thank you, everything's good," but it felt humiliating, very humiliating.

I wanted my dad to bring me into black

manhood; I wanted him to do that. It was very difficult, wanting something from my dad, wanting a race conversation; I wanted him to give me my racial identity.

EUGENE He wanted you to have another identity, other than his.

EARL He wanted me to have a strong English, British identity. He wanted me to get on. All the time, he would say (in a Guyanese accent) "Son, you know this country would shit you out of its ass boy; you're a black boy in this country. They'll shit on you in this country. You got to go to school—a black boy in this country must get an education."

EUGENE You've got to be someone who lives somewhere nice, who's got a lovely house, with white folk all around and keeping your head down.

EARL That's right, and if I ever mentioned black kids in school, he would say: "What have you been doing at school today?" I would say, "I've been playing football with Trevor." "Trevor, is he a black boy?" He would get all suspicious about it, where if I said it was a white person. . . . Now I think about it, it's something positive in his mind; I guess, he wanted me to get on.

EUGENE He was saying it pretty clearly wasn't he? If you're black you get shit on, so be something else. Although what else could you be other than white? If you follow the logic, he's giving you this non-Caribbean identity. He's also belittling himself as a person by saying don't be like me. It's quite a strong message, isn't it? To add to all this, it's not even what you wanted.

Earl's father was faced with a predicament that many parents of color have to face. The choice taken on this occasion was to prioritize a strong white British identity so that Earl would not be overly impacted by racism. The trade-off for this protection, however, is a feeling of alienation on two fronts. The first being alienation from his family's identity, including aspects of his racial self, and the second being the inevitable alienation from the gaze of society who sees him as black.

› › › PAUSE . . . *and breathe* ‹ ‹ ‹

THE CALL TO ACTION AND SPEAKING OUR TRUTH

> *Give yourself permission to be uncomfortable and to make others uncomfortable in your truth.*
>
> WILLIAMS & OWENS, 2016, P. 175

#4

Becoming **race-construct aware** through an active and compassionate exploration of how the race construct impacts our body identity and racial identity.

Developing and reorganizing self-identity within the race construct is essential for developing race-construct awareness. Are you the person that your family and society says you are? Self-identity as a white person is often in conflict with people of color's experience of whiteness. Self-identity as a person of color is often in conflict with expressing the full range of human responses. For both, self-identity is out of alignment with the world as it really is.

"Developing and reorganizing self-identity within the race construct is essential for developing race-construct awareness."

To develop race-construct awareness, we will need to uncover the many ways in which our minds and actions steer us away from the distress, shame, grief, and fear in people of color and toward alleviating suffering, shame, and guilt in white people. We need to notice for ourselves when and how this happens and at the same time not be automatically triggered into attack or defense mode.

It is a profound challenge to reorganize the beliefs you have about yourself and realign your self-identity. With the right support and resources, however, it is possible to make significant shifts. Within racial identity, just like with any other type of identity, the body speaks as well as the mind. We are going to have to listen, but listen with different ears. Mindfulness and bodyfulness are the different ears with which we can listen and, at the same time, not abandon the body's wisdom. Mindfulness and bodyfulness create conditions that are neurologically incompatible with emotional states like judgment and evaluation. To stay with the opening of our awareness and truthfully see who we are through the eyes of others ultimately requires the soothing balm of compassion. We need to develop compassion first for ourselves, and then bring that experience of compassion for ourselves to others. If we can create these conditions while the metaphorical veil is being lifted, we are left with an urgent call to action and a call to speak our truth that is less confusing and less internally conflictual.

"Mindfulness and bodyfulness create conditions that are neurologically incompatible with emotional states like judgment and evaluation."

Shifting Landscapes

White Israeli therapist and counseling trainer Oryan has, at some unknown body level, made a decision not to perpetuate racism. She feels both the pull to withdraw and, at the same time, there is something that does not have words which does not allow that.

ORYAN

In this section of our conversation, Oryan talks about the differences in how race plays out for her in Israel and in the U.K., and she reflects on the realization that she brings something that silences the other.

ORYAN For me, race would also be between Jews and Arabs, which would be Muslim or Christian. For me, race would include that. Some people would relate to it more as religious, but that's the word we use, and that's what I came here [the U.K.] with. Having the race conversation in the U.K. was something like: "You're not using that word right." That's the way I used the word, and that's the reality of where I grew up. So I had what I feel are two very different conversations. The one here and the one I would have in Israel.

EUGENE In the race construct, people are organized around color for the most part. Is that how it plays out in Israel as well?

ORYAN First of all, there are differences of color because "us," the Ashkenazi, come from eastern Europe, and that's within the Jewish people. Also within the Jewish people, there is the other. They would come from North Africa, so their color would be darker, so you can see who belongs to which group, and the hierarchy is pretty obvious in terms of privileges and resources.

The Arabs would belong, in terms of colors, to the darker group and would be three, four, five classes below in terms of the racism that is going on. So, for example, a couple of years ago there was a lot of knifing. Sephardic Jews, who come originally from Arab countries, would say, "They stopped me in the street!" That would be very insulting. People were talking about shaving their beards as they are aware that they may be stopped, even though they're not Arabs. So there's still a difference of color. But not like here in England. Again, there is the Ethiopian group. There's a lot of racism toward them, they are a smaller group, but the color is more heightened there.

EUGENE Although it's always going to be difficult, and no one is going to get it right, the terror that I might experience going into the Israeli situation to have a race conversation, you probably wouldn't feel so much. It sounds like you have a certain level of confidence that you bring to the Israeli situation.

ORYAN Well, I think that was kind of an illusion. Because I thought I knew what I was talking about when I came here [to the U.K.].

EUGENE When I listen to race conversations in Israel, people's positions are quite stark. This probably mirrors the fact that you physically live in either one place or another. In the U.K. there is more of a sense of overlapping, and there's layers of hidden race content that's not noticeable unless you go beneath the surface.

ORYAN If I think about the discourse in Israel, I would say there is a lot more not said there. While here, even though there is the silence and all that, the silence is so much smaller than in Israel. If I think back, I was way too confident there. Because things were not said, you kind of like assume they're not there, but actually, they're there.

EUGENE There is often so much unsaid, which you only discover when the other starts talking.

ORYAN Then I think, am I adequate to have this conversation when I don't know what's not said? How much do I contribute to things not being said because I assume they're not there? Right now, more and more voices are being silenced. Israel is not in a good place.

EUGENE I guess all that feels possible is to remain apart.

ORYAN That's another thing I thought about when I was there. I can decide what I expose myself to and what I don't, some people can't. I can decide if I stay in Israel or I don't. I have the means. Other people don't, so they have no choice.

EUGENE There are a lot of similarities and a lot of differences to the U.K. experience. It sounds like the race conversations you have here in the U.K. have brought you to a different layer of understanding of the race conversation in Israel?

ORYAN I think in some respects I'm still in the same place and, in other respects, I have moved.

I feel very strongly that I have something to give and that I'd like to create discourse. At the same time, I question what has changed. I still think that I can speak about race in a nondefensive way, but, because I don't know what to listen to, then I silence different things. So I can be nondefensive about what's in my awareness, but, because I come from a different reality, then there's quite a lot that is not in my awareness. So some aspects have stayed the same and some have changed.

EUGENE So, what's changed seems to be an awareness that you're bringing something that silences the other.

ORYAN Yeah, both, that I bring something that silences the other and that shared experience is important. They are connected but not the same. I find the awareness quite painful because I keep seeing where I misbehave, mis-think, mis-feel, mis-, mis-, mis-.

That's like a painful awareness, but that's an ongoing shift. I think that my "misses" are somewhat smaller or I'm more aware of them so I can do something about it, but also the pain about feeling them gets bigger.

EUGENE So what's the pain part of that?

ORYAN Recognizing that I'm silencing, recognizing that I can hurt somebody, recognizing that I make racist choices. That's kind of unpleasant. Another feeling I have is a real wish to retract and forget the whole thing and withdraw.

EUGENE So there's a feeling of wanting to withdraw, but something doesn't allow that? What do you think that might be?

ORYAN I don't know yet.

Oryan had made a decision: a nonverbal sense of "getting it," where it was no longer possible to ignore the impact of race on her students and herself. There is also a strong sense through her narrative of sharing experiences that made it possible to orient toward attending to hurt with greater positive regard, curiosity, and compassion.

When They Go Low, We Go High

In this next section of conversation, GB, a mixed-race Caribbean male therapist, talks about his journey to being able to speak his truth. He talks about trusting what his body tells him, opening his heart, and feeling a sense of alignment with his actions and his sense of purpose.

EUGENE What's the first thing that comes to you when you think about having the race conversation? Is it more thoughts, do you have strong feelings, or is it more of a body sensation?

GB I can feel it energetically. I'll feel it in my solar plexus. That's my radar and where I feel another person's energy field. If there's going to be a conversation, then I might get butterflies, but usually I'm just feeling what's around me. I might get that look, and I feel it here [in my solar plexus], and then I have to think, "How am I going to respond?" For me, it's always there, and because I've always grown up with it every day, it kind of gets filtered; so rather than becoming reactive, I would just say it as it is now. I've gone from being nervous about having a conversation, and now I'm in a different space.

EUGENE That's interesting. You still have that initial feeling in the solar plexus though?

GB Yes, and then I just go with my intuition. So if I'm in that situation, depending on the group and the energy, if I think they have an issue, I actually go for the jugular in a very nice way. That's what I do. Before, I used to get nervous, where I couldn't express myself; initially it was like that, absolutely.

EUGENE How do you think about that initial butterfly feeling being there in the first place?

GB That's really about things being triggered by my past. The traumas of not speaking or being suppressed or parents not hearing me. There are two pathways converging into one, where I've worked through my trauma of being able to speak up and be heard, and there is also that underlying narrative that we can't or shouldn't speak up as well.

EUGENE So there's a real experience of not being heard in the past which comes up in the present?

GB Yes, absolutely. Now I'm more confident in myself. If I need to say something, I just say it because I'm more confident in myself. Maybe I'm connecting more to my essence. There is a level there that is true. I usually sense something or someone's feeling awkward, and I think, "OK, how am I going to respond to this situation?" To be honest with you, it depends on whether I'm triggered.

EUGENE And, if you're triggered?

GB If I'm triggered, it will be like ahhh-ahhh. [*laughter*]

When I know there's a truth that needs to be said, and I need to say something, there is a slight nervousness. It's not out of fear, it's like, alright, I need to say this; and then once I say it, I'm more relaxed; more things open. It's about the message that needs to be delivered, that universal conversation that needs to be had. I guess it's taking the moral high ground, but when I sense something in someone, they're scared, they are distressed, I see it. So I have two choices. I either open up with my heart and see them, holding what I feel they have energetically around race and have a relationship with them [or not].

EUGENE You've come through a journey of not feeling quite so confident about it to feeling more confident in holding that space. What moved you from there to where you are now, and what were the important elements of that?

GB As I said earlier on, that's connected to my soul, meaning, and purpose. I think we all have narratives, and we can fulfil those narratives, those stories. I was abused so many times, emotionally . . . physically, racially—parents not being there because of their own traumas. I could either become a victim or say that there is something in me that's trying to push me forward.

EUGENE It sounds like, for you, there has been a merging of racial traumas with other traumas. Then you said you found something. Your purpose? What was it about your journey of purpose that made it possible for you to not feel the fear as much?

GB I always felt I was born for a reason; a lot of people may feel the same way, I don't know. I was fearful of my intuition, that's my voice of consciousness. There was a lot of violence when I was young; that was an external reality. I was racially abused every day for ten years, or bullied or picked on. I've come to know a piece of the gift that I have been born with; we all have our own gifts and talents. I'm more in tune with that right now.

Energetically, if I'm more in tune with who I

am, it doesn't matter what's going on around me because my essence and presence are going to be out there more. So, when I'm speaking my truth, which goes back to being honest or as authentic as I can be, then I'm OK. If I'm not in that space, yes, chaos and ADHD come in, dyslexia comes in. But when I'm in that moment. . . . My point is that the more we work through our stuff and work through the narratives, the more we can be who we are. For me, finding our purpose is the overriding principle.

EUGENE There is certainly a lot of inner work that you have done.

GB What's also very difficult in this process, not just for me but all of us, is that it gets tiring. It's what Michelle Obama says: "When they go low, we go high"—it's tiring. When you look at the stress, which I think is important here, it's demanding that we always have to hold on to it. I feel I've held the moral high ground, and it does get tiring.

EUGENE Yep, it does.

GB What happens is, and you mentioned about the body, it does come into the body. There is a responding and a responding, and even though we might let things go, there is an impact on the body. If something we haven't worked on gets touched, it gets more intensified. Self-care is very important for us as therapists anyway, but there is that extra bit as well. It's tough having to always be on that level.

In reference to Michelle Obama's quote, she explained in *Time* magazine that " 'going high' doesn't mean you don't feel the hurt or you're not entitled to an emotion . . . it means that your response has to reflect the solution" (Bruner, 2018).

Body Talking—Mind Listening

Defensive silence is the kiss of death to a race conversation. Becoming aware of, and even talking about, the sensations and stirrings in your body can be an honest and compassionate way of remaining in contact across the void. Once you become aware of the body's story and what your body is telling you, speaking becomes more possible, either in the moment or arranging to come back to the conversation later.

"Defensive silence is the kiss of death to a race conversation."

The more consciously aware we become of the landscape of the race construct in the mind and in the body, the more we can navigate through its corridors. It is important, however, to keep listening because, as we become more aware, the possibility of consciously or unconsciously manipulating others for personal gain or of acting out of malice increases. For this reason, we need to continually reassess our motives and ethics and continuously ask ourselves why we are doing this and for whom.

STAYING AT THE CONTACT BOUNDARY

> *We are motivated to protect our own existing views. . . . Often, people refer to this as "trusting their gut."*
>
> AGARWAL, 2020, P. 29

#5

To actively find resources that honestly and compassionately support us to stay at the contact boundary of our experience when race is the focus.

During the early part of 2019, when the U.K. government's attempts to find a settlement for exiting the E.U. were in full swing, the European Parliament voted on a momentous resolution. There were 535 votes for, 80 against, and 44 abstentions. This resolution was on the "fundamental rights of people of African descent." The resolution recognized the current situation of structural racism and asked that former colonizing member states follow the call for apologies and compensation for the colonial period, bearing in mind its lasting impact on the present. The resolution was crafted by Claude Ajit Moraes, a British Labour Member of the European Parliament (MEP) of Indian origin. It was based on the experiences of Italian socialist MEP Cécile Kyenge, who experienced a torrent of cyber-racist abuse when she became Italy's first black government minister.

Over a year later, on June 30, 2020, King Philippe of Belgium wrote a letter to President Félix Tshisekedi of the Democratic Republic of Congo (DRC) in relation to the colonial exploitation that took place under the rule and administration of King Leopold II between 1885 and 1908. Belgium's looting of the Congo and the number of deaths that resulted is truly horrifying. It is estimated that about half the Congolese population died from punishment and malnutrition.[3] The letter was sent on the 60th anniversary of Congo's independence from Belgium. It contained the following:

> During the time of the Congo Free State [1885–1908], acts of violence and brutality were committed that weigh still on our collective memory. The colonial period that followed also caused suffering and humiliations. I would like to express my deepest regrets for the wounds of the past, the pain of today, which is rekindled by the discrimination all too present in our society. (Rankin & Burke, 2020)

The letter from King Philippe is a watershed moment in the fight for racial justice and offers regret but stops short of an apology. Regret and an apology might at first appear to be the same thing, but the difference is very significant in relation to Europe's past actions and potential reparations.

In September 2021, Britain and a small number of allies were accused of jeopardizing the United Nations' anti-racism conference by blocking the European Union from issuing a straightforward apology for the transatlantic trade in slavery. Britain, the Netherlands, Spain, and Portugal were prepared only to express "regret" about the slave trade without any specific recognition of responsibility. Odile Quintin, the French director general of the European Commission in 2001, noted: "what we would like to avoid is where an apology leads to concrete commitments. If you have a legal relationship between apology and commitments, it's a problem" (McGreal, 2001). African leaders have called for an unreserved apology and for slavery and colonization to be recognized as a crime against humanity. This recognition is seen as crucial in the journey towards racial justice and repairing the harm caused. Many also believe that reparations are necessary for this process to be complete. Having formally left the European Union on January 31, 2020, the U.K. government, which has a long history of blocking any apology for the slave trade, probably views no longer being tied to the same direction of travel for the fundamental rights of people of African descent as the rest of Europe as another fortunate win.

The reason I've included the apology letter from Belgium to the DRC and the E.U. resolution is to comment briefly on institutional change. Just like individuals, institutions also need to make an internal decision. For institutions and governmental agencies, this usually is in the form of a declaration of intent. In my mind, such a declaration should not just be a statement of wanting to stand side-by-side in unity. A declaration should include an understanding of how the race construct operates to privilege and humiliate and specific actions that will be taken to collaborate with the institute's stakeholders to minimize its future negative impacts. To me, an organizational declaration of intent such as this would be the single most important thing that an organization could do to be part of a movement for undoing racism. For such a document to exist, the organization would need to challenge the fundamental reasons why organizations and individuals do not materially change. This would mean facing the discomfort of examining the racial biases that the race construct dictates we stay away from and also, ultimately, giving up long-held privileges.

Holding Gut Instincts to Account

Even though we have a sense that there is some healing inherent in making contact with each other within the race conversation, there are still pressing demands on us. There are the pressing demands to replay the racial scripts we swallowed whole in childhood and to hold back the energies in our bodies that want to be heard. We intellectualize, we compartmentalize, we dissociate, we get angry, we do anything we can to not stay in the present moment and not stay with the discomfort. In the race conversation, the act of speaking our truth and opening ourselves up to other people's truths about us cuts across what we might feel are our gut instincts. We are then faced with the problem of distrusting our gut instincts or at least holding our gut instincts to account.

Staying at the Contact Boundary

I have entitled this section "Staying at the Contact Boundary," but what does this mean? The *contact boundary* is a term used in gestalt therapy, a psychotherapeutic approach developed by Fritz Perls (Perls, 1992). Contact is the awareness of differences where neither party takes control. The boundary is where that awareness takes place. A metaphor for the contact boundary is the skin: it differentiates me from the other and also connects me to the other. The contact boundary could also be between different aspects of the same person; for instance, where an unconscious bias becomes conscious and meets an ethical part of the self.

An important part of staying at the contact boundary is the idea of being close, but not so close that it overwhelms, and of being separate, but not so separate that you lose connection. If you are defending your position, you are too far away from the contact boundary; if you have merged with the feelings of the other and have become overwhelmed, you have come too close. When working with trauma, little and often is much more integrating than working forcefully and intensely all in one go.

The contact boundary can be disturbed in a number of ways through:

- unconscious biases
- merging with the feelings of the other
- being confused about whose feelings are whose
- holding back on your responses
- finding ways to move away from the subject
- defending your position through intellectualizing

For me, a meaningful or satisfying race conversation with self or other is one where there has been "good enough" staying at the contact boundary with uncomfortable aspects of the self or other and the remaining connected with the hurt race has inflicted on both sides of the black/white divide. However, at the contact boundary, there exist conditions that can give voice to the parts of us that are in denial, feel silenced, or feel rage or shame. Also, both sides can be a witness to the other and themselves be witnessed by the other.

Decoupling

Holding our gut instincts to account and developing a good enough staying at the contact boundary are the conditions needed to *decouple* from the pressing demands of the race construct. Decoupling is a term used in trauma therapies that points to the possibility of being able to unshackle yourself from trauma-driven mental states of fear so that you are more in the driving seat.

Those frozen moments of fear in the race conversation can be almost tangible. The experience seems so real, regardless of whether an actual threat exists. There is a sense of needing to protect ourselves as we become hijacked by the body's implicit memories and nonverbal cues of safety and danger, with seemingly no way out. In the race conversation, decoupling means experiencing the race conversation mental state and, at the same time, creating the conditions where the nervous system remains regulated and the defenses are dampened. There is then a decoupling from the fear-driven mental representations inherent in the race construct while remaining anchored to the reality of it.

Essentially, the purpose of exploring everything we have up to this point is to decouple from the fear. We have looked at coherent narratives of the past, the idea of intergenerational trauma, the concept of the race construct acting upon us—willing participants or not—the concepts of race-construct arousal and race-construct awareness. These ideas lead us to reevaluate safety, lessen hyperarousal, and maintain the capacity for social engagement. For the rest of this section, I will be discussing what we can do to practice staying at the contact boundary of our experience while not being triggered into immobilizing fear. Eventually, our race conversations will have a higher chance of success.

Embodied Filtering Practice

> *I have found that I practice and employ embodied filtering to titrate the intensity of racism and honor, take care of, and remain in contact with the human greatness of this black body.*
>
> SHERRELL, 2018, P. 152

It may be that racism is very present in your everyday life. If this is the case, employing a filtering practice is almost essential. Carla Sherrell, author of *The Oppression of Black Bodies: The Demand to Simulate White Bodies and White Embodiment,* writes about going through what she calls a filtering practice before leaving the house (Sherrell, 2018). She imagines dressing in a particular way. She imagines what the inside material would be made of and also what is on the outside. Once dressed, she pays special attention to how she breathes, her stance, and her balance. The ritual is done in the presence of the ancestors and elders and those who have loved her in this life.

"Who we are is reflected and manifested in the body."

You could make up your own embodied practice to set you up for the beginning of the day. Perhaps you could also design a ritual for when you get home to cleanse your body of the toxins of racism that have built up over the day. You could imagine, and then enact, a scraping away of the toxins with your hands, as if you were covered with mud, making sure each part of your body is attended to.

Body Awareness Practices

A foundational concept of body- and movement-based therapies is that who we are is reflected and manifested in the body, and our experiences shape our patterns of movement. The core aim is to increase awareness of movement and body sensations to gain awareness of habitual patterns, which then opens up intentionality and choice in how we react and how we wish to move through our environments.

Shraboni is a therapist of Indian heritage who uses body- and movement-based therapies in her work. In this section of our conversation, she speaks about both her work with groups and her personal experience of movement-based practices around race.

EUGENE You work with movement and the body in groups around racial identity. How does that work?

SHRABONI The way I structure most workshops is to start with the participants own race–ethnicity identity. Let's go there first, let's look at self. Let's then look at "other," and then look at when the embodied racial self meets the other embodied racial self. The instruction I might give is something like, "How do you carry your racial and ethnic identity?" I will encourage participants to allow their bodies spontaneous movement, or what might be called authentic movement, to inform where they want to move next. With people who are not so familiar with movement work, I might be a bit more explicit so I might say, "Imagine if your ethnicity shapes your body into a sculpture, what might that look like?" So I might be more directive.

I then lead participants to find their way to boundaries previously set up between the space they are in and a different space. As they find their way toward the boundary, I might say, "Notice where your body wants to yield," "Notice if your body wants to resist." Notice, notice, notice. I use words like "yielding" or "resisting" or "pulling" or "pushing" or "caregiving" or "care-seeking." Depending on the context, I'll use different terminology to allow the body to explore. Notice what inhibits your body; notice what creates flow; what stops flow. When they get to the boundary, I do quite a lot around suspending them in that moment. Notice what happens in your body, what happens in your muscles, what happens in the belly, what happens in the organs; notice your blood flow; notice your heartbeat. I use very visceral language. "We are on the brink of stepping into the other place. What's that like for you?"

When the body starts exploring how it carries its race, something powerful gets unlocked. In one workshop, for instance, nobody thought that they would be looking at objects from the [British] Empire that their ancestors had stolen; we hadn't planned that as part of the session, but somehow that story came alive, that narrative came alive through the movement. Other reenactment themes have been around shame and the visceral feelings that your ancestors are behind you, experienced, for example, when paying attention to the "back body" [the area behind us]. There was something that got powerfully reenacted in that room. There is a process not just of noticing a fragment of the present body experience but of moving with it. Once you start to move it, you can follow the story through and then new parts of the story that are implicit can emerge.

The more that people are used to doing authentic or spontaneous movement and allowing the movement of the body to inform them, the easier they can do it. It's like practice helps the journey. It helps the journey the more you do it.

EUGENE What about your personal experience of doing bodywork as an Indian woman?

SHRABONI One of the things that comes up strongly for me, whether the theme is race or not, is my colonized self. What I mean by that is, when I'm moving in a group [that I'm not facilitating], I will be the follower rather than the leader. Often, I would be the one who copies the movement rather than creates my own. Over the years of participating in groups, I have come to recognize that my body has within it this inherent information about being colonized. In the context of talking about race, that is what it feels like. In my family context, it might be about being a girl, or it might be about being a second child, attitudes of my parents and culture. In a political sense, that feeling of my internal, colonized self is really apparent when I move with people. Part of my process over many years has been about noticing and then not trying something new intellectually, but allowing my body to [try it out]; I call it grating, allowing my body to go somewhere that feels like it grates from my familiar place, so it feels uncomfortable. This is the opposite, for me, of blending, which is what I habitually do as a second-generation immigrant. When I try to go into those places, I noticed my body responding. It feels like leaving a cold country, getting on a plane and arriving somewhere in the scorching heat, my body kinda goes "ahh."

EUGENE That's really interesting.

SHRABONI Whatever I seem to be exploring, what comes up is deeply held oppression which I can intellectualize, but in the body it manifests when I'm with others, and particularly with white male others, in the group. If I'm in a mixed group—white, black, and gendered—the place where my body feels the least comfortable is with white males, and particularly if I try to lead in the moving relationship with white males. If I try to encourage my body to be innovative or lead or something like that, I really struggle with that, and it's only in the movement that I notice it. Intellectually, I'm fine. I can talk with whoever and work with whoever; I'm married to a white man. In the body, when the body moves its way through, something else happens, which is also generational, right? The burden of my forefathers who were the colonized in India by the white male, in particular, that's the bit that goes through me and comes out in this work.

EUGENE Despite many years of exploration of your relationship with colonialism and coming to terms with its impact on an intellectual and everyday level, the impact is still there, in your bones almost.

Mindfulness Practice

While writing this book, my meditation practice has been an essential component of my staying at the contact boundary of my experience. All the way through the writing process, I have experienced the stirrings of race-construct arousal, sometimes quite intensely, where, even though intellectually I was still committed to keep writing, my body told a different story. A frequent experience I would have while meditating during one of these periods was an uncontrollable jerking of my arms, sometimes of my whole body. As my mind and body began to settle, these uncoordinated and spontaneous movements would emerge. In exploring these spontaneous movements, several explanations emerged. My body could just be learning to adapt to new levels of concentration. The movements could also be linked to spontaneous movements that sometimes occur during meditation and prayer called Kriya. Kriya is a Sanskrit word that literally means "to move." As I relax in meditation, the overcharged energy in my body gets dumped into my nervous system, which then causes these spontaneous movements. Relaxation therapies, like cranial sacral and reiki, would see these spontaneous movements as a release of old trauma.

I used to be concerned that this spontaneous jerking and shaking experience that I was having in meditation should be controlled. The movements would also happen outside of meditation, when I was just sitting and focusing on settling my nervous system in times of stress. Now, I am more comfortable with these spontaneous movements happening and, for myself, see them as a discharge of built-up energy and stress that enables me to stay more connected to my ethical self.

Also, in my meditation I am occasionally aware of what could be called a dual awareness. I am aware of the inside of me: my breath, the alignment of my body, the way my hands lay on my lap, the contact my feet and legs are making with the ground. I am also aware of the outside of me: the sounds, the light through my eyelids. While in the race conversation, or any stressful situation, I bring that sense of being to mind. Not always, but often I find myself responding in ways that align with my overall values and ethics and, instead of being wracked with shame and guilt, I am left with a bodily experience that is uncomfortable but that I know will soon pass.

Compassion in Action

Celia is a white therapist and, during the time of this podcast conversation, she set up a successful counseling training for students from diverse backgrounds.[4] She grew up in South Africa.

CELIA I think, on a personal level, the journey I have been on, in terms of dealing with my background. . . I think there was a point at which I suddenly moved from fear of being called racist and the need to demonstrate "no I'm not" to just accepting I was highly likely to be racist and that this was the path—I didn't ask for it, but there it is.

EUGENE How did you get there?

CELIA I think I realized that my own fears were getting in the way. Literally, I don't have much insight in being able to recover that process, but I know it was a kind of a decision. If I start from that point, then I am free to explore. And so I think I bring a lot of safety with me into this kind of training, it's not a subject I feel afraid of, although I have anxieties about what I might discover. But I'm less worried now about saying the wrong thing and all the kind of political correctness that was drummed into us here in this country [the U.K.] in the 1980s, particularly. Once I kind of got past that—that never felt satisfying—I think I just got to that point of just deciding, "I'm a white person; there is much that I didn't ask for in my consciousness," and I suppose feeling some compassion for myself helped.

I said, look, this was something that was important to me, it's something that I want to address (Ellis, 2013, 5:15).

Final Conversations

I have included four final conversation sections that continue the theme of staying at the contact boundary. Each conversation speaks for itself but also mirrors the everyday thoughts and reflections of race conversations. The invitation, again, is to listen and reflect on the presence of these themes within yourself.

Beyond Comfortably Uncomfortable

Andy is a white male therapist.

ANDY Something had fundamentally shifted me in life from the place that I thought I was. I thought I was, you know, developed enough. Quite comfortably uncomfortable. You asked about the shift. What drew me was pain and suffering; there is no doubt about that. The pain of the race issue, I've come to realize, is not the pain that I have. It's a different pain, and it's a different suffering. I came thinking, "Well you know, I've been locked up and shackled, marginalized, failed at school," the stupid kid who's ended up with an advanced education and all this kind of stuff. Someone mentioned about young black men being overrepresented in prison or having addictions or finding other ways of coping. I had to cope; I probably wouldn't be here otherwise.

EUGENE You thought you had many allied experiences that seemed to mirror the experience of race.

ANDY I thought so, yeah, and I was unconsciously really drawn around that, somewhat consciously. But I've come to think, no, actually, they're not the same because I can change how I look, really. I can reinvent myself, as I have. My old dealer came into my clinical room for therapy. Many years had past and I was now the professional, and he didn't recognize me. My colleagues where I work in primary care have no idea of what has happened to me. Interestingly, many of my clients knew. They didn't know that they knew, but there was a shared word; something I would know that only someone on the inside would know.

It's a different kind of pain because I have been

able to reinvent myself and I think I underestimated, undervalued, the particular type of pain and suffering in race, also what can be changed and what is probably so scarring that it can't be.

Knowing I was coming here, I have been thinking about identity, change and the rawness. I have my rawness and others have theirs, but I'm not sure it's the same anymore. I used to think it was similar, but I think it's a whole other dimension.

EUGENE It felt like there was some hope [for radicalized others] there and now the hope has gone? What can be done or not done is now in the spotlight.

ANDY I've been able to help and support, but I feel there's a limit. I was giving the boot to some wishful thinking, or delusions perhaps, on my part. It's kind of hard to have that stripped away and look a bit more clearly.

I was with my partner [who is black], and we were in an embrace and about to kiss. I told her she has lovely lips. She said, "What did you say?" her body froze and all that. She thought I said she had rubber lips.

EUGENE Woah!

ANDY I thought F***, this is decades on, generations on, and you recoil from me like—oh it's painful. It's little things like this that make me wonder why I'm here with you, in a sense. The lips thing, my dilemmas, really feeling it in my body; I can't even say whether it's my body, thoughts, or emotions. It feels even deeper, if there is such a thing . . . interrelations stuff. I actually feel a little bit of anger toward you, I have to admit, because I'm wondering, "Why am I part of this conversation?" I'm sitting here wondering that. In the past, I could be part of the conversation and help unpack things. I've been almost disabused of that, in a way, at a deeper level, yet here we are.

EUGENE Yes, here we are.

I believe that there is a certain part of race hurt that can only effectively be met by other people of color who are of like mind. There is equally, I believe, another part of race hurt that can only effectively be met by white people of like mind.

Going Against the Grain

Raj is a Sikh male therapist of south Asian heritage.

EUGENE I'm interested in the important elements that helped you in exploring your racial identity.

RAJ During my first degree, there was a black lady who was important in my life. It was about being understood, and it was someone who showed an interest. Someone realizing there was something wrong and investigated it instead of just letting it lie there. There was someone to dig something up and do something with it.

EUGENE This person saw something in you?

RAJ She started it off. I met other people in my training [as a counselor] who were willing to take risks and not just look externally but internally. That sort of helped. It's been a big journey, when I think about it all.

EUGENE Some people were willing to engage with you at some level to understand you and reflect with you.

RAJ And to be emotionally honest. It can be isolating though. I've been almost going against the grain of my own culture. I want to talk deep to people. I don't want to talk about *EastEnders* [TV series] anymore. I want to talk about how I feel and how I react with you. It's been a hard journey.

Sometimes I feel programmed, and I have had to deprogram myself in some ways. I can never say I'm fully there, and there's no destination, but it feels good.

EUGENE Our cultures definitely program us. It might be the perfect program that fits everything that you naturally are, but, for you, the program didn't quite fit.

RAJ Someone said of counseling, "Don't do it, it's going to affect you, it's going to affect everything." But why would I want to "be" without awareness? It's not that I'm better than anyone else, but this whole system programs you, capitalism programs you. For me, it's been about healing; the healing really sticks out. It's dangerous but good.

EUGENE You wouldn't have had it any other way.

RAJ No.

EUGENE Even though it's been painful and difficult.

RAJ It's more authentic, I think, and more honest.

EUGENE Do you feel the limitation of the race that you are? Have you hit up against them?

RAJ There are internal limitations and external ones. To everybody who's Asian, I'm a doctor or a psychiatrist. Almost straight away, they go to a medicalized version of mental health. Is that because I'm Asian, and a doctor is something that they approve of? In the media, I'm seen as a bit nerdy. Media stereotypes are of Asians being passive, very intelligent, rational, and as being shopkeepers doctors, lawyers, also being successful materialistically. I know a lot of Asians who are, but that does not make them happy, obviously. These are things we feel we have to adhere to. Yes, there are limitations.

EUGENE Where are you now with the race conversation?

RAJ Specifically, the anger's died down. It was something that used to really get me going. "Oh, you want to talk about race? What do you know about it? I know better than you."

I don't know better than anybody; they're their own expert. But when it becomes divisive . . . I'd be prepared to talk about race with people if they are open to listening to me. To take on my experiences and to have a balanced conversation.

Facing the Closed Door

Oryan is a white Israeli therapist and counseling trainer.

EUGENE What would you say helped you to zoom out from your very intense and personalized experience of the race conversation to stepping back a little bit, still having the feelings but not having them to that degree?

ORYAN Time. Speaking with friends. Trying to understand. Making decisions about what I can take from it. The idea that I'm going to translate some of it into action also kind of soothes me, in that I am listening and not just ignoring and saying it's got nothing to do with me.

EUGENE So bringing that experience to other people, trying to talk it through, moving into action.

ORYAN They bring it back to me, and I can start to unpack it in terms of what belongs to whom. Noticing the people I speak with are my support system; they are my network, so they have a specific angle on things.

EUGENE They are people you trust.

ORYAN Yes, they are putting me in mind. For example, when I was talking to my friend, it started off with "What do I do when things go wrong, what do I notice?" One of the things was noticing who speaks more. Sure enough [during the counseling training course], we started the conversation, and in the first 10 minutes, the white people spoke the most. I could then say, let's just see what's going on, and that did create a shift.

So talking to other people, not just in the sense of "yes, you're right" or "you're fine." I don't believe it if it's told like that because I feel there's something wrong. I am trying to identify what is wrong, so if I feel that I silence, then what can I do about it? How can I make that shift? It just gives me a bit more oriention, I guess. I wanted to say "control," but I don't think that would be the right word. It's definitely a bit more like oriention.

EUGENE Yes, that's a good word. You are really active in trying to orient yourself. You're saying it's not about control or trying to get it right, particularly, although you hope to get it more right than wrong.

ORYAN And realizing my own limitations also.

EUGENE That feeling of being out of sync with what is going on, being out of balance, banging into things with people reacting and saying things to you. What have you read or what ideas have you taken on that have helped orient you in a way that sort of feels more helpful than unhelpful?

ORYAN In Israel, I did a course around Jews and Arabs, and we were talking about the white process. The two groups were separated and had time together, which I found very powerful and orienting. You had to deal with both; you deal with belonging to the greater group, you deal with belonging to your racial group or cultural group, and then you deal with not belonging to the other. That process was quite good for me to recognize my Jewishness within that and my whiteness, and I think that's where I began to feel confident. I thought "Yeah,

I'm aware. I'm aware that I'm privileged; I know about that." But coming here [to the U.K.] and having a relatively mixed group was a shock.

As preparation for the training module [at the University], I read Fanon. He is very good, especially the aspect of stepping out of your home. He said that you grow up [as a black person] in a certain reality, and then when you step out into the world there is a different reality. When I step out of my home, the reality is still the same. The two systems support one another, so that was one idea that helped.

Another was Jane Elliot, the schoolteacher in the States who did class experiments with race. There is this 15-minute video,[5] and there's this white girl that's walking out and this idea that she needs to apologize because other people can't just walk out. That's an experience that I know—being ignored by the native British people in my neighborhood in the U.K. All my friends would be Bulgarian, Polish, Portuguese, all immigrants.

Being estranged from the British has helped a little bit in my understanding. I also grew up belonging to the dominant group, so I think it's not easy to unbalance me in terms of my self-identity. I can see it and it's problematic, but it's not that I feel I need to adapt myself.

So it's Fanon, Elliott. I read your article with Niki Cooper in *Therapy Today* (Ellis & Cooper, 2013). I've read other things and taken in other ideas, but those are the main things.

EUGENE Anything else you would like to add?

ORYAN There is a thing that I still grapple with that was also in Israel. It's when there isn't a wish for a discourse. So, for example, last year, a student said we don't need to hear about white privilege, we know about white privilege. I thought, "Well, the dominant group has to be part of the discourse if you want things to change. If there isn't a wish to share your experience and to hear the other person's experience, then . . ." again, I'm disoriented. I don't know what to do with that.

EUGENE You're saying that position is understandable but doesn't help move things forward.

ORYAN There was this quote from Sartre (1948). I'll paraphrase—What did you expect when you take away the shackles, and the person raises their eyes; you expected to find gratitude? No, you will find anger. I'm thinking, "Okay, fair enough, it's legitimate," but then we're stuck; I still don't know what to do with it. What helps me is to be active and do something about it. If I can't, I'm a bit more lost.

EUGENE What to do when the door is closed? You make an offering, and it's rejected.

ORYAN And you don't know whether to make another offer or just to back off.

EUGENE When there is a willingness, even though it might be messy and horrible, you can say "Well, at least we're getting somewhere." When the door closes, there is so much history that you're butting up against, although it doesn't feel very historical at that moment. It's the weight of the past that comes slamming into the present.

ORYAN It's very difficult to remember that in the moment.

EUGENE Yes, we all have nervous systems, and we all get into protection mode, but we can recover and reorient.

The Race Conversation—So Much More Than Race

Patrick is a black male therapist.

EUGENE Is there anything else you would like to add about your experiences of the race conversation that you feel are important?

PATRICK There are times, when it comes to those race conversations, that I think, "Am I giving this thing too much of my time and energy? Just let it go, let it go."

EUGENE Don't respond to it, you mean?

PATRICK Yeah, don't respond; but again, is it because of how painful it is? Perhaps that's a way of responding to the pain. Let it go and leave it. Life is too short! Yeah.

EUGENE Have there been moments when you've had race conversations which have been satiating; where you kind of feel like, "Yeah, that was the business"?

PATRICK Yeah, many of those, many of those. With one of my closest friends, when we were in our late twenties to thirties, two black men. Every other weekend, my man has got his little tent out, and he's out by the sea somewhere up north. I would say, "Boy, you know you're different"—but I love him to bits. What we would do is say, right, bang, we're gone. We would just get away for a weekend or a whole day in the country. We'd get a map and just walk. It was just talking, reflecting, just the two of us walking, through the wilderness at times. The conversations we had touched on race and, for me, I was learning that the race conversation isn't a thing within itself—it's all connected to so many other things. That position has come out of some of those conversations with him. Having a race conversation, and focusing on it, on its own, for me now, I wonder how useful or reflective or accurate it is.

So, it's not just about race; it's about class as well. It's about internalizing processes; it's about issues around self-identity and masculinity. The race conversation, to me, on its own arguably is a bit of a misnomer. It's connected to so many other things. Going back to the question you asked, yes, there were conversations that included race with him that felt really good.

I read something recently, a Buddhist-type thing, I can't remember exactly what it was, but it's so true for me. When we read something, the absorption of it occurs when we're not actually reading, but during the pauses. I'm beginning to think that's so true. I went through a process whereby I would read and read and read [about race] and thought well I'm not getting it, I'm not getting it, I'm not getting it, I'm not getting it; but maybe I'm not supposed to get it, you know what I mean?

Maybe I'm supposed to leave it and allow the pause for absorbing. But again I'm still chasing that carrot! There are still those moments when chasing the carrot, how do I describe it: it's satisfying; difficult, frustrating, but satisfying.

CONNECTING OPPRESSIONS

Although we have been focusing predominantly on race, it is also vital that we connect racial oppression with other oppressions. Racial oppression is part of the bigger picture of harm that humans inflict on each other and on the planet; for instance, the assault on the planet's biodiversity and the rapid acceleration of species extinction. All of these harms are driven by the psychological drivers of wealth accumulation to quench the fear-driven need for material comfort and security and also an unwillingness to stay with the discomfort of seeing ourselves as we truly are.

It might at first appear that developing awareness of ourselves as we are—our greeds, our hatreds, and our delusions—will make us unhappy and that the work of awareness is yet another demand on our time and energy. There is, however, something deeply satiating about aligning our outer behaviors with our inner human values of liberty and individual freedom that make the journey worthwhile.

"There is something deeply satiating about aligning our outer behaviors with our inner human values of liberty and individual freedom."

It needs to again be emphasized that we cannot really hope to do this work by ourselves. We need to join with others of like mind, and when we do so, much is possible, even though we may see only occasional glimpses of hope. If we are doing the work of awareness, we need to trust that change is happening in the world, even though we can never really know the extent of the influence we are having.

I want to end this guide to the race conversation with a quote from the incomparable social justice icon Angela Davis that mirrors the potential for change that I have witnessed in others and myself:

> People accuse me of being an inveterate optimist, but I always think we have to find something that holds a promise and that way we look toward the future. A great deal of change has happened. The very fact that we are able to imagine connections between struggles against racism, imperialism, and homophobia, discrimination against people who are differently-abled, against trans-people; this is an indication that we've moved forward. (Baker, 2016, 71:30)

APPENDICES

1. Legal and Ideological Timeline for the Organization of the Race Construct

2. Race-Construct Awareness Diagram

1. LEGAL AND IDEOLOGICAL TIMELINE FOR THE ORGANIZATION OF THE RACE CONSTRUCT

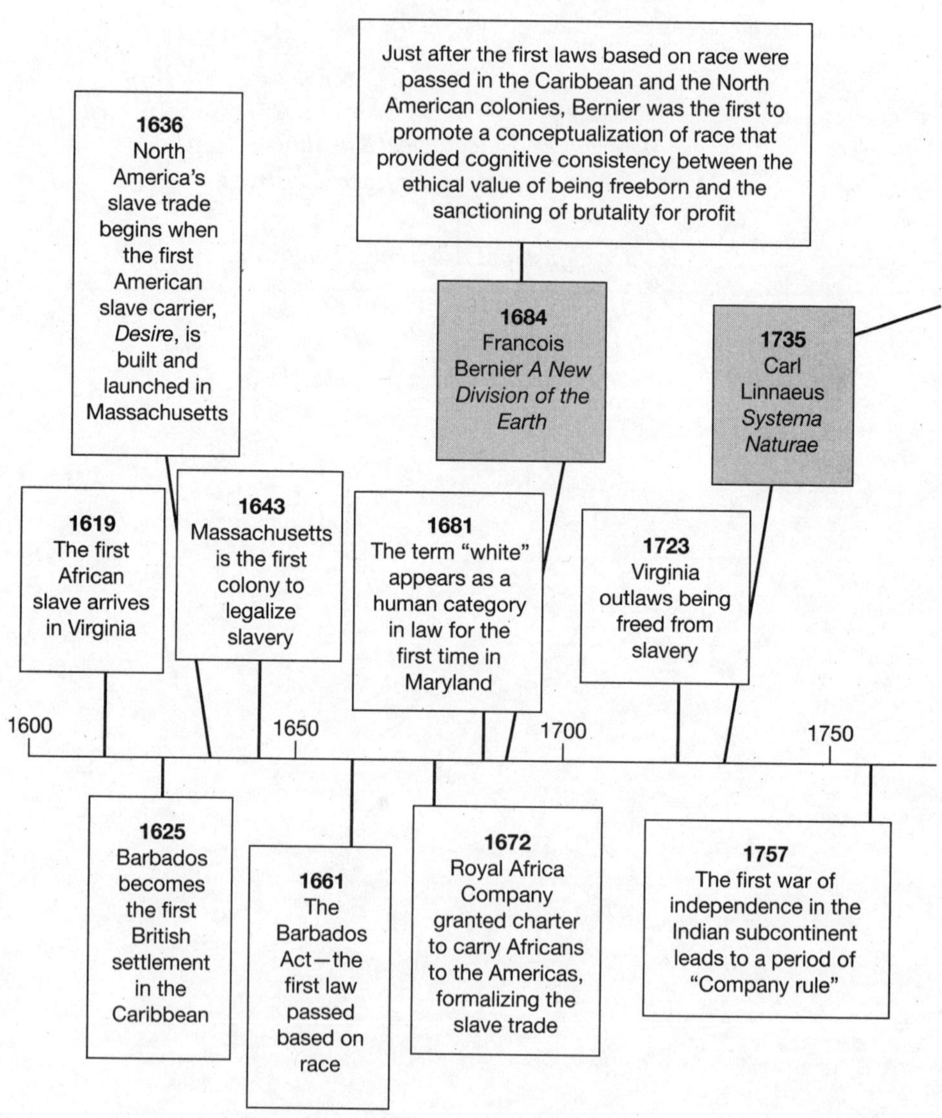
Just after the first laws based on race were passed in the Caribbean and the North American colonies, Bernier was the first to promote a conceptualization of race that provided cognitive consistency between the ethical value of being freeborn and the sanctioning of brutality for profit
1636 North America's slave trade begins when the first American slave carrier, Desire, is built and launched in Massachusetts
1684 Francois Bernier A New Division of the Earth
1735 Carl Linnaeus Systema Naturae
1619 The first African slave arrives in Virginia
1643 Massachusetts is the first colony to legalize slavery
1681 The term "white" appears as a human category in law for the first time in Maryland
1723 Virginia outlaws being freed from slavery
1600
1650
1700
1750
1625 Barbados becomes the first British settlement in the Caribbean
1661 The Barbados Act—the first law passed based on race
1672 Royal Africa Company granted charter to carry Africans to the Americas, formalizing the slave trade
1757 The first war of independence in the Indian subcontinent leads to a period of "Company rule"

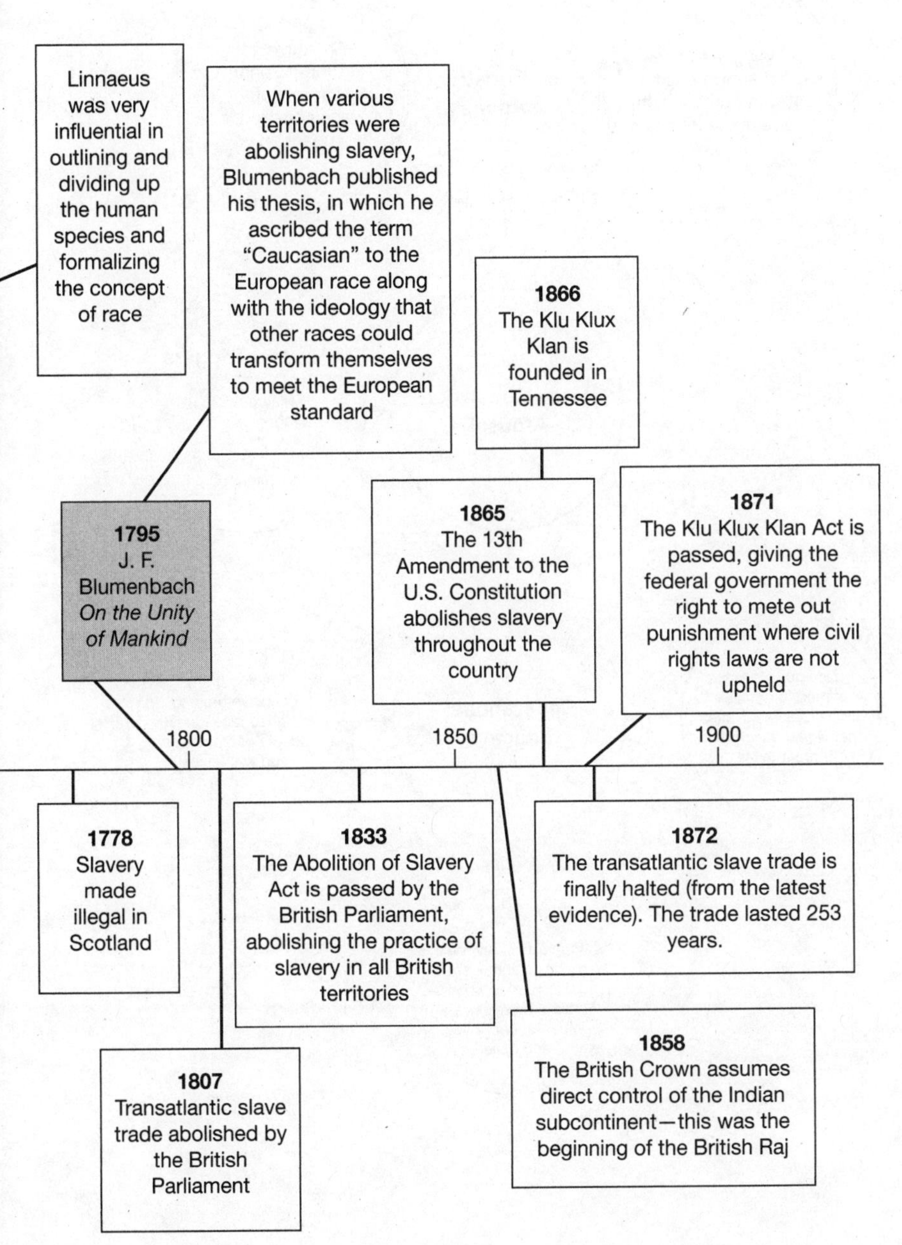
Linnaeus was very influential in outlining and dividing up the human species and formalizing the concept of race
When various territories were abolishing slavery, Blumenbach published his thesis, in which he ascribed the term "Caucasian" to the European race along with the ideology that other races could transform themselves to meet the European standard
1866 The Klu Klux Klan is founded in Tennessee
1795 J. F. Blumenbach *On the Unity of Mankind*
1865 The 13th Amendment to the U.S. Constitution abolishes slavery throughout the country
1871 The Klu Klux Klan Act is passed, giving the federal government the right to mete out punishment where civil rights laws are not upheld
1800
1850
1900
1778 Slavery made illegal in Scotland
1833 The Abolition of Slavery Act is passed by the British Parliament, abolishing the practice of slavery in all British territories
1872 The transatlantic slave trade is finally halted (from the latest evidence). The trade lasted 253 years.
1858 The British Crown assumes direct control of the Indian subcontinent—this was the beginning of the British Raj
1807 Transatlantic slave trade abolished by the British Parliament

2. RACE-CONSTRUCT AWARENESS DIAGRAM

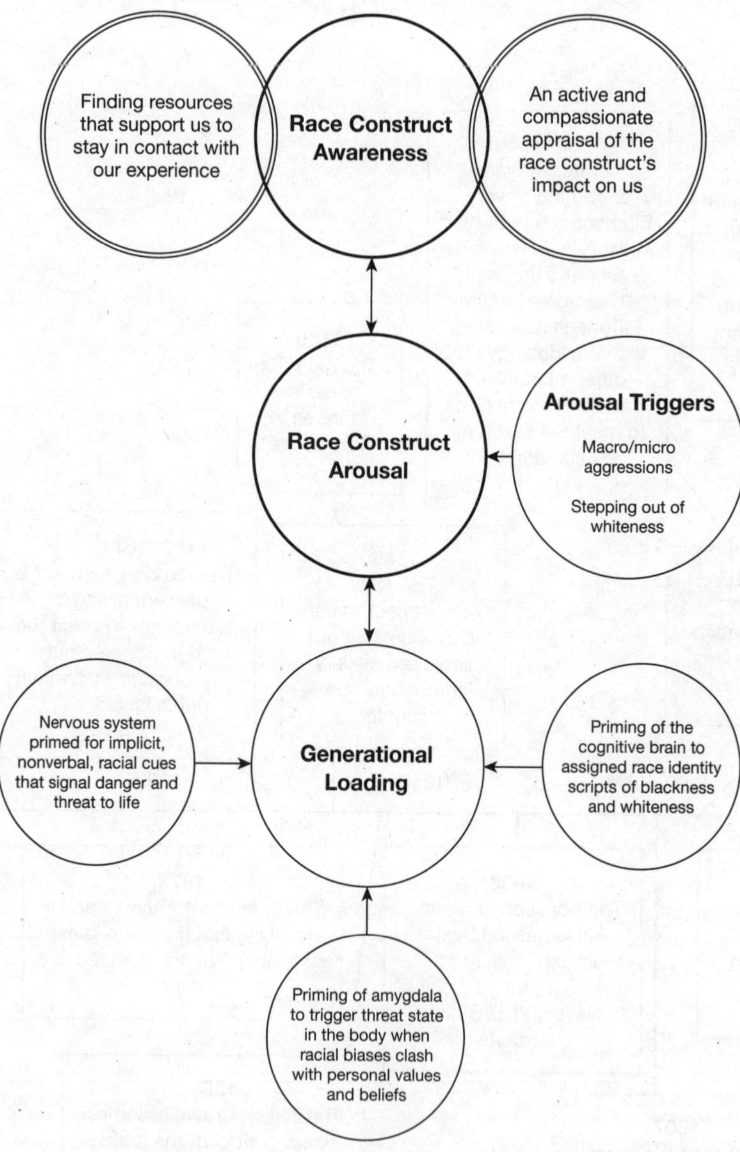

NOTES

CHAPTER 1

1 Dan Siegel (1999) was the first to describe the "window of tolerance."

2 James Baldwin, from the film *I Am Not Your Negro* (Peck, 2016).

3 Frances Cress Welsing (1991) was a black psychiatrist and social and psychological theorist who put forward ideas to understand European thought and behavior and challenged western social sciences.

4 bell hooks, from www.lionsroar.com. bell hooks is the pen name of Gloria Jean Watkins; bell hooks is intentionally not capitalized so as to put the focus on her ideas rather than her name.

5 Jay Smooth (2011), *How I Learned to Stop Worrying and Love Discussing Race*, is available on YouTube.

6 The People in Harmony online resource is an excellent source of information about the mixed-race experience in the U.K. and how to interact confidently with the subject. https://pih.org.uk/

7 *The Infinite Monkey Cage* (2016) is available on BBC iPlayer.

8 Blog post by Ta-Nehisi Coates entitled "What we mean when we say race is a social construct," an argument that racial labels referring to natural differences in physical traits doesn't hold up.

9 "Feeling Free" from the Soul II Soul album *Keep on Moving*, 1989.

10 A love-based approach to helping children with severe behaviors.

11 Keating, F., Robertson, D., McCulloch, A., & Francis, E. (2002). Breaking the circles of fear: A review of the relationship between mental health services and African and Caribbean communities. *Social Care Online*. Sainsbury Centre for Mental Health. Report is available online.

CHAPTER 2

1 In "Silenced: The Black Student Experience" (Ellis & Cooper, 2013), Eugene Ellis and Niki Cooper discuss some of the reasons why black and Asian counseling students often complain that their difference and experience is ignored in counseling training.

2 Porges (2015), "Making the World Safe for Our Children." Porges talks about the Polyvagal Theory he proposed in 1995 and why feeling safe

requires a unique set of cues to the nervous system that are not equivalent to physical safety or the removal of threat. Like many concepts where science meets psychology, this theory is disputed by some. There are many people who derive therapeutic benefit from adopting the polyvagal model, but there are also evolutionary biologists who note that no direct evidence has been found.

3 The Race Test has been completed over 5 million times and takes only a few minutes to complete; it can be found on the Project Implicit website: https://implicit.harvard.edu/implicit/user/agg/blindspot/indexrk.htm

4 From Stephen Porges's lecture, "The Transformative Power of Feeling Safe: A Master Class on the Polyvagal Theory," May 20 and 21, 2017, Regent's University, London.

5 This journal article gives more information about Porges's Polyvagal Theory in a relatively easy to digest format. If you are feeling up to further reading, you can also read his book on the Polyvagal Theory (Porges, 2011).

CHAPTER 3

1 Reni Eddo-Lodge (2017) is a British journalist who, in her book, talks about structural racism and racial disparities in our institutions as a threat to human potential.

2 The Nation of Islam, sometimes referred to as the "Black Muslims," converted thousands of African American men and women to Islam during the height of the civil rights movement with the aim of improving their spiritual, mental, social, and economic conditions.

3 Michael Parkinson's interview with Muhammad Ali shows the boxer's powerful statement on racism. Journalist Roisin O'Connor wrote an article about Ali's response to white men in America being the devil. The article also includes a short video clip of Ali's response. https://www.independent.co.uk/news/people/muhammad-ali-dead-michael-parkinson-interview-shows-boxer-s-powerful-statement-on-racism-a7067656.html. Ali's views on black politics can be found between 9:55 and 26:37 in the full interview, which is available to view online at https://www.dailymotion.com/video/x16z2ff.

4 In the story of *Tar Baby*, the character Janine has transcended suffering through assimilation. The character Song transcends suffering through identification securely with African culture. With these choices, however, they did not achieve transcendence; instead, they were disturbed by the feeling and the state of alienation.

5 African American author Touré (2011), in his book *Who's Afraid of Post-Blackness?*, put forward the theory of post-blackness, in which he proposes that if there is a right way to do blackness, there must be a wrong way, and that this type of thinking inhibits the full exploration of black humanity.

6 Creole refers to any person, whether black, white or mixed race born in a British colony. Over time this has tended to be thought of as referring to someone of mixed race.

7 The "Rivers of Blood" speech is read in its entirety by Ian McDiarmid and then reflected on in a Radio 4 broadcast entitled "50 Years On: Rivers of Blood"; see https://www.bbc.co.uk/programmes/b09z08w3

8 Additional reading for those interested in further exploring mixed-race dynamics are: Anderson (2011), "The Eurasian Problem in Nineteenth Century India"; Song (2015), "What Constitutes Intermarriage for Multiracial People in Britain?"; Poston (1990), "The Biracial Identity Development Model: A Needed Addition"; Root (2003), "Five Mixed-Race Identities: From Relic to Revolution"; Song and Aspinall (2012), "Is Racial Mismatch a Problem for Young "Mixed Race" People in Britain?"; Song and Gutierrez (2015), "Keeping the Story Alive: Is Ethnic and Racial Dilution Inevitable for Multiracial People and Their Children?"; Ifekwunigwe (2004), *'Mixed Race' Studies.*

9 Also of interest might be *Black Rage Confronts the Law* by Paul Harris (1999). Harris traces the origins of the black rage defense in various legal cases since 1846. In 1971, Harris pioneered the modern version of the black rage defense when he successfully defended a young black man charged with armed bank robbery.

CHAPTER 4

1 There is no citation source for this quote. This quote is a statement of folk law.

2 Professor Kofi Awoonor appears in the documentary Britain's slave trade (Timeline, 2017).

3 Akbar, N. (1996). *Breaking the chains of psychological slavery.* Mind Productions & Associates.

4 James Walvin appears in the BBC documentary *Coolies: How Britain Re-Invented Slavery* (Girmitunitedorg, 2012).

5 You can watch a dramatized version of King's address at the end of the Selma to Montgomery March in the film Selma. The film was based on Martin Luther King's 1965 Selma to Montgomery voting rights marches. A transcript is also available at Standford University; see https://kinginstitute.stanford.edu/our-god-marching

6 Source: "British Involvement in the Transatlantic Slave Trade," Abolition Project, retrieved June 19, 2018, from http://abolition.e2bn.org/slavery.html

7 In the podcast "Transcending Intergenerational Trauma—Dr. Aileen Alleyne," Aileen Alleyne talks about the work of transcending intergenerational trauma and introduces us to a model she has developed which acts as a guide toward the emergence of the true self.

8 This Guardian Newspaper article is a useful overview of the subject with useful links for further study: Thomson, H. (2015). Study of Holocaust survivors finds trauma passed on to children's genes. *The Guardian*. Retrieved May 29, 2018, from https://www.theguardian.com/science/2015/aug/21/study-of-holocaust-survivors-finds-trauma-passed-on-to-childrens-genes.

9 Yehuda et al.'s (2016) "Holocaust Exposure Induced Intergenerational Effects on FKBP5 Methylation," is a paper describing a genetic study of 32 Jewish men and women who had either been interned in a Nazi concentration camp where they witnessed or experienced torture or who had to hide during the Second World War.

CHAPTER 5

1 Refer to Chapter 4, "Race, Class, and Gender."

2 Refer to Chapter 4, "Race and the Law."

CHAPTER 6

1 Refer to Chapter 2 for an explanation of neuroception.

2 Refer to Chapter 2 for an explanation of how the amygdala triggers the body.

3 Refer to Chapter 8, "Staying at the Contact Boundary."

CHAPTER 7

1 Refer to Chapter 2 for a discussion of implicit memories.

2 Headspace is a smartphone app of guided meditations and contemplations.

3 Stephen Porges, taken from the video recording The Science of Compassion.

4 "Summary of Stages of Racial Identity Development" can be found on the Racial Equity Tools website: www.racialequitytools.org.

CHAPTER 8

1 Therapists and trainee therapists discuss their work and clients on a regular basis with a supervisor, who is a more experienced therapist, and they may specialize in an area they are interested in. This forms part of good practice and self-care.

2 The golliwog is a doll-like character widely considered a racist caricature of black people, which appeared in children's books in the late 19th century. The character had great popularity in the Southern United States, the U.K., South Africa, and Australia into the 1970s.

3 Noted in National Geographic website, Belgian King Establishes Congo Free State, producer Mary Crooks, 2023.

4 Celia Levy gave an interview in a podcast called "Beyond Silence—Black Issues in the Therapeutic Process" (Ellis, 2013).

5 Video of this experiment is available on YouTube entitled "Brown Eyes and Blue Eyes Racism Experiment Children Session."

BIBLIOGRAPHY

Ababio, B., & Littlewood, R. (Eds.). (2019). *Intercultural therapy: Challenges, insights and developments.* Routledge.

Adamson, A. H. (1972). *Sugar without slaves: The political economy of British Guiana, 1838–1904.* Yale University Press.

Afuape, T. (2011). *Power, resistance and liberation in therapy with survivors of trauma: To have our hearts broken.* Routledge.

Agarwal, D. P. (2020). *Sway: Unravelling unconscious bias.* Bloomsbury Sigma.

Alberge, D. (2024, January 4). Transatlantic slavery continued for years after 1867, historian finds. *The Guardian.* https://www.theguardian.com/world/2024/jan/04/transatlantic-slavery-continued-for-years-after-1867-historian-finds

Allen, T. W. (1997). *The invention of the white race: Vol. 2. The origins of racial oppression in Anglo-America.* Verso.

Ellis, E. (Host). (2012, June 21). *Transcending intergenerational trauma—Dr. Aileen Alleyne* (No. 4) [Audio podcast episode]. In *The BAATN Podcast.* BAATN. https://soundcloud.com/baatnpodcast/transcending-intergenerational-trauma-episode-4

An Act for the Better Ordering and Governing of Negroes, Barbados. (1661). Public Record Office, Kew, United Kingdom, CO 30/2/16–26, 25–8, 32–3.

Anderson, C. (2017). *White rage: The unspoken truth of our racial divide.* Bloomsbury.

Anderson, V. (2015). *Race and power in British India: Anglo-Indians, class and identity in the nineteenth century.* Bloomsbury Publishing.

Anthony, F. (1969). *Britain's betrayal in India: The story of the Anglo-Indian Community.* Allied Publishers. Digital Library of India Item 2015.111609. Retrieved August 12, 2019, from http://archive.org/details/in.ernet.dli.2015.111609

Appiah, K. A., Gutmann, A., & Wilkins, D. B. (1998). *Color conscious.* Princeton University Press. (Original work published 1996)

Baker, D. (Director). (2016). *The house on Coco Road* [Documentary].

Peck, R. (Director). (2016). *I am not your negro* [Film]. Magnolia Pictures.

Banaji, M. R., Greenwald, A. G. (2013). *Blindspot: Hidden biases of good people.* [Illustrated ed.]. Delacorte Press.

Battalora, J. (2013). *Birth of a white nation: The invention of white people and its relevance today.* Strategic Book Publishing & Rights Agency, LLC.

Battalora, J. (2014, July 10). *Birth of a white nation* [Video]. YouTube. Retrieved July 7, 2019, from https://www.youtube.com/watch?v=riVAuC0dnP4

Batts, V. (2017, November 22). *Is reconciliation possible? The question remains: Bridging troubled waters.* Visions, Inc. Retrieved October 1, 2023, from https://visions-inc.org/wp-content/uploads/2017/09/is-reconciliation-possible-july-2017-3.pdf

Bean, R. B. (1906). Some racial peculiarities of the negro brain. *American Journal of Anatomy, 54*, 353–432.

Blumenbach, Johann. F. (2009). *On the unity of mankind*, from Rice, Stanley. A. (2009). *Encyclopedia of Evolution.* Infobase Publishing. (Original work published 1795)

Boakye, J. (2019). *Black, listed: Black British culture explored.* Dialogue Books.

Bruner, R. (2018, November 20). Michelle Obama Explains What 'Going High' Really Means. *Time.* https://time.com/5459984/michelle-obama-go-high/

Caldwell, C. (2016) Body identity development: Definitions and discussions, body, movement, and dance in psychotherapy (pp. 1–15), DOI: 10.1080/17432979.2016.1145141

Caldwell, C. (2018). Body identity development: Who we are and who we become. In C. Caldwell & L. Bennett Leighton (Eds.), *Oppression and the Body: Roots, Resistance, and Resolutions* (pp. 40–51). North Atlantic Books.

Campion, K. (2017). *Making mixed race: Time, place and identities in Birmingham* [Unpublished doctoral dissertation, University of Manchester]. Retrieved August 11, 2019, from https://www.research.manchester.ac.uk/portal/en/theses/making-mixed-race-time-place-and-identities-in-birmingham(9e0f3a3d-667c-4970-8197-f0a4a6ae7557).html

CaribNation TV. (2015, April 29). *The Caribbean East Indians, part 1 of 2* [Video]. YouTube. https://www.youtube.com/watch?v=oxFrQd6lVzA

Cayoun, B. A., Francis, S. E., & Shires, A. G. (2018). *The clinical handbook of mindfulness-integrated cognitive behavior therapy: A step-by-step guide for therapists.* Wiley-Blackwell.

CCARE at Stanford University. (2012). *The science of compassion: Origins, measures, and Interventions—Stephen Porges, PhD* [Video]. YouTube. Retrieved August 27, 2019, from https://www.youtube.com/watch?v=MYXa_BX2cE8

Chakravorty, S. (2019a, June 19). *How the British reshaped India's caste system.* BBC News. Retrieved August 23, 2019, from https://www.bbc.com/news/world-asia-india-48619734

Chakravorty, S. (2019b). *The truth about us: The politics of information from Manu to Modi.* Hachette India.

Coates, T.-N. (2013, May 15). *What we mean when we say "race is a social construct."* The Atlantic. Retrieved April 28, 2019, from https://www.theatlantic.com/national/archive/2013/05/what-we-mean-when-we-say-race-is-a-social-construct/275872/

Craton, M. (1982). *Testing the chains: Resistance to slavery in the British West Indies.* Cornell University Press.

Crenshaw, K. (1991). Mapping the margins: Intersectionality, identity politics, and violence against women of color. *Stanford Law Review, 436*, 1241–1299.

DeGruy, J. (2005). *Post traumatic slave syndrome: America's legacy of enduring injury and healing.* Joy DeGruy Publications.

Deyoung, P. A. (2015). *Understanding and treating chronic shame: A relational/neurobiological approach.* Routledge.

DiAngelo, R. (2017, December 6). Why it's so hard to talk to white people about racism [News Blog]. *HuffPost.* https://www.huffpost.com/entry/why-its-so-hard-to-talk-to-white-people-about-racism_b_7183710

DiAngelo, R. (2018). *White fragility: Why it's so hard for white people to talk about racism.* Beacon Press.

Eddo-Lodge, R. (2017). *Why I'm no longer talking to white people about race.* Bloomsbury.

Ellis, E. (Host). (2012, June 21). *Transcending Intergenerational Trauma—Dr. Aileen Alleyne* (No. 4) [Audio podcast episode]. In *The BAATN Podcast.* BAATN. https://soundcloud.com/baatnpodcast/transcending-intergenerational-trauma-episode-4

Ellis, E. (Host). (2013, August 2). Beyond silence—Black issues in the therapeutic process—pt 1 (No. 14) [Audio podcast episode]. In *The BAATN Podcast.* BAATN. https://soundcloud.com/baatnpodcast/beyond-silence-black-issues-in-the-therapeutic-process-pt-1-episode-14

Ellis, E., & Cooper, N. (2013). Silenced: The black student experience. *Therapy Today, 2410*, 14–19.

Engerman, S. L., Drescher, S., & Paquette, R. L. (Eds.). (2001). *Slavery.* Oxford University Press.

Ensler, E., & hooks, b. (2014). *Strike! Rise! Dance! Lion's Roar.* Retrieved May 5, 2019, from https://www.lionsroar.com/strike-rise-dance-bell-hooks-eve-ensler-march-2014/

Equiano, O. (2017). *The interesting narrative in the life of Olaudah Equiano.* CreateSpace. (Original work published 1789)

Faber, R. (1966). *The vision and the need: Late Victorian imperialist aims.* Faber & Faber.

Fanon, F. (1986). *Black skin white masks* (C. L. Markmann, Trans.). Pluto

Classics. (Original work published 1952) http://archive.org/details/BlackSkinWhiteMasksPlutoClassics_201501

Fletchermen-Smith, B. (2003). *Mental slavery: Psychoanalytical studies of Caribbean people* (2nd ed.). Karnac.

Fonagy, P., & Target, M. (1997). Attachment and reflective function: Their role in self-organization. *Development and Psychopathology, 9*, 679–700.

Forbes, H. T., & Post, B. (2014). *Beyond consequences, logic, and control: A love-based approach to helping children with severe behaviors.* Beyond Consequences Institute.

Fryer, P. (1993). *Aspects of British black history.* Index Books.

Garrett, A. (2000). Hume's revised racism revisited. *Hume Studies, 26*(1), 171–177.

Girmitunitedorg. (2012, November 11). *Coolies: How Britain reinvented slavery* [Video]. YouTube. Retrieved July 31, 2019, from https://www.youtube.com/watch?v=oxl4q_jfDPI

Gordon, G. (2007). *Towards bicultural competence: Beyond black and white.* Trentham Books Ltd.

Grier, W. H., & Cobbs, P. M. (1968). *Black rage.* Basic Books.

Guest, Y. (2019). Between black and white. *Therapy Today, 303*, 26–29.

Harris, P. (1999). *Black rage confronts the law.* NYU Press.

Henry, W. (2007). *Whiteness made simple: Stepping into the grey zone.* Nu-Beyond Ltd.

Hesse, E. (1999). The adult attachment interview: Historical and current perspectives. In *Handbook of Attachment: Theory, Research, and Clinical Applications.* Guilford Press.

hooks, b. (1992). Representing whiteness in the black imagination. In L. Grossberg (Ed.), *Cultural Studies* (pp. 338–346). Routledge.

Hooper, N., & Romeo, B. (1989). Feeling free [Song]. Soul II Soul. On *Keep on Moving.* Virgin.

Hope, D. (2011). From browning to cake soap: Popular debates on skin bleaching in the Jamaican dancehall. *Journal of Pan African Studies, 44*, 165–194.

Ifekwunigwe, J. O. (Ed.). (2004). *"Mixed race" studies, A reader.* Routledge.

Jefferson, T. (2006). *Notes on the state of Virginia* [Electronic ed.]. https://docsouth.unc.edu/southlit/jefferson/jefferson.html (Original work published 1788)

Jordan, W. D. (1968). *White over black: American attitudes toward the negro, 1550–1812* (2nd ed.). University of North Carolina Press.

Kendall, F. (2013). *Understanding white privilege: Creating pathways to authentic relationships across race* (2nd ed.). Routledge.

Keval, N. (2016). *Racist states of mind.* Routledge.

Lawrence, W. (1822). *Lectures on physiology, zoology and the natural history of man: Delivered at the Royal College of Surgeons.* James Smith.

Linnaeus, C. (2009). *Systema Naturae*, from Rice, Stanley. A. (2009). *Encyclopedia of Evolution*. Infobase Publishing. (Original work published 1758)

Locke, J., (2010). *Two treatises on government*. Bartleby.com. Retrieved July 31, 2022, from https://www.bartleby.com/169/101.html (Original work published 1821)

Main, M. (1991). Metacognitive knowledge, metacognitive monitoring, and singular (coherent) vs. multiple (incoherent) model of attachment: Findings and directions for future research. In C. M. Parkes, J. Stevenson-Hinde, & P. Marris (Eds.), *Attachment across the Life Cycle* (pp. 127–159). Tavistock/Routledge.

McGreal, C. (2001, September 3). Britain blocks EU apology for slave trade. *The Guardian*. https://www.theguardian.com/world/2001/sep/03/race.uk

McIntosh, P. (2003). White privilege: Unpacking the invisible knapsack. In S. Plous (Ed.), *Understanding prejudice and discrimination* (pp. 191–196). McGraw-Hill.

Mckenzie-Mavinga, I. (2009). *Black issues in the therapeutic process*. Palgrave Macmillan.

Mckenzie-Mavinga, I. (2016). *The challenge of racism in therapeutic practice: Engaging with oppression in practice and supervision* (2nd ed.). Palgrave.

Menakem, R. (2017). *My grandmother's hands: Racialized trauma and the pathway to mending our hearts and bodies* [Illustrated ed.]. Central Recovery Press.

Morrison, T. (1997). *Tar baby*. Vintage.

Nakashima, C. L. (1996). Voices from the movement: Approaches to multiraciality. In M.P.P. Root (Ed.), *The multiracial experience: Racial borders as the new frontier*, pp. 79–97. Sage Publications, Inc. https://psycnet.apa.org/record/1996-97566-003

Ogden, P. (2009). Emotion, mindfulness, and movement: Expanding the regulatory boundaries of the window of affect tolerance. In D. Fosha, D J. Siegel & M F. Solomon (Eds.), *The healing power of emotion: Affective neuroscience, development & clinical practice*, pp. 204–231. W. W. Norton & Company.

Ogden, P., & Fisher, J. (2015). *Sensorimotor psychotherapy: Interventions for trauma and attachment*. W. W. Norton & Company.

Okri, B. (1998). *A way of being free*. Phoenix.

Okri, B. (1999). *Mental fight*. Phoenix.

Parkinson, M. (Interviewer). (1971). *Parkinson Interviews Muhammad Ali*. BBC. https://www.dailymotion.com/video/x16z2ff

Perls, F. S. (1992). *Gestalt therapy verbatim* (2nd, Rev. ed.). Gestalt Journal Press.

Phelps, E. A., & Thomas, L. A. (2003). Race, behavior, and the brain: The role of neuroimaging in understanding complex social behaviors. *Political Psychology*, *244*, 747–758.

Pierce, C. (1970). Offensive mechanisms. In F.B. Barbour (Ed.), *The black seventies*, pp. 265–282. Boston.

Porges, S. W. (2009). The polyvagal theory: New insights into adaptive reactions of the autonomic nervous system. *Cleveland Clinic Journal of Medicine, 76*(Suppl 2), S86–S90.

Porges, S. W. (2011). *The polyvagal theory: Neurophysiological foundations of emotions, attachment, communication, and self-regulation.* W. W. Norton & Company.

Porges, S. W. (2015). Making the world safe for our children: Down-regulating defense and up-regulating social engagement to "optimize" the human experience. *Children Australia, 402*, 114–123.

Poston, W. C. (1990). The biracial identity development model: A needed addition. *Journal of Counseling & Development, 692*, 152–155.

Premack, D., & Woodruff, G. (1978). Does the chimpanzee have a theory of mind? *Behavioral and Brain Sciences, 1*(4), 515–526.

Rajan, A. (2018, Apr. 14). *50 years on: Rivers of blood* [Radio episode]. BBC Radio 4. Retrieved August 23, 2019, from https://www.bbc.co.uk/programmes/b09z08w3

Rankin, J., & Burke, J. (2020, June 30). Belgian king expresses 'deepest regrets' for brutal colonial rule. *The Guardian.* https://www.theguardian.com/world/2020/jun/30/belgian-king-philippe-expresses-profound-regrets-for-brutal-colonial-rule

Roediger, D. R. (1991). *The wages of whiteness: Race and the making of the American working class* (Rev. ed.). Verso.

Root, M. P. P. (2003). Five mixed-race identities: From relic to revolution. In L. I. Winters & H. Debose (Eds.), *New Faces in a changing America: Multiracial identity in the 21st century*, pp. 3–20. Sage Publications, Inc.

Sainsbury Centre for Mental Health. (2002). *Breaking the circles of fear: A review of the relationship between mental health services and African and Caribbean communities.* Sainsbury Centre for Mental Health. Retrieved April 28, 2019, from https://www.scie-socialcareonline.org.uk/breaking-the-circles-of-fear-a-review-of-the-relationship-between-mental-health-services-and-african-and-caribbean-communities/r/a11G0000001802YIAQ

Sartre, J.-P. (1948). *Black Orpheus.* French & European Publications Inc.

Schacter, D. L., & Graf, P. (1986). Effects of elaborative processing on implicit and explicit memory for new associations. *Journal of Experimental Psychology: Learning, Memory, and Cognition, 123*, 432–444.

Sellers, R. M., & Shelton, J. N. (2003). The role of racial identity in perceived racial discrimination. *Journal of Personality and Social Psychology, 84*, 1079–92.

Sherrell, C. (2018). The oppression of black bodies: The demand to simulate white bodies and white embodiment. In C. Caldwell & L. Bennett Leighton (Eds.), *Oppression and the body: Roots, resistance, and resolutions.* North Atlantic Books.

Siddique, S. (2014). Hidden in plain sight. *Therapy Today*, *25*(1), 45. https://www.bacp.co.uk/bacp-journals/therapy-today/2014/february-2014 [available on subscription]

Siegel, D. J. (1999). *The developing mind: Toward a neurobiology of interpersonal experience.* Guilford Press.

Silva Parker, C., & Willsea, J. (2011). Summary of stages of racial identity development. Retrieved November 2, 2020, from https://www.racialequitytools.org/resourcefiles/Compilation_of_Racial_Identity_Models_7_15_11.pdf

Singer, T., & Klimecki, O. M. (2014). Empathy and compassion. *Current Biology, 2418*, R875–R878.

Smith, W. A., Hung, M., & Franklin, J. D. (2011). Racial battle fatigue and the miseducation of black men: Racial microaggressions, societal problems, and environmental stress. *Journal of Negro Education, 801*, 63–82.

Song, M. (2015). What constitutes intermarriage for multiracial people in Britain? *The Annals of the American Academy of Political and Social Science, 6621*, 94–111.

Song, M., & Aspinall, P. (2012). Is racial mismatch a problem for young "mixed race" people in Britain? The findings of qualitative research. *Ethnicities, 126*, 730–753.

Song, M., & Gutierrez, C. O. (2015). Keeping the story alive: Is ethnic and racial dilution inevitable for multiracial people and their children? *Sociological Review, 633*, 680–698.

Staats, C. (2014). State of the science: Implicit bias review. Kirwan Institute for the Study of Race and Ethnicity, Ohio State University. Retrieved December 12, 2023, from https://www.studocu.com/en-gb/document/durham-university/introduction-to-english-law-and-legal-method/kirwan-2014-implicit-bias/76530125

Sue, D. W., Capodilupo, C. M., Torino, G. C., Bucceri, J. M., Holder, A. M., Nadal, K. L., & Esquilin, M. (2007). Racial microaggressions in everyday life: implications for clinical practice. *The American psychologist*, *62*(4), 271–286. https://doi.org/10.1037/0003-066X.62.4.271

Sweatt, J. D., Meaney, M. J., Nestler, E. J., & Akbarian, S. (2012). *Epigenetic regulation in the nervous system: Basic mechanisms and clinical impact.* Academic Press.

Tang et al., (2015). A unique gene regulatory network resets the human germline epigenome for Development. *Cell, 161*(6), 1453–1467. https://doi.org/10.1016/j.cell.2015.04.053

TEDx. (2011, November 15). *Jay Smooth: How I learned to stop worrying and love discussing race* [Video]. YouTube. https://www.youtube.com/watch?v=MbdxeFcQtaU

The Infinite Monkey Cage. (2016). *What is race?* [Radio broadcast]. BBC Radio 4. Retrieved April 28, 2019, from https://www.bbc.co.uk/programmes/b06ybg84

Timeline. (2017). *Britain's slave trade* [Documentary]. YouTube. https://www.youtube.com/watch?v=Uas4hGFXFZM

Touré, (2011). *Who's afraid of post-blackness? What it means to be black now.* Free Press.

Vrana, S. R., & Rollock, D. (1998). Physiological response to a minimal social encounter: Effects of gender, ethnicity, and social context. *Psychophysiology, 354*, 462–469.

Wallin, D. J. (2007). *Attachment in psychotherapy.* Guilford Press.

Weisner, T. S. (2018). The socialization of trust: Plural caregiving and diverse pathways in human development across cultures. In H. Otto & H. Keller (Eds.), *Different faces of attachment: Cultural variations on a universal human need* (pp. 263–277). Cambridge University Press.

Welsing, F. C. (1991). *The Isis papers: The keys to the colors.* Third World Press.

Williams, A. K., & Owens, L. R. (2016). *Radical dharma: Talking race, love, and liberation.* North Atlantic Books.

Williams, P. (1997, February 25). *The emperor's new clothes* [Radio broadcast]. Retrieved November 1, 2020, from https://www.bbc.co.uk/programmes/p00gwb37

Wu, A. (2015). The four kinds of self-negativity. *de-Label Ourselves.* Retrieved May 2, 2019, from https://medium.com/de-label-ourselves/the-four-kinds-of-self-negativity-2cea5844b4e2

Yehuda, R., Daskalakis, N. P., Bierer, L. M., Bader, H. N., Klengel, T., Holsboer, F., & Binder, E. B. (2016). Holocaust exposure induced intergenerational effects on FKBP5 methylation. *Biological Psychiatry, 80*(5), 372–380. https://doi.org/10.1016/j.biopsych.2015.08.005

INDEX

ABOUT THE AUTHOR

Eugene Ellis is the director and founder of the Black, African, and Asian Therapy Network (BAATN), the United Kingdom's largest independent organization to specialize in working therapeutically with black, African, Caribbean, and South Asian people. He trained as an integrative arts psychotherapist and has worked for many years with severely traumatized children and their families in the field of adoption and fostering. He has special interests in body-oriented therapies and in facilitating self-healing through the use of metaphor and the imagination.

Eugene is particularly interested in facilitating race conversations with the therapeutic community in the U.K. through articles and podcasts. He is also active in facilitating a dialogue around race as it relates to the body within organizations and in psychotherapy training.